A Shining City on a Hill

PRAEGER SERIES IN POLITICAL COMMUNICATION

Robert E. Denton, Jr., *General Editor*

Speak No Evil: The Promotional Heritage of Nuclear Risk Communication
Louis M. Gwin, Jr.

Enacting Political Culture: Rhetorical Transformations of Liberty Weekend 1986
David E. Procter

Within These Walls: A Study of Communication Between Presidents and Their Senior Staffs
Patricia D. Witherspoon

Continuity and Change in the Rhetoric of the Moral Majority
David Snowball

Mediated Politics in Two Cultures: Presidential Campaigning in the United States and France
Lynda Lee Kaid, Jacques Gerstlé, and Keith R. Sanders

Crime and the American Press
Roy Edward Lotz

The Cold War As Rhetoric: The Beginnings, 1945–1950
Lynn B. Hinds and Theodore O. Windt, Jr.

Presidential Perspectives on Space Exploration: Guiding Metaphors from Eisenhower to Bush
Linda T. Krug

Political Campaign Communication, Second Edition
Judith S. Trent and Robert V. Friedenberg

Ethical Dimensions of Political Communication
Edited by Robert E. Denton, Jr.

Cordial Concurrence: Orchestrating National Party Conventions in the Telepolitical Age
Larry David Smith and Dan Nimmo

Political Empiricism: Communication Strategies in State and Regional Elections
Rita Kirk Whillock

For our parents:
You weren't just marking time;
you made a difference.
You made the city stronger,
freer, and left it in good hands.

Library of Congress Cataloging-in-Publication Data

Kiewe, Amos.
A shining city on a hill : Ronald Reagan's economic rhetoric, 1951–1989 / Amos Kiewe, Davis W. Houck.
p. cm.—(Praeger series in political communication)
Includes bibliographical references (p.) and index.
ISBN 0–275–93634–1 (alk. paper)
1. Communication in politics—United States—History—20th century. 2. Economics—United States—History—20th century. 3. English language—Rhetoric. 4. United States—Economic policy—1945– 5. Reagan, Ronald. I. Houck, Davis W. II. Title. III. Series.
JK271.K44 1991
353.03′23′092—dc20 91–9595

British Library Cataloguing in Publication Data is available.

Library of Congress Catalog Card Number: 91–9595
ISBN: 0–275–93634–1

First published in 1991

Praeger Publishers, One Madison Avenue, New York, NY 10010
An imprint of Greenwood Publishing Group, Inc.

Printed in the United States of America

The paper used in this book complies with the Permanent Paper Standard issued by the National Information Standards Organization (Z39.48–1984).

10 9 8 7 6 5 4 3 2 1

A Shining City on a Hill

Ronald Reagan's Economic Rhetoric, 1951–1989

Amos Kiewe
and Davis W. Houck

Praeger Series in Political Communication

PRAEGER

New York
Westport, Connecticut
London

Contents

About the Series

Those of us from the discipline of communication studies have long believed that communication is prior to all other fields of inquiry. In several other forums I have argued that the essence of politics is "talk" or human interaction.[1] Such interaction may be formal or informal, verbal or nonverbal, public or private but always persuasive, forcing us consciously or subconsciously to interpret, to evaluate, and to act. Communication is the vehicle for human action.

From this perspective, it is not surprising that Aristotle recognized the natural kinship of politics and communication in his *Politics* and *Rhetoric*. In the former, he establishes that humans are "political beings [who] alone of the animals [are] furnished with the faculty of language."[2] And in the latter, he begins his systematic analysis of discourse by proclaiming that "rhetorical study, in its strict sense, is concerned with the modes of persuasion."[3] Thus, it was recognized over two thousand years ago that politics and communication go hand in hand because they are essential parts of human nature.

Back in 1981, Dan Nimmo and Keith Sanders proclaimed that political communication was an emerging field.[4] Although its origin, as noted, dates back centuries, a "self-consciously cross-disciplinary" focus began in the late 1950s. Thousands of books and articles later, colleges and universities offer a variety of graduate and undergraduate coursework in the area in such diverse departments as communication, mass communication, journalism, political science, and sociology.[5] In Nimmo and Sanders's early assessment, the "key areas of inquiry" included rhetorical analysis, propaganda analysis, attitude change studies, voting studies, government and the news media, functional and systems analyses, technological changes, media technologies, campaign techniques, and research techniques.[6] In a survey of the state of the field in 1983 by the same authors and Lynda Kaid, they found additional, more specific areas of concerns such as the presidency, political polls, public opinion, debates, and advertising, to name a few.[7] Since the first study, they also noted a shift away from the rather strict behavioral approach.

Today, Dan Nimmo and David Swanson assert that "political communication has developed some identity as a more or less distinct domain of scholarly work."[8] The scope and concerns of the area have further expanded to include critical theories and cultural studies. While there is no precise definition, method, or disciplinary home of the area of inquiry, its primary domain is the role, processes, and effects of communication within the context of politics broadly defined.

In 1985, the editors of *Political Communication Yearbook: 1984* noted that "more things are happening in the study, teaching, and practice of political communication than can be captured within the space limitations of the relatively few publications available."[9] In addition, they argued that the backgrounds of "those involved in the field [are] so varied and plurist in outlook and approach, . . . it [is] a mistake to adhere slavishly to any set format in shaping the content."[10] And more recently, Swanson and Nimmo call for "ways of overcoming the unhappy consequences of fragmentation within a framework that respects, encourages, and benefits from diverse scholarly commitments, agendas, and approaches."[11]

In agreement with these assessments of the area and with gentle encouragement, Praeger established in 1988 the series entitled "Praeger Series in Political Communication." The series is open to all qualitative and quantitative methodologies as well as contemporary and historical studies. The key to characterizing the studies in the series is the focus on communication variables or activities within a political context or dimension. Scholars from the disciplines of communication, history, political science, and sociology have participated in the series.

I am, without shame or modesty, a fan of the series. The joy of serving as its editor is in participating in the dialogue of the field of political communication and in reading the contributors' works. I invite you to join me.

Robert E. Denton, Jr.

NOTES

1. See Robert E. Denton, Jr., *The Symbolic Dimensions of the American Presidency* (Prospect Heights, IL: Waveland Press, 1982); Robert E. Denton, Jr., and Gary Woodward, *Political Communication in America* (New York: Praeger, 1985, 2d ed.,

1990); Robert E. Denton, Jr., and Dan F. Hahn, *Presidential Communication* (New York: Praeger, 1986); and Robert E. Denton, Jr., *The Primetime Presidency of Ronald Reagan* (New York: Praeger, 1988).

2. Aristotle, *The Politics of Aristotle*, trans. Ernest Barker (New York: Oxford University Press, 1970), 5.

3. Aristotle, *Rhetoric*, trans. Rhys Roberts (New York: The Modern Library, 1954), 22.

4. Dan Nimmo and Keith Sanders, "Introduction: The Emergence of Political Communication as a Field," in *Handbook of Political Communication*, ed. Dan Nimmo and Keith Sanders (Beverly Hills, CA: Sage, 1981), 11–36.

5. Ibid., 15.

6. Ibid., 17–27.

7. Keith Sanders, Lynda Kaid, and Dan Nimmo, ed., *Political Communication Yearbook: 1984* (Carbondale, IL: Southern Illinois University: 1985), 283–308.

8. Dan Nimmo and David Swanson, "The Field of Political Communication: Beyond the Voter Persuasion Paradigm," in *New Directions in Political Communication*, ed. David Swanson and Dan Nimmo (Beverly Hills, CA: Sage, 1990), 8.

9. Sanders, Kaid, and Nimmo, *Political Communication Yearbook*, xiv.

10. Ibid., xiv.

11. Nimmo and Swanson, "Field of Political Communication," 11.

Series Foreword

In 1980, Ronald Reagan came to Washington with a strong social and economic ideology. According to Gary Wills, it was not a social agenda but inflation that elected Reagan.[1] By constantly quizzing "Are you better off now than you were four years ago?", Reagan ultimately asked people to vote their pocketbooks. Not since Franklin Roosevelt in 1933 had a newly elected president publicly proclaimed to alter the nation's fundamental economy and economic policy.

Ronald Reagan might have been the "great communicator," but the fact of the matter is that the administration did implement policy. Reagan's economic ideology was based upon the belief in free markets, free enterprise, and laissez faire. His strategy was to cut taxes first, accept federal deficits, and use them to prod Congress into cutting the budget, eliminating wasteful social governmental spending. As Reagan expresses in his autobiography, "I believed that if we cut tax rates and reduced the proportion of our national wealth that was taken by Washington, the economy would receive a stimulus that would bring down inflation, unemployment, and interest rates, and there would be such an expansion of economic activity that in the end there would be a net increase in the amount of revenue to finance the important functions of government."[2]

In many ways, the 1981 federal income tax cuts were the culmination of a nationwide revolt that began with California's infamous Proposition 13. Reagan's tax reform was actually a revenue cap resulting in a 5 percent difference between spending and revenues that generated a deficit of nearly $200 billion a year.[3] Yes, such deficits stimulated business activity, and by 1984, everyone was feeling great. The federal deficit was never an issue, except for Walter Mondale. Reagan's early policy can best be summarized as "spend, spend, don't tax, don't tax."[4]

In addition to tax cuts, the other essential element of his strategy was the theory of "supply-side economics."[5] For most Americans, the first time we ever heard of "supply-side economics" was from George Bush in the primary campaign against Reagan in 1980, who characterized the theory as "voodoo economics." In theory, at least, supply can never outrun demand since demand is infinite. Supply responds to the type of demand stimulated. Thus, the solution is not to give more money to consumers but to give capital to producers who can produce more to stimulate demand. In the end, the winners were the "producers" for two reasons. They received all the tax credits and benefits as well as higher profits. Supply-side economics appealed to Ronald Reagan because the theory trusts the free market, distrusts government, and espouses unlimited growth.

Of course, we know now that the plan simply did not work.[6] In reality, he attempted an ambitious growth of defense spending while simultaneously reducing tax revenues. The rich got richer. Poverty and economic inequality increased. There was early evidence of this provided by David Stockman. But for Reagan, philosophy was more important than specific results. For "true believers," failure is not possible. Only more time is needed to achieve the goal. What Reagan did is obvious. But *how* did he do it?

As the "great communicator," it was up to Reagan to explain, to sell, to defend, and to justify his economic policy. Amos Kiewe and Davis Houck provide a comprehensive rhetorical biography of Reagan's economic rhetoric. Their analysis traces the development and progression of Reagan's economic rhetoric beginning in 1951 as well as the various strategies of policy implementation through 1988. The authors are right in their observation that Reagan's economic rhetoric influenced his rhetoric on other issues such as foreign policy, national defense, and the environment. Thus Reagan's political ideology and agenda were "conditioned" by his self-defined, common-sense economic viewpoint.

The value of this outstanding study is fourfold. First, as a rhetorical study, it excels at demonstrating the role of rhetoric in discovering ideology and in defining and implementing public policy. The authors recognize that economics is not so much a science as an interpretative art or philosophy of "market interaction." Second, as a political study, Kiewe and Houck explain the development and essence of Ronald Reagan's political ideology. The authors challenge the assumption that Reagan's experiences somehow contributed to his conversion to a more conservative political philosophy. Rather, the authors effectively argue that Reagan's philosophy evolved very early based upon several key assumptions about the role of economics in a democratic society. Thus this book serves as an excellent study of the economic policy of the Reagan administration. Indeed, the economic policies of the era not only changed the economic structure of our society but also left a legacy that will impact future generations of Americans. Finally, the study enlightens us about the presidency and the process of governing a nation through words and deeds.

In many ways, Kiewe and Houck offer a new look at the Reagan presidency. In essence, we see that the Reagan legacy is more than an image, a strong military, or renewed national pride. The Reagan legacy is "Reaganomics"—a personal ideology where nearly all issues of national and international concern can be addressed through pragmatic economic principles. The debate of Reaganomics will continue well into the next decade. Without doubt, a cornerstone of the debate is the work of Amos Kiewe and Davis Houck.

Robert E. Denton, Jr.

NOTES

1. Gary Wills, *Reagan's America: Innocents at Home* (New York: Doubleday, 1987), 362.
2. Ronald Reagan, *An American Life* (New York: Simon & Schuster, 1990), 231.
3. Richard Reeves, *The Reagan Detour* (New York: Simon & Schuster, 1985), 85.
4. Ibid., 86.
5. Although in his autobiography Reagan denies adopting the theory of supply side economics, it is the term that his economic advisors frequently used. Reagan explains that it is just "common sense." Reagan, *An American Life*, 232.
6. Kevin Phillips, *The Politics of Rich and Poor* (New York: Random House, 1990).

Acknowledgments

This book is an outgrowth of an Independent Study begun in September 1988 that initially culminated in an article published by *Communication Studies* in the summer of 1989. After completing the article, we both realized that we had only begun to scratch the surface of a much larger topic, that being a longitudinal study of Ronald Reagan's economic discourse beginning during his Hollywood years.

Through the entire process several people had a direct hand in influencing its contents. Jennifer McGee, Greg Rumberg, and Sarah Thomas, all from the College of Wooster, spent many much-appreciated hours rummaging through countless articles, speeches, and books to make this manuscript complete. Joanne Yoder of the College of Wooster worked her editorial magic on seemingly endless drafts of earlier chapters. We would also like to acknowledge the following people for their valuable input on drafts of earlier chapters: Carole Blair, Mark Bruner, Dan Buehler, and Joanne Gribble from the University of California, Davis, Enrico Pucci from the Pennsylvania State University and Greg Dickinson from the University of Southern California.

A special thank you goes out to Mary Stuckey from the University of Mississippi for generously loaning several hard-to-find texts of Ronald Reagan's speeches. Without these speeches, Chapter 4 would still be a formless abstraction.

We would also like to thank our respective institutions: Temple University and the University of California, Davis for their support in seeing this project through.

Writing a book puts a halt to many activities. Saying "no" got to be a common refrain for both of us over the past year. For this we offer our apologies to those affected by our hermitlike behavior. Additionally, anyone who has written a book knows of the emotional roller-coaster such a project entails. Invariably, those closest to us often suffer from our "book phobias." For this we apologize to our close family and friends, who, in spite of our preoccupations and anxieties, remained supportive and understanding throughout.

Last, a special mention is in order to the second author's loving Grandmother, Eila Lee Coffeen, who recently told a disbelieving Grandson of a blind date with a "polite young man who went by the name Dutch" at a mid-afternoon tea dance in Des Moines, Iowa. Over 50 years after the date, she still vividly recalls Dutch's charm and affable personality, the same attributes that would eventually endear Dutch Reagan to the American people.

Introduction

Some have labeled him the "great communicator." Others have seen fit to refer to him with such flattering names as the "great persuader" and the "great rhetorician."[1] The "him" we are referring to is Ronald Wilson Reagan, the 40th president of the United States. Regardless of how historians choose to chronicle the Reagan years, no one can deny Reagan's gift for the spoken word. Perhaps no other president in the electronic age has so successfully "gone public" as this actor-turned-politician.[2]

As one might imagine, given Reagan's legacy as a rhetorical president, rhetoricians have spent considerable attention attempting to explain, interpret, and evaluate Reagan's presidential discourse.[3] However, in examining his presidential rhetoric, rhetoricians have largely ignored Ronald Reagan's pre-presidential discourse.[4] Essentially, Reagan did not become the "great communicator" through some mystical transformation while in the confines of the White House. Rather, Reagan was first publicly recognized for his communicative appeal following his 1964 speech "A Time for Choosing." This speech, addressed to a national television audience in support of Barry Goldwater's presidential bid, elevated stump orator Reagan to political candidate Reagan almost overnight.[5]

Reagan's knack for the rhetorical, however, dates back much earlier than "A Time for Choosing," all the way back to Reagan's freshmen year at Eureka College in Illinois. It was then that Reagan gave a speech in support of a student-sponsored strike, intended to oust the college's president. Reagan's speech overwhelmed the assembly, resulting in a unanimous vote for the student's strike. Bert Wilson, the college's president, resigned shortly afterward.[6]

The reader will recognize by the title of the book that our emphasis is on Reagan's economic rhetoric. Our reasons for focusing exclusively on this topic involve several considerations. First, underlying our emphasis on Reagan's economic rhetoric is the conditioning influence that economics had on other issues. Reagan saw the world largely through economic lenses. As we will attempt to illustrate in the ensuing chapters, Reagan's economic rhetoric conditioned much of his rhetoric on such issues as foreign policy, national defense, and the environment, to name a few. Hierarchically considered, economic issues were at the pinnacle of Reagan's political agenda, not only as president but also during his gubernatorial and pre-gubernatorial years.

Second, attempting to examine all of Reagan's discourse would confine us to saying very little about a lot. In the words of Martin J. Medhurst, "the explanation that accounts broadly for everything, accounts specifically for nothing."[7] This is especially true for Reagan. Over the 38 year period we will be examining, Reagan spoke literally thousands of times. Thus, due to Reagan's propensity for speaking as well as the many topics he spoke on, we do not feel we could "do justice" to such a vast corpus of discourse.

A third reason for our attention to economic rhetoric is not germane to Ronald Reagan. As Donald McCloskey has argued in his book *The Rhetoric of Economics,* economics is not a purely scientific discipline. Rather, economics exhibits many rhetorical dimensions. Furthermore, the fusion of economics with politics creates a most interesting "rhetorical situation."[8] Regardless of the mathematical validity and the intricate graphical analysis of a given economic philosophy, the successful politician must translate his/her economic philosophy into words; more specifically, words that are persuasive.

THE RHETORICAL ACT

Few words in the English language have been as misused and misunderstood as the word "rhetoric." Ironically, the increased demand for a knowledge of rhetoric, spawned by the media's pervasiveness, has paralleled the demise of the word. Instead of attempting to grapple with political discourse, news commentators delight in dismissing the politician's "mudslinging rhetoric" or the "heated rhetoric" generated by partisan issues.

Given this confused conception of rhetoric, what is the meaning of the word? Bernard L. Brock and Robert L. Scott define rhetoric as "the human effort to induce cooperation through the use of symbols."[9] Kenneth Burke defines rhetoric as *"the use of language as a symbolic means of inducing cooperation in beings that by nature respond to symbols.*"[10] As both definitions imply, rhetoric is a purposeful act: "A *rhetorical act,* . . . is an intentional, created, polished attempt to overcome the obstacles in a given situation with a specific audience on a given issue to achieve a particular end."[11]

For our purposes we will be using the word "rhetoric" to refer to the discursive attempt by a rhetor to persuade. Emphasis is placed on the word "attempt" insofar as one cannot, in good judgment, account for the effect of a given rhetorical act. Whether persuasion actually takes place or not is for the social scientist or pollster to determine. As Edwin Black claims, "Whether a given discourse actually exerts an influence has no bearing on whether it is rhetorical."[12]

RHETORICAL CRITICISM

As Burke noted over fifty years ago, "all living organisms interpret many of the signs about them."[13] Burke argued that even a trout has some semblance of a critical apparatus based on previous experience. That the trout's critical apparatus is inherently inferior to the human capacity to construct critical judgments is of no great significance. Suffice it to say, as Carroll C. Arnold has, that "we are all 'critics' at some point during almost any given day."[14] Whether our criticism operates on a very simplistic level or on a complex one, all humans share in "the critical impulse."[15]

What is it then that we humans critique? Specifically, we critique the products of humans.[16] Given that language is an intrinsically human product, the human use of language becomes one of the many products that humans attempt to criticize. And insofar as language fulfills a suasive function, the criticism of persuasive discourse has become the domain of rhetorical critics. Though rhetorical criticism is not exclusively confined to the spoken word, for our purposes we will narrow our critical task to Reagan's spoken discourse.

As critics of rhetoric, we do not claim to be "objective" in our analyses and the conclusions we draw. Clearly, objectivity and rhetorical criticism are a highly incongruous pair. Because our medium is language, an inherently ideologically charged medium, we can offer the reader only our efforts to remain as impartial as our discourse will permit.[17]

If not objectivity, then what becomes the critic's stance? One of the primary values of rhetorical criticism (if performed constructively and responsibly) is its attempt to understand humanity, as well as contemporary events.[18] In this sense, rhetorical criticism functions not only as something scholars spend their time doing, but also something that has the potential for serving important social, political, and pedagogic functions.[19]

RHETORICAL PERSPECTIVE

Rhetorical critics, like scholars in other disciplines, incorporate certain perspectives or methods to guide their inquiries. A list of perspectives often incorporated by rhetorical critics include: Aristotelian, neo-Aristotelian, dramatism, fantasy theme, ideological, metaphor, narrative, postmodern, and textual, to name a few. In analyzing Reagan's economic rhetoric, we chose not to label our approach but rather to highlight the important constituents of our analysis. Of importance to us is the analysis of ideas and their rhetorical development. In understanding the suasive nature of words and ideas, we look at their substance as well as their style and developmental pattern. This approach permits and encourages us to consider the rhetorical nature of ideas through several different perspectives. Using one specific perspective would greatly limit our critical task and the resulting insights. We are in agreement with Burke that "the main ideal of criticism . . . is to use all that there is to use."[20]

PURPOSE

In a free and democratic society, economics, like foreign policy or social issues, is a political subject-matter in need of persuasive discourse to secure successful implementation and adherence. Market interaction does not get set in motion by some omnipotent being. Rather, rhetorical forces play a significant role in advancing economic matters. Thus one of our goals in this project is to examine Ronald Reagan's economic "words" and how these words functioned within an economic framework.

In order to provide a coherent structure and purpose to our undertaking we have raised several questions that we will use as touchstones: (1) what rhetorical strategies were evidenced in Reagan's economic discourse?; (2) did these strategies coincide with or contradict other strategies?; (3) how, if any, did Reagan's role(s) affect his rhetorical strategies?; (4) what do these strategies tell us about Reagan?; (5) did shifts occur in Reagan's economic discourse over time and, if so, how can one account for these shifts?; (6) what influence did certain situations exert on Reagan's economic rhetoric?; (7) and did Reagan's economic rhetoric undergo a certain development or progression? At the most basic level, we are attempting to write a chapter in Reagan's rhetorical biography. Hopefully, our study will encourage others to write additional chapters.

LIMITATIONS OF STUDY

One of the primary disadvantages in analyzing speech texts is the inability of the critic to account for the visual dimensions of the discourse. This is an important concern especially relative to Ronald Reagan. Without a doubt, Reagan's acting background enhanced the public's perception of him. An analysis of Reagan's "visual text" could be a full study in its own right.[21] However, for our purposes, we will be focusing exclusively on the verbal texts of Reagan's speeches. The visual dimension is less important in this study, for we are not attempting to account for Reagan's general rhetorical effectiveness; rather, we advance an account of the character and development of his economic rhetoric.

A second limitation is that many of the speeches selected for analysis have likely undergone editing by government sources, campaign committees, and book editors. Thus the speeches we will be analyzing are not necessarily the identical speeches that Reagan delivered. Such a disparity, however, is unavoidable. Reagan's speeches come primarily from six sources: three anthologies of Reagan's speeches: *Speaking My Mind, A Time for Choosing,* and *Ronald Reagan Talks to America*; press releases issued by the governor's office; speeches issued by the Republican National Committee; and *The Public Papers of the U.S. President* and the *Weekly Compilation of Presidential Documents.*

OUTLINE

We have proceeded chronologically, beginning with a speech in 1951 and concluding in 1989 with Reagan's Farewell Address to the nation. However, it should be noted that in Chapters 2, 3, 5, and 6 we have subdivided each period into various economic topics. We have structured the book this way so that the reader can easily distinguish the topics that were important in a given phase as well as to aid us in identifying similarities and differences in how Reagan approached various economic topics.

Chapter 1 analyzes four speeches Reagan gave between 1951 and 1964. Several important findings emerge from this chapter: the originations of Reagan's economic ideology, Reagan's alternative to the progressive income tax—a proportional income tax that Reagan warranted biblically, the effect that the ideological orientation of his auditors had on Reagan's economic discourse, the conditioning influence that economic prosperity exerted on noneconomic issues, and the implications of Reagan's predominantly negative economic rhetoric.

Chapter 2 follows Reagan's economic rhetoric during his first term as governor of California (1967–1970). Several conclusions emerge including Reagan's scapegoating tactics, his repeated emphasis on shifting the responsibility for effective state governance onto the citizens of the state, the projection of "symbolic economies" due to the Reagan administration's lack of legislative success, the oftentimes contradictory rhetorics stemming from Reagan's two personae—the ideological and the pragmatic politician—and Reagan's attempts to redefine potentially detrimental fiscal occurrences to his political advantage.

Chapter 3 examines Reagan's economic discourse during his second term as governor (1971–1974). Conclusions drawn from this period include the rhetorical implications of supply-side logic observed in Reagan's discourse, Reagan's extreme interpretations surrounding his campaign for Proposition 1, Reagan's emphasis on "real" economies spawned by significant legislative reforms, and the redemptive powers free enterprise embodied for Reagan.

Chapter 4 concludes the pre-presidential section of the book by examining Reagan's economic discourse during the presidential campaigns of 1976 and 1980. Conclusions emerge concerning the three distinct rhetorics Reagan employed during the 1976 campaign, Reagan's defense of supply-side tax cuts as not just a pro-wealthy proposal, the Carter-led economic conspiracy, the consequences of Reagan's actualized prophecies during the 1980 campaign, and Reagan's move away from specifics to more generalized rhetorical appeals.

Chapter 5 discusses Reagan's economic discourse during his first presidential term. In promoting a "New Beginning," Reagan sought to implement radical economic programs including a massive tax-rate cut and reforms in various government programs. Reagan was successful during 1981 in passing important legislation but the recession throughout 1982 minimized earlier achievements. Reagan maintained an optimistic rhetorical posture during the recession while after the recession his discourse turned redemptive. Overcoming the economic recession proved to be Reagan's biggest asset in confidently campaigning for a second term.

Chapter 6 examines Reagan's economic rhetoric during his second presidential term. During this period, Reagan sought to complete his economic agenda, calling for a second American Revolution. A massive tax overhaul in 1986 as well as welfare reform and an important trade bill late in his presidency highlighted Reagan's second term. The economy performed well though the growing budget deficit and national debt threatened the prosperity of the moment. Reagan's rhetoric was confident, deflecting any notion of potential economic downturn or loss to international competition. Reagan left political office reaffirming America's greatness and promising an even better future.

Chapter 7 presents a reflection on Reagan's economic rhetoric spanning over four decades. Here, an assessment of Reagan's economic rhetoric is offered, highlighting rhetorical progressions, recurrent themes, unique features, and characteristics.

NOTES

1. Gregg Phifer, "Two Inaugurals: A Second Look," *Southern Speech Communication Journal* 48 (1983): 385; and William K. Muir, Jr., "The Primacy of Rhetoric," in *Leadership in the Modern Presidency*, ed. Fred I. Greenstein (Cambridge: Harvard University Press, 1988), 278.

2. This phrase was coined by Kernell in Samuel Kernell, *Going Public* (Washington, D.C.: Congressional Quarterly Press, 1986).

3. Walter R. Fisher, "Romantic Democracy, Ronald Reagan, and Presidential Heroes," *Western Journal of Speech Communication* 46 (1982): 299–310; Ernest G. Bormann, "A Fantasy Theme Analysis of the Television Coverage of the Hostage Release and the Reagan Inaugural," *Quarterly Journal of Speech* 68 (1982): 133–45; Sarah Russell Hankins, "Archetypal Alloy: Reagan's Rhetorical Image," *Central States Speech Journal* 34 (1983): 33–43; Gary C. Woodward, "Reagan as Roosevelt: The Elasticity of Pseudo-Populist Appeals," *Central States Speech Journal* 34 (1983): 44–58; Phifer, "Two Inaugurals: A Second Look," 378–85; Richard E. Crable and Steven L. Vibbert, "Argumentative Stance and Political Faith Healing: 'The Dream Will Come True,' " *Quarterly Journal of Speech* 69 (1983): 290–301; Robert L. Ivie, "Speaking 'Common Sense' about the Soviet Threat: Reagan's Rhetorical Stance," *Western Journal of Speech Communication* 48 (1984): 39–50; C. Thomas Preston, Jr., "Reagan's 'New Beginning': Is It the 'New Deal' of the Eighties?" *Southern Speech Communication Journal* 49 (1984): 198–211; David Zarefsky, Carol Miller-Tutzauer, and Frank E. Tutzauer, "Ronald Reagan's Safety Net for the Truly Needy: The Rhetorical Uses of Definition," *Central States Speech Journal* 35 (1984): 113–19; Martin J. Medhurst, "Postponing the Social Agenda: Reagan's Strategy and Tactics," *Western Journal of Speech Communication* 48 (1984): 262–76; G. Thomas Goodnight, "Ronald Reagan's Re-formulation of the Rhetoric of War: Analysis of the 'Zero Option,' 'Evil Empire,' and 'Star Wars' Addresses," *Quarterly Journal of Speech* 72 (1986): 390–414; Janice Hocker Rushing, "Ronald Reagan's 'Star Wars' Address: Mythic Containment of Technical Reasoning," *Quarterly Journal of Speech* 72 (1986): 415–33; Richard L. Johanneson, "Ronald Reagan's Economic Jeremiad," *Central States Speech Journal* 37 (1986): 79–89; David E. Procter, "The Rescue Mission: Assigning Guilt to a Chaotic Scene," *Western Journal of Speech Communication* 51 (1987): 245–55; David S. Birdsell, "Ronald Reagan on Lebanon and Grenada: Flexibility and Interpretation in the Application of Kenneth Burke's Pentad," *Quarterly Journal of Speech* 73 (1987): 267–79; William F. Lewis, "Telling America's Story: Narrative Form and the Reagan Presidency," *Quarterly Journal of Speech* 73 (1987): 280–302; Amos Kiewe and Davis W. Houck, "The Rhetoric of Reaganomics: A Redemptive Vision," *Communication Studies* 40 (1989): 97–108; Mark P. Moore, "Reagan's Quest for Freedom in the 1987 State of the Union Address," *Western Journal of Speech Communication* 53 (1989): 52–65; Roger C. Aden, "Entrapment and Escape: Inventional Metaphors in Ronald Reagan's Economic Rhetoric," *Southern Speech Communication Journal* 54 (1989): 384–400.

4. Aside from articles dealing with his campaign rhetoric, which would technically be considered pre-presidential rhetoric, we found only three sources that examined Reagan's rhetoric prior to 1980: Kurt W. Ritter, "Ronald Reagan and 'The Speech': The Rhetoric of Public Relations Politics," *Western Speech* 32 (1968): 50–58; Paul D. Erickson, *Reagan Speaks: The Making of an American Myth* (New York: New York University Press, 1985); Mary E. Stuckey, *Getting into the Game: The Pre-Presidential Rhetoric of Ronald Reagan* (New York: Praeger, 1989).

5. Lou Cannon, *Reagan* (New York: G. P. Putnam's Sons, 1982), 217.

6. Anne Edwards, *Early Reagan* (New York: William Morrow, 1987), 90–92.

7. Martin J. Medhurst, "Public Address and Significant Scholarship: Four Challenges to the Rhetorical Renaissance," in *Texts in Context: Critical Dialogues on Significant Episodes in American Political Rhetoric*, ed. Michael C. Leff and Fred J. Kauffeld (Davis: Hermagoras, 1989), 33.

8. The term "rhetorical situation" comes from Lloyd F. Bitzer, "The Rhetorical Situation," *Philosophy and Rhetoric* 1 (1968): 1–14.

9. Bernard L. Brock and Robert L. Scott, "An Introduction to Rhetorical Criticism," in *Methods of Rhetorical Criticism: A Twentieth-Century Perspective*, ed. Bernard L. Brock and Robert L. Scott, 2d ed., rev. (Detroit: Wayne State University Press, 1980), 16.

10. Kenneth Burke, *A Rhetoric of Motives* (Berkeley: University of California Press, 1969), 43 (Burke's emphasis).

11. Karlyn Kohrs Campbell, *The Rhetorical Act* (Belmont, CA: Wadsworth, 1982), 7 (Campbell's emphasis).

12. Edwin Black, *Rhetorical Criticism: A Study in Method* (New York: Macmillan, 1965), 15.

13. Kenneth Burke, *Permanence and Change*, 3d ed. (Berkeley: University of California Press, 1984), 5.

14. Carroll C. Arnold, *Criticism of Oral Rhetoric* (Columbus: Charles E. Merril, 1974), 10.

15. Brock and Scott, *Methods of Rhetorical Criticism*, 13.

16. Ibid.

17. For a discussion concerning the ideological biases contained in language see Hans-Georg Gadamer, "Semantics and Hermeneutics," in *Philosophical Hermeneutics*, trans. and ed. David E. Linge (Berkeley: University of California Press, 1976), 82–94; Stuart Hall, "The rediscovery of 'ideology': return of the repressed in media studies," in *Culture, society and the media*, ed. Michael Gurevitch, Tony Bennett, James Curran, and Janet Woollacott (London: Methuen, 1982), 56–90.

18. Black, *Rhetorical Criticism*, 9.

19. Ibid., 6.

20. Kenneth Burke, *The Philosophy of Literary Form*, 3d ed. (Berkeley: University of California Press, 1973), 23.

21. For example see Jane Blankenship, Marlene G. Fine, and Leslie K. Davis, "The 1980 Republican Primary Debates: The Transformation of Actor to Scene," *Quarterly Journal of Speech* 69 (1983): 25–36; Bormann, "A Fantasy Theme Analysis of the Television Coverage of the Hostage Release and the Reagan Inaugural," 133–45.

Chapter One

Finding the Rest of Himself

When analyzing Ronald Reagan's economic discourse, one is tempted to begin with Reagan's election as governor of California. It was, after all, during this period of time when Reagan actually began to formulate economic legislation. However, to have begun our study with Reagan's victory over Edmund (Pat) Brown in the fall of 1966 would have meant ignoring a very significant portion of Reagan's ideological development, especially Reagan's evolving economic ideology. It becomes apparent when looking back over Reagan's rhetoric prior to his election in 1966 that his experiences both in Hollywood as well as his eight-year stint with General Electric greatly influenced his economic views. To bypass these formative years would be analogous to a biographer skipping over his/her subject's childhood years.

Four speeches have been selected for analysis in this chapter: a 1951 speech to the Kiwanis; a 1958 speech delivered to the House Ways and Means Committee; and two different versions of "The Speech"—the right-wing version delivered in 1961 and the moderate version delivered in 1964.[1] Reagan gave thousands of speeches during this time period; unfortunately, very few speech texts remain.[2] However, these four speeches particularly aid us in understanding the formation of Reagan's economic discourse.

"THE BASIC HOLLYWOOD SPEECH"

June 21, 1951

Although comparatively short by Reagan's later standards, this speech provides some revealing details about Reagan's political and economic philosophies. More important, the reader can begin to understand some of the origins of these beliefs. Another important reason for singling out this speech is that it set the tone for Reagan's later speeches that addressed more "political issues." Reagan himself noted that "it's from this plain little acorn of a speech that my political speechmaking grew" (18).[3]

Reagan, whether purposefully or not, misled the reader by referring to this speech and others like it as "my basic Hollywood speech" (18). Reagan did discuss the topic of Hollywood and the filmmaking industry, but this speech was not as much about Hollywood as it was an attack on the federal government's discriminatory tax policies imposed on the wealthy. This speech was delivered to the Kiwanis International Convention held in St. Louis, Missouri, on June 21, 1951.

At the beginning of the speech Reagan argued that the press had portrayed the people of Hollywood as being "crazy," "extravagant," "immoral," and "fickle." Also, he suggested that anyone interested in politics in the Hollywood community was labeled a communist. To correct this misperception and misrepresentation, Reagan attempted to identify the Hollywood community with mainstream America. Reagan stated that actors and actresses "have to go to work in the morning like everyone else, and they come home in the evening like everyone else. They have lawns to mow and they own their own homes"(19). However, Reagan also specified that 70 percent of actors and actresses were high-school graduates or better, 79 percent were married (70 percent to their first husband or wife), 70 percent had children, and 61 percent of them were regular church members. Reagan attempted to create a further cleavage between the two groups by alluding to Hollywood's moral victory in "holding back the flood of propaganda from the other side of the Iron Curtain" (20).

Though Reagan initially attempted to identify the members of Hollywood with "everyone else," he purposefully fell short of his goal. Reagan portrayed the Hollywood community as being more generous, more intellectual, more capitalistic, and possessing greater morality in their daily living. Reagan's tactic of simultaneously identifying and dissociating actors and actresses from mainstream America becomes more obvious in the second half of the speech.

Reagan asserted that the film industry was the most sacred capitalistic industry in America because the Kremlin labeled it as "The worst enemy of the people," and therefore it "must be destroyed." (20). By claiming that the Kremlin aimed to "destroy" the film industry, Reagan implied that his occupation represented the living embodiment of the capitalist ideal.

After attempting to legitimate the film industry based on its devout capitalistic spirit, Reagan made a transition into more political concerns. Reagan began this transition with the following statement:

> Because there is so much apathy about us, certain enemies of ours—enemies of democracy and our way of life—think they have found a leak in the dike. They have found a way to attack some of our American institutions and our American principles by way of the motion picture industry (20).

Note the lack of a clear antecedent in the preceding statement. On first glance one would presume that Reagan was here referring to communists. However, "they" were made explicit in the following statement:

> The Communists have tried to invade our industry and . . . we now have them licked. But there are other more insidious and less obvious inroads being made at our democratic institutions by way of the motion picture industry. For example, no industry has been picked for such discriminatory taxes as have the individuals in the industry of motion pictures (20).

Though Reagan never explicitly stated it, the federal government was the villain, more insidious than even the communist villain whose aim was nothing short of overthrowing capitalism. One word in particular is worthy of singling out in the above quote—the word "picked." Based on his word choice, Reagan was claiming that the members of the film industry had been specifically *targeted* by the federal government. It sought to discriminate against not only the wealthy, but more important, against the single most capitalistic industry in the United States. Thus Reagan's claim of an intragovernmental conspiracy was warranted by the discriminatory rates of taxation imposed on the acting community.

Why, then, was he appealing to mainstream America for their sympathy and support? Reagan answered, "The reason I want to say all of this to you . . . is because we feel that we are operating in the best manner of free enterprise" (21). Capitalism, rather than statistics on church membership, or monetary generosity, was the film industry's redeeming feature. Hollywood, by acting in the best tradition of free enterprise, was absolved of any wrongdoing stemming from the federal government's symbolic punishments (i.e., discriminatory taxes).

Why, then, did Reagan attempt to both identify and differentiate mainstream Americans from the acting community? The answer, in part, is found in Reagan's final persuasive appeal:

> We feel that you people should join us now in the struggle to preserve some of these freedoms, some of these American principles that are being nibbled away through our industry. In short, we would like to invite you to be on our side because we feel that we have been on your side for a very long time (21).

By demonstrating the superior moral quality of the Hollywood community and by emphasizing the capitalistic spirit shared by all Americans, Reagan was in a position to "win them over" to the side of virtue and morality. By joining Hollywood's side, the average citizen was identified not only with the capitalistic spirit, but also with a morally superior agent whom Reagan had cast as the symbolic underdog in this struggle of good and evil. More important, because of the common link with capitalism, Reagan's invitation for the audience to join "his side" effectively created a situation whereby the average citizen could participate in a moral battle. For Reagan's listeners the choice was a simple one: either side with the Hollywood community or stand in opposition to "the American way." Reagan had framed the choice in such a way that the former was the moral and proper thing to do, the latter more insidious than communism.

Two economic themes are central to this speech: the sanctity of the free enterprise system and the federal government's attack on freedom by means of high tax rates. Economic issues were placed within the context of morality, hence Hollywood capitalism, not military might, was holding back the flood of Soviet propaganda and thus saving the world from communist influence. In this context, actors and actresses took on the role of saviors, singlehandedly capable of defeating communists at home. Second, according to Reagan, the federal government was attempting to undermine American capitalism and freedom by singling out the Hollywood community for exceedingly high tax rates. By connecting these two themes, Reagan implied that Hollywood's economic morality warranted lower taxes. This argument was to be the central focus of Reagan's 1958 speech to the House Ways and Means Committee.

"ON TAXATION"

January 27, 1958

Reagan "testified" as an expert on the negative effects of high tax rates on the acting profession before the House Ways and Means Committee on January 27, 1958. Perhaps the most intriguing aspect of this speech was its political foreshadowing. Two instances are particularly revealing: Reagan's proposal that the federal government should undergo an across-the-board spending cut and that by decreasing tax rates on the wealthy the federal government's revenues would actually increase.

Nearly nine years to the day in 1967, Governor Reagan announced that each department of California's state government would undergo a 10 percent across-the-board cut. Just as Reagan based this cut on the grounds that "well run" businesses and corporations periodically made these cuts in 1958, in 1967 Reagan would offer the same grounds for his proposed cutbacks.

The second instance of political foreshadowing was even more noteworthy. One cannot soon forget Reagan's presidential promises in 1981 to balance the federal budget by 1984 despite draconian tax rate cuts and massive increases in defense spending. Reagan's belief that a tax cut would stimulate savings and investment and ultimately government revenues was not a new conviction when he expressed it in the late 1970s. As this speech will make clear, Reagan was preaching "supply-side" theology well before Kemp-Roth was ever dreamed up.

In addition to the two instances of political foreshadowing, this speech reveals Reagan's views on taxation, specifically his proposal for an "equitable" income tax structure and how this view was conditioned by his Hollywood experiences.

Following a brief introduction describing the organizations he was representing, Reagan set the tone immediately: "We believe the schedule of surtaxes in the personal income tax structure is unrealistic, confiscatory, and contrary to the principles of free enterprise" (1981).[4] The problem, however, was not limited to the structure of surtaxes, but also included "high tax rates" and "the capital gains structure." Reagan claimed that the entire tax system was biased unfavorably against those employed in the film industry. In order to make this claim Reagan had to effectively debunk the myth that all Hollywood actors and actresses were financially well-off. No doubt, Reagan faced a rhetorical constraint due to the perceived wealth of actors and actresses. In other words, Reagan could not afford to come across as attempting to get a tax break for the wealthy. To have done so would have been self-defeating. Thus Reagan used several tactics designed to remove this perception.

First, Reagan depicted the acting profession as atypical with regard to work conditions and traditional supply and demand economics: "Our business is peculiar in that way. We have no assembly line operation where so many units must be made to meet a predetermined market demand" (1981). Reagan attempted to gain the sympathy of his auditors by claiming that the film industry had to create its own demand, hence the industry was largely outside of traditional free market economics.

Second, Reagan portrayed the film industry as economically deprived relative to the economic conditions of the country. "It is a strange paradox that in these last several years of prosperity in our Nation, the workers in the motion-picture industry have known unemployment and hardship" (1981).

Third, Reagan portrayed actors', actresses', and tradespeoples' lifestyles as a lonely and anxious existence, contingent solely on the whims of others higher up in the industry: "When a picture is ready to roll, the telephones start ringing and the lucky ones go to work. Then, when the picture is finished, they are again unemployed and back all alone by the telephone'' (1981).

Fourth, the financial payoff was not all it was cracked up to be according to Reagan. While people could ''make a lot of money. . . . it is a feast or famine existence'' (1982). Armed with a plethora of statistics, Reagan reported, ''Last year, of the 11,704 members of the Screen Actors Guild, 85 percent of them grossed less than $7,500, and 65 percent grossed less than $3,000. Now, note that I did not say they averaged this. They grossed less than those two figures'' (1982).

While Reagan's profession suffered economically for reasons inherent to the profession, the federal government had compounded the problem through taxation:

> He gets virtually no return on his output for a long time, and then he scores, lightning strikes, and he jumps into a top earnings bracket and he also jumps into a top tax bracket. Because of this high tax bracket, he cannot really cash in on his windfall in the way that a businessman could (1982).

Reagan asserted that the federal government was discriminating against the acting profession. The businessman could keep his earnings from a profitable venture, but the actor ''by condensing his earnings into 1 year has put himself into a tax bracket often as high as 91 percent'' (1982). Autobiographically, Reagan noted, ''It is not unusual for a performer to go from a 6-figure income to 1 or 2 years of no employment at all'' (1982).

Reagan detailed the effects of high tax rates on the motion-picture industry, yet he also noted the consequences for the federal government:

> The producer, faced with the risk of no return on his investment, seeks to minimize the gamble by featuring one of these artists of proven box office value. The artist in a 75 to 91 percent tax bracket raises his price because the only way he can keep a dime is to make a dollar. Or, if he has done his 1 or 2 pictures, he turns down the picture entirely. The result is unemployment in our industry, and it is also a loss of tax revenue to the Government (1983).

The obvious reason for Reagan's newfound concern for the coffers of the government involved his audience. More clearly, it would have been detrimental to Reagan's purposes to have attacked the federal government in the presence of a Congressional committee holding hearings on taxation.

The solutions that Hollywood had sought to the problem of high taxes had not worked either, according to Reagan. In fact, they made the problem worse. One of these solutions was to film movies in foreign countries. While there were tax advantages to filming overseas, the costs outweighed the benefits: ''It must be stressed that when a picture is made overseas, only 1 or 2 Hollywood artists are employed in that picture. The entire shooting crew, administrative personnel, and supporting cast are from the foreign industry, and for every one of the foreigners so employed there is an American worker unemployed" (1983).

In alluding to other problems of filming movies abroad, Reagan was at his patriotic best. Hollywood, in the best practice of free enterprise, had captured 70 percent of all the playing time of movie theaters around the world. This was of major importance because "in capturing this world market, the people of the world have seen America" (1984). People from all over the world had been able to see "our backgrounds" and to observe "store windows filled with wares." In short, the world had the opportunity to view on a daily basis the fulfillment of the American dream, as told by Hollywood. But Reagan did not stop here as he proceeded to translate American media imperialism into basic economic terms: "This is, of course, selling America at its best, and we know how much money our Government is spending in an effort to sell America throughout the world. Here is probably the greatest good-will ambassador we have, and it is provided free as far as the Government is concerned" (1984). In public finance terms, the federal government was a "free rider," reaping both the pecuniary and nonpecuniary benefits of Hollywood's success abroad without incurring any monetary costs. Also, American movies sold American products: "I do not think anyone could challenge the statement that the American motion picture has probably been the greatest salesman on the world market for American goods and material of all types" (1984).

Proof of Hollywood's sales ability was reinforced by the attempted communist takeover of the film industry. The Kremlin's motivation for capturing the motion picture industry was due to Hollywood being "the most potent weapon of decadent capitalism" (1985). In other words, due to Hollywood's capitalistic spirit and its promotion of the American way of life and of American products, the members of the film industry deserved a tax break. Furthermore, the federal government was shooting its own foot because more and more movies were being made in foreign countries, thus potential tax revenues were being forfeited. Reagan reminded his auditors, though, that communism did not force Hollywood abroad; "this has been done by our own income tax structure" (1985). Reagan was careful not to specifically blame the government for the Hollywood exodus; rather, the blame was on the income tax structure.

Reagan moved to strengthen his argument in the next section of his speech by moving away from the adverse effects of taxation on Hollywood to the negative effects of taxation on the entire country. Through this topical expansion, Reagan transformed himself from Hollywood actor to national politician. "We believe the tax problems besetting us are shared by our fellow citizens in all lines of endeavor, varying only in the manner in which the taxes adversely affect them and curb their initiative" (1985). In deploring the tax system, Reagan again chose his words carefully:

> We have decided that probably one of the things wrong with this topheavy tax structure has resulted from the attempt on the part of various industries and groups to create some loophole or some protective shelter for themselves. We feel that the basic evil is in the overall structure itself, particularly the progressive rates of surtax; and so we have dedicated ourselves to doing what we can to see if this cannot be altered (1985).

Government was not to blame for the topheavy tax structure; industries and groups were. Reagan clearly blamed the federal government for the imposition of high tax rates on the wealthy in his speech to the Kiwanis. However, given his audience, Reagan modified his accusations so as not to alienate his auditors.

Paradoxically, in the next section of the speech, Reagan implied that a federal conspiracy was underway. The visible manifestation of such a conspiracy was in the taxes imposed on the middle class. Reagan stated that "we cannot help but recognize that the steepest rate of increase in the surtax, from 22 to 50 percent, occurs right through the low and middle income brackets. And we remember that Karl Marx said, and Lenin echoed, that the way to impose socialism on the people would be to first tax the middle class out of existence" (1985). Note the omission of the word "communism." Clearly, Marx and Lenin were associated with communism. But to have implied that the federal government was perpetuating a communist conspiracy directly to the House Ways and Means Committee would have been antithetical to Reagan's purposes. Implicitly, though, Reagan associated the federal government's system of taxation, and therefore the federal government itself, with a communist conspiracy.

Reagan's word choice in this section of the speech is also noteworthy. He stated, "When the individual is penalized a half of [*sic*] three-fourths or nine-tenths of the dollar he earns by his own effort and ability, it is imperative that some relationship exist between the individual's sacrifice and the Government's fiscal needs" (1985). Reagan's use of the word "penalized" is of particular interest. To be penalized one typically must do something in opposition to a perceived authority. Taxes, Reagan implied, were a direct penalty for work. Viewed thus, taxes were not so much a means for government's effective functioning, but a penalty serving as a disinclination towards productive effort. This view of taxation holds considerable importance for later years, particularly in Reagan's first year as president.

Before offering his solutions to the problem, Reagan inserted one last factual piece of evidence to support his cause: "The Government's entire income from personal surtax is around $4 billion. Above the 34 percent bracket it is less than $2 billion. And when it gets above 65 percent, it drops to less than a quarter of a billion dollars" (1986). Reagan's argument had changed from one concerned with productivity to one of dollars and cents. He implied that because the federal government was making such a relatively small amount of money from the wealthy, they should, at minimum, cut back or revoke high surtaxes.

Following his thorough analysis of the problem, Reagan offered his solution. Reagan's "theory of taxation" was derived directly from the Old and New Testaments of the Bible. Tithing, where one gives 10 percent of his/her income to the church, was Reagan's simple answer to a complex problem. Instead of a progressive tax, Reagan advocated a proportional income tax based on one's ability to pay. In explaining tithing to his audience Reagan declared "that if the Lord prospers you 10 times as much, you are to give ten times as much" (1986). Reagan's theory of taxation is significant for two reasons. First, it is difficult to refute. To effectively argue with Reagan, one would have to refute the Scriptures, hence God. Second, if proportional taxation had its legitimacy in God, from where, then, did a progressive income tax derive its legitimacy? Dialectically considered, the progressive income tax would be of a satanic nature. In this sense, income taxation was reduced to an ultimate good and an ultimate evil. Proportional income taxing was morally warranted; progressive income taxing was morally wrong.

In a tactic to demonstrate concern for those lower on the socioeconomic scale, and thus divorcing himself and his profession from being perceived as self-interested, Reagan discussed the merits of several bills in Congress, the Sadlak-Herlong bills, which the film industry supported. According to Reagan, these bills would benefit the lower- and middle-classes more than the upper-income class. One of the concerns about these bills, though, was the loss of tax revenues to the federal government caused by lower tax rates. However, Reagan claimed that no revenues would be lost; in fact revenues would be increased.

> It is our belief that no revenue will be lost. This belief, incidentally, is supported by most of the leading economists of our Nation. The normal growth of our economy plus the stimulant to business and investment will actually result in the Government's share of the national income increasing rather than decreasing (1986).

This statement could well have been uttered in 1981 when Reagan was actively campaigning for implementation of supply-side tax cuts. Garry Wills has argued that Reagan became a convert to supply-side only in the late 1970s under the influence of Jack Kemp.[5] However, based on Reagan's beliefs expressed in this speech, Reagan was not a convert to supply-side in the late 1970s; rather, he was one of its spokespersons as early as 1958.

Big business' influence on Reagan was also evident: "Periodically, well-run corporations and business firms have to check this trend. They do it by ordering an across-the-board percentage cut in the cost of operation" (1987). This also proved to be a prophetic statement, for it was in Reagan's first budget in 1967 that he ordered a 10 percent across-the-board reduction in each department of California government.

Returning to the acting profession, Reagan offered one last solution to the current tax system, that of tax averaging. Such a proposal, according to Reagan, would go a long way in alleviating the tax burden of the "lucky" actor or actress who struck it rich in one year and fell on hard times the next. "A person earning $10,000 per year for 10 years pays in that time a tax of about $27,000. If he earns the same amount, $100,000, in 1 year and should not earn anything in the other 9 years, he pays $67,000 tax" (1987).

Not only was tax averaging warranted numerically, but Reagan also relied on the expert testimony of one J. S. Seidman, general chairman of the American Institute of Accountants. Reagan, paraphrasing Seidman, claimed that "the individual with fluctuating income is likely to be a person of enterprise and of creative or artistic ability whose contributions to the national welfare are of great value and who should be encouraged, not pelalized [sic]" (1987–1988). Reagan's paraphrasing of Seidman functioned to further legitimate the acting profession while simultaneously delegitimating the tax system.

Reagan concluded this speech on a "good vs. evil" theme that again invoked the conspiratorial sentiment.

> Like all our fellow citizens, we are . . . in support of our system based on individual freedom and liberty, the sacredness of the individual if you please, as against a philosophy of statism and collectivism. Yet at the same time that we have pledged ourselves to this all-out fight, it seems ironic that we are subject here to a tax with many features that can only be defended by endorsing the principles of the Socialism we are sworn to oppose (1988).

Reagan's position was that the government had contradicted itself by going against the sacredness of the individual in favor of socialism. And if socialism caught on, communism would inevitably follow.

Reagan's persuasive appeal consisted largely of framing matters of taxation within an ideological battle. By equating the tax system with socialism and communism, Reagan attempted to garner support for his tax proposals not only on their economic merits, but also on their ideological merits. With the onset of the cold war, anything merely resembling communism was viewed suspiciously. By framing matters of taxation within an ideological context, capitalism vs. socialism, Reagan capitalized on the "good vs. evil" theme of cold war rhetoric.

After concluding his speech, Reagan was asked to clarify and explain the details of some of his proposals. Most of the questions provided Reagan with the opportunity to merely reiterate his proposals. However, a question concerning the fairness of a tax break for the wealthy directly addressed Reagan's notion of the American dream.

> I think there is a thing called the American dream, and even the man who knows that he has probably reached, somewhere later in his life, his economic level, and that the American dream is not going to happen for him, that he is not going to find a pot of gold at the end of the rainbow, transfers that dream to his children. He saves his money to send his son to school to learn a profession so that he can do better. [T]he American dream is that anyone in our country, regardless of his start, can get rich. I think that the average American objects to a ceiling that literally says to him, "Stop dreaming, because neither you nor your children can ever get rich" (1990).

Implicitly, Reagan claimed that the wealthy were not selfish, but that they were merely fulfilling a dream unique to Americans. The wealthy members of Hollywood were not simply self-interested capitalists out to make a buck; rather, they were fulfilling their destiny as Americans. This fulfillment was possible only in America. And by making the dream come true, the wealthy citizen was a symbol of all that America stood for. In this context, the wealthy, by fulfilling their destiny as Americans, were heroes worthy of emulation.

Measuring effect is an entirely subjective practice, yet the effect of Reagan's speech was extremely favorable. Reagan's auditors made such comments as, "Mr. Reagan, I want to compliment your industry for having selected you as its spokesman. You have been a very fine witness," and "Mr. Reagan, you have convinced me of one thing which I have long suspected, and that is that you are engaged in a very hazardous profession," and "Mr. Reagan, you have given very interesting and effective testimony in behalf of the lowering of the ceiling on personal income tax. You have put your story across in great shape." Perhaps most revealing of all were the comments made by Representatives Byrnes and Mason. Byrnes noted, "May I make a comment that I think Mr. Reagan ought to run for Congress because we need more of his philosophy and persuasiveness here in Congress." Mason added, "Particularly the persuasiveness" (1988, 1991, 1993). Little did Mason realize that Reagan would later take such sentiments to heart.

"ENCROACHING CONTROL"

March 30, 1961

"Encroaching Control" delivered by Reagan to the Phoenix Chamber of Commerce on March 30, 1961, represented the right-wing version of "The Speech." Describing this version, Kurt W. Ritter noted, "The right wing version of 'The Speech' differed from the moderate version by explicitly citing Communism as an exterior enemy to whose philosophy our nation might unwittingly succumb through 'voluntary slavery' to a 'controlled economy' and a 'proliferation of bureaucratic agencies.' "[6]

Reagan's speeches from this period until his election as governor contained a great deal of repetition. Lou Cannon noted five characteristics of "The Speech": economic individualism; an admiration and imitation of Franklin D. Roosevelt; an invocation of American democratic ideals; a "bundle" of statistics; and a strong anti-communist theme.[7] This genre of speeches may have contained a remarkable degree of topical similarity, yet Reagan's rhetorical strategies and tactics often varied from speech to speech. In addition to the theme of communist domination, specific economic events and signs provided Reagan with "tangible proof" of the United States' gradual advance towards socialism. More significantly, Reagan's economic ideology offered a solution to the threat of communism. Thus, economic issues were central to "The Speech."

Reagan established the tenor for the rest of the speech by stating, "The inescapable truth is that we are at war, and we are losing that war simply because we don't, or won't realize that we are in it" (23).[8] Since there was little, if any, perceived exigence by his auditors, Reagan attempted to create an artificial exigence by using the metaphor of war.[9] Reagan, however, did not explicitly identify who the country was at war with. From the context of the statement, one could plausibly conclude that the war was being waged against communism of the Soviet variety. However, implicit in Reagan's war metaphor was the notion that the country was at war with itself. This war was an ideological one in which those of the "liberal persuasion" were siding with evil (Soviet Union). Republicans, on the other hand, held the truth about the conspiracy and thus assumed the role of virtue in this ideological war.

For Reagan, the communist invasion of the United States was inextricably linked to economic issues and events. It was through economic recession that communism would gain entry and ultimately acceptance in the United States. Reagan gave support to this view by employing a quote from Nikolay Bulganin: "The American working man is too well fed; we cannot appeal to him, but when through inflation America has priced herself out of the world market and unemployment follows—then we will settle our debt with the United States' " (24). According to

Reagan, economic prosperity was at the heart of a strong national defense. Implicit in the quote was Reagan's view that Americans were ideologically unsettled. That is, they were willing to compromise their democracy in times of economic hardship. Reagan's view of "the people" in 1961 stood in stark contrast to Reagan's view of "the people" during his gubernatorial and presidential years.

Proof of the communist conspiracy was manifested in what Reagan termed "foot in the door" legislation perfected by those of the "liberal persuasion." The first policy Reagan indicted was government-paid medicine. A move toward socialized medicine existed in two different areas: Veteran Administration hospitals and government-paid medical and hospital care for those of Social Security age, known as the Forand Bill.

A second area illustrative of the federal government's "foot in the door" legislation was Social Security. According to Reagan, the Social Security system was not so much an insurance program as it was an inefficient welfare program. Not only was the system a deception, but it ran a huge deficit and was counter to Reagan's view of free-market capitalism: "And what of our sons—the young man joining the work force in the next few years? . . . If he would have his Social Security tax to invest in private insurance, it would provide for almost double the benefits provided by Social Security" (28). The individual was a superior economic decisionmaker than the federal government, according to Reagan.

A third illustration of "foot in the door" legislation was the National Education Act of 1958. Reagan offered his audience statistics to support the claim that local governments had been adequately handling the influx of students. With federal aid to education, Reagan envisioned a grim scenario for parents and their children whereby federal aid would be the first step in a federal school system with teachers and subjects removed from parental control. Reagan created the illusion that in the near future parents would no longer have control of raising their sons and daughters, that the federal government would play the role of parent or guardian. Parenting would become obsolete, with the federal government assuming the role of parent as well as turning out educational clones. Explicitly, then, federal aid amounted to federal control.

A fourth proof of the federal government's "foot in the door legislation" involved a more central economic issue, that of government subsidization of the agricultural industry, or what Reagan termed the "farm mess." Reagan framed the problem as having a simple and obvious solution:

> All of the "farm mess" is concerned with the 20 percent of agriculture coming under government regulation and subsidy. Eighty percent of our agricultural

> economy is out in the free market of supply and demand. It would seem that the answer to the "farm mess" would be to free the other 20 percent of governmental regimentation (30–31).

Reagan, by framing the problem in this manner, was able to draw the only common-sense solution available: freeing the other 20 percent of the farm economy.

Not only did the federal government desire to nationalize the farm industry, but they had made inroads into nationalizing other industries, owning more than 19,000 enterprises. These industries were losing billions of dollars and they were also competing unfairly against the nation's own citizens, claimed Reagan. By operating tax-free, dividend-free, and rent-free, the federal government had great advantages over private industries, yet the nationalized industries continued to lose money.

In relating some of the possible solutions to the problem, Reagan's choice of metaphor was revealing: "Don't forget to . . . say 'well done' to your Representative when he has acquitted himself well on the firing line" (32). The "firing line" metaphor implied a life and death struggle of good vs. evil. The federal government collectively was the executor, forcing compliance, with the ever-present threat of termination. Only by revealing the ongoing conspiracy would representatives be acquitted from the symbolic death of having complied with the enemy.

As mentioned in the previous analysis, the composition of Reagan's audience influenced Reagan's rhetoric on taxation. Basically, Reagan could afford some degree of extremism before a Republican audience. Reagan's use of hyperbole on matters of taxation aptly illustrated this point: "We have received this progressive tax directly from Karl Marx who designed it as the prime essential of a socialist state" (33). Reagan implied that Marx himself had instituted the 16th amendment to the Constitution. Furthermore, because the steepest rates of surtax occurred through the middle class—the people Marx said should be taxed out of existence—Reagan added more "proof" of the communist conspiracy. Reagan's rhetoric on the progressive income tax had shifted from his 1958 speech to the House Ways and Means Committee. In that address Reagan claimed that "various industries" and "groups" were to blame for the "topheavy" or progressive income tax structure. In "Encroaching Control," however, the federal government was to blame for the progressive income tax. Reagan's two very different audiences may help account for his disparate statements on who was to blame for progressive tax rates.

Reagan's solution to the progressive income tax, as it was in his 1958 speech, was a tax of proportionality. The justification for such a tax resided both in the notion of tithing and "that those better able to pay should remove some of the burden from those least able to pay" (33). Notice that Reagan claimed the federal government would not be removing the burden of taxation; those better able to pay would. In so doing, the middle and upper classes would become the saviors of the lower class. In actuality, the federal government would be removing the burden, not the middle and upper classes.

Once again, Reagan framed the discussion on taxation as a moral issue. Explicitly, the progressive income tax was evil. According to the Ultimate Authority, the federal government's take should be no more than the morally justified amount of 10 percent. To take any more would be akin to stealing, itself an immoral act.

Not only did the progressive income tax subvert capitalism, according to Reagan, but so too did inflation, in particular "deliberate" inflationary policies planned by the federal government. Reagan indicted the federal government for purposefully and deliberately advocating inflationary policies that, according to Lenin, would "destroy Capitalism." While Reagan claimed that the citizenry was earning twice as much, the progressive tax was based on dollars earned and not the value of the dollar. Thus, one would have to earn more than double one's 1940 wages to break even. Reagan noted that "by 1975, the $5,000-a-year man will have to earn $33,000 and the $10,000-a-year man will have to earn $84,000 just to maintain their 1940 standard of living" (35). Through numeric illustrations, Reagan attempted to create an exigency that spelled the doom of capitalism and the symbolic end of the nation.

Discussing inflation, Reagan again made use of the metaphor of war: "*Here is the main battleground! We must reduce the government's supply of money and deny it the right to borrow* (Reagan's emphasis, 35). There existed other important battles to be won, but the main battleground, and thus where the war would eventually be won or lost, concerned monetary policy. There existed two symbolic villains in this all-important battle: the federal government and the Federal Reserve Board. Only by suppressing the uncontrolled power of these two villains could the conspiracy be subverted.

Not only had inflation, coupled with the progressive income tax structure, undermined capitalism, but the federal deficit was Reagan's final piece of incriminating evidence. Alluding to the dangers of deficit spending, Reagan stated that "there can be little security any place in the free world if there isn't fiscal stability in the United States" (36–37). Reagan's notion of a strong national defense had its roots only partially in military apparati. Because matters of national defense were contingent on economic prosperity or the lack thereof, any issue other than economic-related issues assumed a subsidiary role in Reagan's ideological agenda.

Reagan stated that victory was the only way to end the war. The audience was not told to which war he was referring, either the war against communism or the war against the federal government. Regardless, the nation, according to Reagan, had only ten years to determine whether the world would be entirely free or entirely enslaved.[10] For Reagan, there was no in between, no compromises could be made with the enemy; to compromise with the enemy was to legitimatize the enemy.

"Encroaching Control" offers a glimpse of Reagan the extremist, and it was this extremist label that he fought until he was elected president. Perhaps we should answer a fundamental question: what rhetorical elements in Reagan's discourse illicited the extremist label? There are two such elements: his claim of a federal government–led communist conspiracy and the ensuing vision of the end of the world. Aside from his own extreme discourse, Reagan was also a victim of guilt by association. Specifically, such infamous right-wingers as Robert Welch, founder of the John Birch Society, espoused the same communist conspiracy and apocalyptic visions as did Reagan.[11] Additionally, Reagan's association with another designated extremist, Barry Goldwater, did little to deter the extremist tag. After all, it was none other than Ronald Reagan who gave the most effective address in support of Goldwater's 1964 presidential bid, the focus of the next analysis.

"A TIME FOR CHOOSING"

October 27, 1964

Perhaps Reagan's most famous speech is "A Time for Choosing," the moderate version of "The Speech," given to a national television audience in support of Barry Goldwater's 1964 presidential campaign on October 27, 1964. This speech was the only positive note in a thoroughly humiliating defeat for the Republican party, particularly its conservative faction. The immediate reaction to the speech was extremely favorable as millions of dollars were raised for the Republican party. Not only did this speech provide a financial windfall for the Republican party, but it established Reagan as the heir apparent to Barry Goldwater, thus launching his own political career. Reagan confirmed that this speech and the reaction it received "soon changed my entire life."[12]

This speech is also significant because of the audience Reagan was addressing. Due to the national television audience, and thus the heterogeneity of his auditors, Reagan took a much more moderate rhetorical stance relative to other addresses delivered to predominantly Republican audiences. Also, given the fact that Goldwater had been targeted as an extremist during the campaign, Reagan could ill afford to come across as a "grenade-chucking" right-wing extremist and thus cause further damage to Goldwater's already beleaguered presidential campaign.

In this speech, what was not said was more instructive than what was said, specifically the omission of the communist conspiracy being advanced by the liberals in the federal government. Communism and its evils did occupy a major part in this speech, but the threat of a communist takeover was portrayed largely as an external threat rather than an internal one.

As was "Encroaching Control," "A Time for Choosing" was not solely an economic address. Yet, economic events and issues unified the various themes running throughout the speech. The importance of economic issues was manifested immediately following Reagan's abrupt introduction: "The line has been used, 'We've never had it so good!' But I have an uncomfortable feeling that this prosperity isn't something upon which we can base our hopes for the future" (561).[13]

According to Reagan, the rosy economic scenario was nothing but an aberration, a peak in a typical business cycle soon to be followed by economic hardship. Reagan's "uncomfortable feeling" was legitimized relative to several economic statistics: the high tax burden, the unbalanced budget, the expanding debt limit that permitted increased government spending, foreign claims on the United States' supply of gold, and the diminished value of the dollar. Of note in Reagan's refutation of a prosperous economy were the words he used to refer to the federal government. Instead of naming the federal government, Reagan used the metaphor of the "tax collector" as his referent. Such a referent has fairly obvious religious connotations, typically portraying the tax collector as the godless Pharisee, the villain of the citizens of the state.

One of Reagan's tactics in this speech involved the creation of a dichotomy between the country's Founding Fathers and the federal government. That is, Reagan attempted to utilize the typical plot line of "good vs. evil." Reagan stated, "This is the issue of this election, whether we believe in our capacity for self-government or whether we abandon the American Revolution" (562). The nation's Founding Fathers stood for capitalism and the inherent morality of self-determination, while the federal government was in direct opposition to the freedoms won during the American Revolution, professed Reagan.

In an attempt to further delineate virtue from vice, Reagan again employed metaphors associated with religion: "I would like to suggest that there is no such thing as a left or right. There is only up or down . . . and, . . . those who would trade our freedom for security have embarked on this downward course" (562). Implied by this statement was that liberally backed fiscal programs, motivated by security, would lead the citizenry figuratively to Hell. Meanwhile, capitalism, motivated by freedom, would lead the citizenry upward to a Heaven-like utopia. Furthermore, freedom conditioned security and not vice versa.

For Reagan, controlling the economy was not evil in itself. The evil of a controlled economy involved the "force and coercion to achieve its purposes" and "controlling people" (563). This, he emphasized, was not his opinion, it was the view espoused by the Founding Fathers. Additionally, Reagan, paraphrasing the Founding Fathers, claimed that "government does nothing as well or as economically as the private sector of the economy" (563). Proof of these claims made by the Founding Fathers was warranted by the federal government's interference with the agricultural economy. Reagan's statistics had changed in three years, but his underlying premise, that government interference in agriculture bred inefficiency and waste, had not. The ultimate proof of the government's failings in the farm economy resided in the basic economic theory of supply and demand: "Now the price of bread goes up; the price of wheat to the farmer goes down" (564). The farm economy, thanks to the federal government's intervention, defied the economic logic of supply and demand.

Further proof that the federal government did not know basic economic theory was evidenced by the government's handling of unemployment: "For three decades we have sought to solve the problems of unemployment through government planning, and the more the plans fail, the more the planners plan" (564). Not only had the planners been unable to solve the problem, but according to Reagan's logic planning itself was the cause of unemployment. The obvious solution to the problem would be to get rid of the planners since they were merely exacerbating the unemployment problem.

For Reagan, the federal government's lack of business sense was clearly illustrated by the $298 billion deficit run by Social Security. The answer to the problem involved a combination of using business sense and introducing voluntary features for those people who had already made provisions for their nonearning years.

Interestingly, Reagan coupled Social Security with the issue of inflation primarily because Barry Goldwater had "been getting kicked all over the place on the issue."[14] Reagan asked, "Was Barry Goldwater so irresponsible when he suggested that our government give up its program of deliberate planned inflation so that when you do get your Social Security pension, a dollar will buy a dollar's worth, and not 45 cents worth?" (566). Attempting to appeal to those of Social Security age, Reagan framed Social Security in terms of inflation. Implied was the notion that whatever reforms Goldwater would make in the Social Security system, nothing could be worse than the federal government's planned inflation, which literally robbed the elderly of their hard-earned pensions. Thus Reagan attempted to turn a negative into a positive by framing the issue of Social Security within the larger issue of government-planned inflationary policies.

The conspiracy theme emerged near the end of Reagan's speech, though in a muted form. Reagan claimed that the United States was "creating bureaucracy, if not socialism, all over the world" (567). Instructive is Reagan's connection between bureaucracy and socialism. According to Reagan, the former inevitably created the latter. Proof of conspiracy was rampant: "We set out to help 19 countries. We are helping 107. We spent $146 billion. . . . 52 nations have bought $7 billion of our gold, and all 52 are receiving foreign aid from us" (567). The federal government was not just spending huge sums of money abroad, but the money was being put to little if any productive use. No longer did Reagan explicitly claim that socialism was being practiced at home; rather, the United States was exporting socialism abroad. Thus, Reagan attempted to blunt his extremism by deemphasizing the socialist conspiracy at home in favor of claiming that the United States' foreign policy had precipitated socialism abroad.

Perhaps the most revealing evidence of the prime importance Reagan placed on economics was the clustering of three key terms near the conclusion of "A Time for Choosing": "He [Khrushchev] has told them [Soviets] that we are retreating under the pressure of the cold war and some day . . . our surrender will be voluntary because by that time we will have weakened from within spiritually, morally and economically" (570).[15] For Reagan, capitalism took on religious dimensions. Statistics were not the final judgement of a given economic issue. Any economic event or theory that purported to grant the federal government more power over the individual was not merely faulty for statistical reasons. It was faulty because of the inherent immorality of denying the individual freedom in his/her daily economic endeavors. Additionally, an economic event or theory that granted the individual autonomy in making economic decisions was warranted purely on moral and spiritual grounds, statistical information aside. By framing events in this manner, Reagan had largely "bulletproofed" his economic ideology. To attack Reagan's views on free market capitalism was an attack on God and the Founding Fathers.

Thematically, "A Time for Choosing" is very similar to "Encroaching Control." Economic issues such as agriculture, Social Security, unemployment, inflation, taxation, the federal deficit, and the growth of the federal government were mentioned throughout both speeches. However, the causes for these economic problems changed radically. Instead of the federal government purposefully staging a socialist conspiracy, the federal government had caused these problems out of sheer stupidity. Additionally, when Reagan did allude to a conspiracy in "A Time for Choosing" it was being asserted by someone else (that is, Nikita Khrushchev, Nikolay Bulganin). Such a strategy served to underscore Reagan's moderate political views.

CONCLUSION

Collectively, these four speeches offer a fairly comprehensive account of Reagan's economic philosophy developed between 1951 and 1966. Of particular interest is the origination of Reagan's economic ideology. Based on the four speeches analyzed, his economic views on taxation were greatly influenced by his experiences in the acting profession. Cannon confirms that Reagan's interest in the tax laws during his Hollywood years grew concomitantly with his increasing income.[16]

Reagan's audience greatly influenced the content and strategies contained in his discourse. In his 1951 speech to the Kiwanis, Reagan attempted to garner support and empathy for the acting profession by indicting the federal government of tax discrimination. In 1958, Reagan advocated new tax laws, while his attacks on the federal government were muted for his Congressional audience. In fact, Reagan portrayed the federal government in a neutral role. It was no longer the villain conspiring to overthrow capitalism; rather, Reagan even offered his advice as to how the federal government could generate greater tax revenues. "Encroaching Control" represents the right-wing version of "The Speech." Given to a partisan Republican gathering, Reagan's extremist economic rhetoric charged the federal government with purposefully instigating a conspiracy that would spell the end of capitalism. Last, "A Time for Choosing" represented the moderate version of "The Speech." While economics was central to this speech, the federal government's purposeful conspiracy had been edited for obvious political purposes.

We have noted seven fairly recurrent tactics, strategies, and lines of reasoning that pervaded Reagan's economic rhetoric: (1) the use of the Judeo-Christian tradition to ground many of his economic beliefs; (2) the use of war metaphors in order to elicit an exigence in the economic situation; (3) equating the federal government's fiscal and tax policies to a socialist conspiracy; (4) blame placed on liberals for the nation's economic maladies; (5) apocalyptic visions reinforcing the economic exigence; (6) framing potentially complex economic problems such that there existed only one common-sense answer; (7) and framing economic issues in dialectical pairs so as to create a clear distinction between good and evil.

On a macro level, one of the most distinct features of Reagan's economic rhetoric was its "anti-ness." That is, Reagan's economic ideology was transmitted by a negative rhetoric. With the exception of portions of his 1958 speech, in which he was lobbying for specific legislation, Reagan's economic ideology was only vaguely discernible by what it was not. Specifically, it was not pro-government regulation, pro-progressive taxation, pro-government intervention, or pro-socialism.

Reagan's listeners were largely forced to draw inferences about his economic beliefs through a simple equation: whatever Reagan was opposed to, he was in favor of the opposite. Clearly this equation was extremely tenuous. That is, one of the problems encountered by Reagan's anti-economic rhetoric is one of identity. One can make an unambiguous determination of what, economically speaking, Ronald Reagan opposed. The opposite, however, does not hold true. Aside from a few isolated instances (i.e., proportional taxation), one can only conjecture at this point as to what Reagan really advocated. We can say confidently that Reagan supported a proportional income tax structure and lower rates of surtax on middle- and upper-income classes. We cannot, however, conclude with equanimity that Reagan favored less government spending. We can only say for certain that Reagan favored less government spending on certain programs, not all of them. We cannot even conclude with certainty that Reagan favored free-market economic principles to the exclusion of all others. For an entirely "free" market would be devoid of any government interference whatsoever. Thus the ideological picture one gets of Reagan during this period is at best hazy and at worst distorted.

NOTES

1. "The Speech" was the standard oration Reagan developed during his employment with General Electric. While the content of the speech was very similar, Reagan's strategies and tactics across speeches were not. For a discussion noting the distinction between the versions see Kurt W. Ritter, "Ronald Reagan and 'The Speech': The Rhetoric of Public Relations Politics," *Western Speech* 32 (1968): 50–58.

2. Excluding his gubernatorial campaign speeches during 1966, Stuckey lists 24 extant speeches from the period 1951–1965 (This number does not include brief statements and interviews). See Mary E. Stuckey, *Getting into the Game: The Pre-Presidential Rhetoric of Ronald Reagan* (New York: Praeger, 1989), 143–45.

3. All references to this speech are from Ronald Reagan, *Speaking My Mind* (New York: Simon & Schuster, 1989), 18–21.

4. All references to this speech are from Congress, House of Representatives, Committee on Ways and Means, *General Revenue Revision*, 85th Cong., 2d sess., January 27, 1958, 1980–93.

5. Garry Wills, *Reagan's America: Innocents At Home* (Garden City, NY: Doubleday, 1987), 365.

6. Ritter, "Ronald Reagan and 'The Speech,' " 54–55.

7. Lou Cannon, *Reagan* (New York: G. P. Putnam's Sons, 1982), 70.

8. All references from this speech are from "Encroaching Control," in *A Time for Choosing: The Speeches of Ronald Reagan, 1961–1982*, ed. Alfred A. Balitzer (Chicago: Regnery Gateway, 1983), 21–38.

9. For a discussion concerning the creation of artificial exigences see Carole

Blair, "From 'All the President's Men' to Every Man for Himself: The Strategies of Post-Watergate Apologia," *Central States Speech Journal* 35 (1984): 250–60.

10. For the definitive treatment of the Radical Right's use of apocalyptic visions see Richard Hoftstadter, *The Paranoid Style in American Politics and Other Essays*, Phoenix ed. (Chicago: University of Chicago Press, 1979).

11. Robert Welch, *The Blue Book of the John Birch Society* (Copyright by the author, 1961).

12. Reagan, *Speaking My Mind*, 24.

13. All references to this speech are from Anne Edwards, *Early Reagan* (New York: William Morrow, 1987), 561–70.

14. Reagan, *Speaking My Mind*, 24.

15. For a description of a cluster analysis see Carole A. Berthold, "Kenneth Burke's Cluster-Agon Method: Its Development and an Application," *Central States Speech Journal* 27 (1976): 302–9.

16. Cannon, *Reagan*, 96.

Chapter Two

The Creative Society: Part One

Consistent with the conservative national trend, Ronald Reagan defeated Edmund (Pat) Brown in the Fall of 1966 by nearly a million votes.[1] Unfortunately for Reagan, this was to be his last major political victory for quite some time.

Nineteen sixty-seven was a difficult year for the new governor, especially relative to matters of fiscal and tax policy. Upon entering office, Reagan found the state's finances in desperate straits as California's deficit for fiscal year 1966–67 exceeded $400 million. In addition to the deficit, several other economic-related issues plagued Reagan throughout his first year: (1) the state's first $5 billion budget; (2) a Reagan-sponsored $1 billion tax hike; (3) Reagan's call for tuition at both the state's college and university systems; (4) Reagan's plan to lay off 3,700 workers in the Department of Mental Hygiene; (5) Reagan's proposed 10 percent across-the-board cuts in each department of state government; (6) the mounting deficit run by the state's Medi-Cal program; (7) and the underfunding of the State Water Project.

In all fairness to Reagan, several of these problems he encountered in 1967 were the legacy of Pat Brown. Reagan, however, frequently compounded his inherited problems by displaying his ineptitude as a politician. Specifically, his proposed economies affecting higher education and the Department of Mental Hygiene (part of his 10 percent cuts) met with strong opposition from both California's legislature and the press.

Coupled with the inherited and self-inflicted economic damage he encountered in 1967, Reagan also faced a "new" rhetorical constraint. Up until his term as governor officially began, Reagan was the consummate ideologue, preaching the virtues of less government, lower taxes, less government spending, and more freedom for the individual. In other words, Reagan's rhetoric was not constrained or conditioned by the "give and take" required by effective governance. Reagan's role prior to 1967 was one of outspoken critic, not pragmatic politician. This all changed shortly following Reagan's election as governor. No longer could Reagan, in good judgment, continue to appeal to only one constituency (Republicans); rather, given his presidential aspirations, Reagan had to "tone down" his rhetoric, making it more palatable to a heterogeneous constituency. This politically advantageous rhetoric, however, did not altogether silence Reagan's ideological or right-wing rhetoric. In fact, as we will illustrate, Reagan's two personae (the pragmatic politician and the ideologue) were often evident within the same speech, giving rise to oftentimes contradictory rhetorics.[2]

Thus, California's sorry fiscal condition, his unpopular attempts at economies, and his new role as governor combined to make 1967 a truly unforgettable year for Ronald Reagan.

"PUTTING OUR FISCAL HOUSE IN ORDER"

January 5, 1967

Reagan inaugurated his administration with a speech that has since become known simply as the "Creative Society."[3] This title was to serve as the theme of Reagan's eight years as governor.[4]

Reagan defined his new role explicitly in his *Inaugural Message*: "We are of the people, chosen by them to see that no permanent structure of government ever encroaches on freedom or assumes a power beyond that freely granted by the people. We stand between the taxpayer and the taxspender" (2).[5] Not only did Reagan identify himself as being "of the people," but, more significantly, Reagan defined his new role relative to taxation, as being a protector of the taxpaying citizen, a heroic defender of sorts.

Reagan also defined the collective role of the citizenry. In fact, Reagan repeatedly stressed the roles that the citizens of California must assume if the state was to prosper:

> Government is the people's business. . . . It demands much of those chosen to govern, but also from those who did the choosing. . . . Government will lead, of course, but the answers must come from all of you. . . . You will have all the information you need to make the decisions which must be made. This is not just a problem for the administration; it is a problem for all of us to solve together (2, 3, 10).

The repetition of Reagan's role definition for the people is cause for suspicion. By repeatedly emphasizing the responsibility of the citizens, Reagan concomitantly de-emphasized his own responsibilities; government's "proper" role was only to lead, the people were to provide the answers. Thus the man who was to become known as the "Teflon president" for his ability to extricate himself from "sticky" situations earlier attempted to at least partially remove himself from responsibility for California's future.

Economic issues occupied a central position in this speech. Specifically, Reagan addressed welfare, taxation, unemployment, and the fiscal situation inherited from Pat Brown. The last of these economic concerns, fiscal responsibility, was to occupy a central place in Reagan's discourse not only in this speech, but throughout much of 1967.

Trying to avoid increasing taxes during a campaign year, Brown's administration had changed accounting procedures, which payed for 12 months of governmental goods and services with 15 months of revenue. Brown's accounting practices resulted in a deficit that totaled more than $400 million by the end of fiscal year 1966–67. Reagan not only faced a huge deficit, but he was forced by constitutional mandate to submit a balanced budget by January 31. This situation, coupled with Reagan's campaign promises to cut taxes and reduce government spending, posed a major problem for the governor. Obviously, upon being elected as a self-proclaimed fiscal conservative, raising taxes was the last thing Reagan wanted to do. To rectify the political implications of his actions, Reagan pinned the blame on Pat Brown.

> Very simply, it was just another one-time windfall—a gimmick that solved nothing but only postponed the day of reckoning. We are financing the 12-month spending with 15-month income. All the tax revenues for the first quarter of next year . . . will be used to finance this year's expenses up to June 30th (8).

Further compounding the economic situation was Reagan's campaign promise to decrease property taxes. To finance property tax relief, the deficit, and the projected increases in government spending due to increases in population and inflation required close to a billion dollars that the state did not have. Reagan's tentative answer to the deficit was to "squeeze and cut and trim until we reduce the costs of government" (9). Raising taxes would be a last resort "only if it becomes clear that economies alone cannot balance the budget" (9). By cutting the costs of government, Reagan could at least partially fulfill some of his campaign promises.

Thus, while this speech served as an introduction to Reagan's "Creative Society," the issue of responsibility was Reagan's central concern. By putting the burden on the people to solve the state's problems, in addition to blaming Brown for California's fiscal situation, Reagan tried to remove himself from both present and future responsibility.

February 5, 1967

The economic situation had grown more urgent in the month following Reagan's inaugural message. "Bluntly, we have gone to the fiscal well once too often in California and that well is now dry," observed Reagan (1).[6] Using Brown as his scapegoat, Reagan claimed that he had no other choice but to increase taxes, "to dig a little deeper in your pockets" (2). Reagan, however, attempted to counter the bad news with the good:

> I'm sure you know that once a government agency gets used to a certain level of spending, it is something of a revolution to cut that back; but we are going to do it. Next year's budget will total $4.6 billion, which is actually $251 million less than is being spent this year (2).

For Reagan, cutting the growth of government was translated as a revolution, of which he was the symbolic leader. However, Reagan's revolution never materialized as the budget Reagan eventually signed for fiscal year 1967–68 exceeded $5 billion.

The proposed $251 million in budget cuts were not enough, stated Reagan: "These economies still leave us roughly $250 million short of balancing the budget" (2). Reagan's answer for the revenue gap was "new or increased taxes on cigarettes, liquor and in other specialized areas" (2). As it turned out, these "other specialized areas" consisted of increases in bank and corporate taxes as well as increases in the state income tax.

Reagan's tax bill also called for a reduction in the "confiscatory" property tax. Oddly enough, Reagan's call for a property tax reduction was to be financed by a tax increase: a 1 percent increase in the sales tax. Even Reagan was not oblivious to the logic of decreasing taxes in order to raise them: "Now some people have charged that we are robbing Peter to pay Paul if we talk about adding a tax to replace a tax. This is not completely true" (2).

As mentioned, Reagan began this speech by metaphorically likening California's fiscal situation to a dry well. Reagan, however, changed metaphors midway through the speech. He observed, "We are like a family facing an unexpected emergency. The household budget must be cut and we have to put the new TV set off for another year and make the old car do for a while" (3). The fiscal situation had changed from the urgency of a dry well to a much more moderate, temporary "family emergency"—an emergency infused with middle/upper-class values and spending habits. This metaphorical transformation perhaps reflected Reagan's own uncertainty as to the seriousness of the fiscal situation.

Returning to where the $251 million in economies would be affected, Reagan concluded that elementary and secondary education and welfare were off limits to budget cuts. Instead, in a move that Reagan paid a high political price for, he advocated budget cuts in the state's college and university systems. Reagan also proposed that tuition be charged by both systems claiming that "education on that level is not compulsory. It is a gift to a limited number of our young people, paid for by all of us" (3). Reagan also justified his call for tuition based on low graduation rates: "Only about one-third of those who enter the University are ever graduated. Perhaps the responsibility of paying tuition would be the inspiration many of these dropouts . . . need to complete their studies" (4). However, Reagan's arguments justifying his call for tuition were to change. Reagan's discourse legitimizing his budget cuts was, ironically, apologetic: "But we must face one basic fact . . . this year the money just isn't available to do all the things we would like to do in education or in welfare or anywhere else" (4). Based on his promise to "squeeze, cut and trim" in his inaugural message, one would have expected Reagan to champion his cuts instead of apologizing for them.

Shifting the responsibility onto the people as well as to the legislature, Reagan stated,

> We need and must have your support in this time of crisis. [T]he Legislature and the pressure groups need to know where you stand . . . whether you stand on the side of fiscal reality and sanity, or whether you wish to retreat along the path that leads to more and more spending and onward to more and more taxes. [N]ot taxes that just 'soak the rich,' but taxes that cut across the board and hit all our incomes and purchases of the every-day items we all must buy (Reagan's ellipses, 5).

One may note the contradiction in Reagan's description of the path leading to fiscal insanity. Specifically, Reagan had earlier advocated increasing the sales tax by a penny to fund property tax relief. Yet according to the above description of fiscal insanity, a sales tax would affect the purchase of "every-day items." Thus, within the context of a single speech Reagan advocated increasing the sales tax and claimed that such methods of taxation should be considered a retreat, a solution to be avoided at all costs.

April 16, 1967

In his second televised *Report to the People* Reagan attempted to summarize the accomplishments of his administration's first 100 days as well as to discuss tuition, mental health, his tax bill, and income tax withholding. In this address Reagan tried to portray himself as a fiscal conservative, despite the fact that his proposed budget for fiscal year 1967–68 had increased from $4.6 billion to $4.89 billion.[7] Also, Reagan's optimistic projection of creating $251 million in economies had been nearly cut in half, to the sum of $127.6 million.

Not only were the budget numbers continuing to swell, but Reagan was taking a beating in the press on two other issues: his plan to implement tuition at both the state college and university systems, and his call to lay off 3,700 state employees in the Department of Mental Hygiene.

Not surprisingly, Reagan tried to downplay his administration's first 100 days: "There is nothing magic about the first 100 days, especially in a case such as California's where the Legislature is controlled by one party and the Executive by the other. Under those circumstances no great miracles or instant legislation should be expected" (1).[8]

Despite the increased budget numbers, Reagan tried to create the perception that he was still a fiscal conservative by drawing attention to the smaller number of state employees, cuts in out-of-state travel, freezes on state automobile purchases, departmental cuts of 10 percent, and the creation of a large money-saving task force. Not only was Reagan attempting to come across as a fiscal conservative through these "symbolic economies" that added up to very little, but he was also trying to cast the legislature in a negative light by contrasting all of his accomplishments with the lack of legislation in the first 100 days.

The tuition issue was to plague Reagan throughout 1967. Reagan changed some of his arguments concerning the need for tuition to manage the crisis. Specifically, Reagan chose not to dwell on college education being a gift, as he had in his February 5 *Report to the People*. Rather, Reagan claimed that tuition would provide funds for loan and scholarship programs, "which would assure needy students of [sic] the financing they must have to get an education" (3). Reagan also argued that tuition would reduce some of the costs to the taxpayer, who may or may not have had offspring enrolled in California's higher education system. Instead of being antagonistic, Reagan opted for a fairness argument in order to legitimatize his tuition proposal.

Not only did the tuition issue raise a furor in the press, but so did Reagan's call for drastically reducing the number of employees in the state's mental health program. According to Reagan, the cuts were warranted because of the sharp decline in the number of patients being treated: from 37,000 to 22,000. Reagan also emphasized that cuts at the state level would be offset by increased funding for care centers at the county level, where Reagan claimed that patient care would be just as good or better than care at the state level. Ironically, it was Reagan who would later take great pride in the increased funding for these county care centers.

Reagan also presented a detailed list of why California needed $865 million more in revenue for fiscal year 1967–68 and where this money would come from. More interesting than the numerical breakdown was Reagan's revenue proposal to raise the $865 million. It included a 1 percent sales tax increase, a 75 cent increase in the tax on distilled spirits, a 3.5 cent increase in the tax on cigarettes, a 25 percent increase in the tax on cigars and smoking tobacco, a 1 percent increase in the bank and corporation franchise tax, and last, increased state income taxes "according to a specific formula" (6). These last two revenue enhancing measures are particularly noteworthy since they both ran counter to Reagan the ideologue's pro–big business and anti-tax rhetoric. This was the first of several instances in which Reagan the ideologue and Reagan the pragmatic politician were at odds with one another.

Reagan spelled out his revenue package much more clearly in his March 8 *Tax Message* given to the legislature. Specifically, Reagan advocated narrowing the bracket structure, increasing the maximum rate to 10 percent, and adopting various tax credits in favor of tax exemptions.[9] Reagan even explicitly spelled out the financial implications of his proposed revenue bill to the legislature: "This amendment would eliminate the tax liability of people at the bottom of the present taxable income scale, and would reduce the amount of tax for others in the lower brackets."[10] Thus the burden of the tax would fall on the middle- and upper-income classes. Realizing that proportional taxation was politically unrealistic, Reagan the pragmatic politician advocated a more progressive income tax rate structure in order to raise revenues.

The last issue Reagan addressed in this speech was income tax withholding; an issue that would come back to haunt him. In 1967, Reagan was adamantly opposed to income tax withholding, a measure in which the state automatically withholds a person's income tax liability. Reagan's opponents were in favor of such a measure largely because of its revenue generating potential. Reagan's aversion to withholding stemmed from several considerations: low income people would be overtaxed and would likely not seek to get the lost revenue back; the average taxpayer, claimed Reagan, did not cheat on his taxes; and withholding was "too painless." Addressing the "painlessness" of withholding, the conspiratorial theme resurfaced in Reagan's discourse:

> Withholding is a painless way of extracting your money. And the very fact that it is painless means government is always willing to ask for more. [W]ithholding means you don't watch so closely where your tax money is going because it removes your consciousness of the fact that you are paying (7).[11]

Reagan would later claim that "taxes should hurt," reflecting his firm belief that the taxpayers should be fully cognizant of the large amount of money that was going to finance state government.

Reagan concluded this speech by noting that his administration's first 100 days was "a period during which we have sought to reverse the trend of 30 years towards bigger, more expensive, more powerful government" (7). Paradoxically, it was Reagan who sponsored a tax bill that would generate close to two billion dollars in increased revenues during fiscal years 1967–68 and 1968–69.

May 6, 1967

In one of his first addresses to a highly partisan gathering after his election, Reagan the ideologue was highly visible. One of Reagan's primary objectives in this speech was to "set the record straight here and now" on his billion dollar tax bill. Attempting to separate himself from the responsibility of the tax bill, Reagan blamed former governor Pat Brown:

> Roughly half of that tax increase is necessary simply to pay off this year's deficit and put us on a pay-as-you-go basis. Half of the remainder is not a new tax so much as a broader based substitute tax to give, . . . direct property tax relief. . . . [T]he remainder . . . is for the normal increase to keep pace with population growth and increased prices and wages resulting from the federal government's policy of planned inflation (2).[12]

The blame for the tax bill was on Brown as well as the federal government. However, Reagan was the sole cause for cutting back the growth of government to 7 percent. Clearly, Brown and the federal government were the villains; Reagan projected himself as the hero.

Reagan also attempted to rationalize why he could get only $127 million in economies when he had initially promised over $250 million: "We tried for some $250 million in economies in the budgets requested by all the divisions of government. We ended up with more than $127 million. I'm just stubborn enough to think we got the $127 million because we tried for $250 million" (2). Interestingly, Reagan did not claim this in his April 14 *Report to the People*, where his audience was much more diverse. Reagan clearly felt more comfortable in announcing his "stubbornness" to a relatively small gathering of Republicans. Such a strategy underscores Reagan's extremism; in the future he would knowingly try for more economies than he knew were possible.

Reagan also downplayed his revenue bill as a "cure-all" for California's fiscal problems. For Reagan, taxes were anything but a symbolic "cure" for the sickness of California's fiscal situation. Rather, the real "cure," the one that would mean lasting health for California's economy was "by making government more economical, more frugal, more workable" (2). In this highly symbolic scenario, Reagan fancied himself as the doctor, capable of both diagnosing the problem and providing the cure.

Proving that he was keeping his campaign promises, Reagan drew considerable pride from referring to the living embodiment of his Creative Society: 152 of "the best and most successful" business and industrial leaders were busy trying to implement "modern business practices" in California's government. Reagan was to refer time and again to the vast sums of money he had saved the taxpayers due to his task force. Such a task force served to draw attention to Reagan's promise to "squeeze, cut, and trim" while detracting attention from his record budget.

Reagan was perceptive enough to realize that he had to at least attempt to temper his tough talk on spending cuts by showing some conciliation for those whom he labeled as "the truly needy." Thus Reagan trumpeted his administration's spending increases for crippled children, state employees, teachers' pensions, and job placement for unemployed state employees. Collectively, this group of people comprised Reagan's "truly needy" in 1967.

Reagan also warned his fellow Republicans of the federal government and that part of his duties were to create "an effective bulwark between the people and an ever-encroaching federal government" (7). Reagan added, "I still believe that government is best which remains closest to the people, but almost daily the Goliath that is the federal government moves to gather more power unto itself and to minimize the functions of both the Congress and the states" (7). If the federal government was Goliath, then Reagan viewed himself and his role as David, capable of defeating the enemy despite being a heavy underdog.

Reagan concluded this speech by depicting the Republican party as being engaged in a "battle" of epic proportions. What is more instructive than Reagan's use of war metaphors to situate a partisan drama was his prophetic statement concerning freedom and security. Reagan noted, "Because there can be no freedom without law and order, every act of government must be approved if it makes freedom more secure and disapproved if it offers security instead of freedom" (9). Reagan, in this instance, greatly reduced any complexity on legislative matters; either it was pro-freedom or pro-security—nothing existed in between.

July 9, 1967

Shortly following Reagan's signing of the biggest budget in the history of California ($5.08 billion), he went to the people, proclaiming his innocence: "It is not a budget that reflects my philosophy or the approach this administration intends to take to government or government spending. . . . I've submitted the biggest budget in our state's history and I still think the government of California costs the people of California too much'' (1).[13]

Not only did Reagan attempt to blame both Pat Brown and the legislature, he also contended that ''we can only cut in that portion of the cost that has to do with operations and administrative overhead. The rest of the budget is controlled by legislation enacted into law and it will take action by the Legislature to change these programs'' (2).

Reagan, realizing the potentially damaging perceptions caused by the record budget, attempted to combat this fiscally loose image with a fiscally prudent one. In a repeated effort, Reagan referred his audience to the 79 percent reduction in state travel, the reduction in the state's consumption of gasoline, improved maintenance procedures, and the reduced numbers of state employees. According to Reagan, these savings would amount to millions of dollars. However, Reagan did not stop with just the savings on costly items as he detailed savings achieved in the purchases of typewriter ribbons.

Reagan also used another strategy to symbolize his conservative fiscal nature: emphasizing the ''record'' he had set in 1967. ''Incidentally, there was another record broken besides size of the budget. The $43.5 million blue pencilled was the largest cut ever made by a Governor in a California budget'' (4). In his very next utterance, however, Reagan proudly announced the $18 million that his administration had added to the budget. Specifically, Reagan attempted to prove his humanitarian nature by detailing increased funding to mental health, state salary increases, and that the budget had not been cut for the state's system of higher education. One can hardly help but notice Reagan's efforts to assuage the public on the two issues that he had come under the most fire for: cutbacks in both the Department of Mental Hygiene and California's system of higher education.

Reagan concluded this speech by also attempting to divorce himself from the tax bill: ''I will tell you now—this tax bill, like the budget, does not represent my philosophy. I do not like it and I regret the circumstances that make it necessary'' (7).

MEDI-CAL

September 20, 1967

The first half of 1967 was, from an economics perspective, an extremely difficult one for Reagan. The record budget, the billion dollar tax hike, the call for tuition, and the controversy centering around the massive layoffs in the Department of Mental Hygiene combined to make a miserable start to Reagan's Creative Society. However, the second half of 1967 proved to be much less troublesome for Reagan, with one exception: welfare. Specifically, the state's Medi-Cal program threatened to "bankrupt" the state, according to Reagan. The major problem surrounding the state's Medi-Cal program was that it was underfunded by over $100 million: "Our Medi-Cal program implementation of Article Nineteen was budgeted at $746,000,000 for its first sixteen months, but costs for that same period was $876,000,000" (1).[14] Even worse than the large overrun was the ruling by California's attorney general "that this newly discovered deficit must be paid out of the current year's budget" (1).

Given the huge tax bill that he already signed, another tax hike was out of the question since California was already "one of the highest taxpaying states in the union" (1). Reagan's alternative solution was "to see if we cannot make these programs workable at a realistic price" (1). Reagan again portrayed himself as a victim of circumstance; both the legislature and the attorney general (a Democrat) were responsible for the underfunding of Medi-Cal and the strain on the budget for fiscal year 1967–68.

Reagan claimed that California's budget, given the current tax structure, could only increase 8 percent a year; an amount insufficient to cover the growing increases in the Medi-Cal program. Reagan, in an effort to win back some of the support he had lost on the tuition issue, stated, "Obviously, if we are to continue to provide other government services, including education, this program will have to be radically changed" (2). Reagan framed the issue such that he was the defender of education, protecting it from its enemy, welfare.

Reagan offered three solutions to the Medi-Cal problem: changing eligibility requirements, changing the services to be provided, and "to revise our entire concept of aid and medical aid for the poor" (2). Part of this last solution involved a semantic change: "The poor have always been with us, while the disadvantaged, the deprived, only joined us with the advent of the 'Great Society' " (2). The problem, as Reagan interpreted it, was that the Great Society was a purely political undertaking, designed to buy votes through the creation of expensive welfare programs. Thus, in an indirect way, Reagan implicated Lyndon Johnson as the culprit for California's increasing welfare payments.

The way in which Reagan defined welfare largely colored his perceptions of it. For example, Reagan stated, "I don't believe that just giving the poor a handout is of any great service to them, whether it be money or medical care. . . . They may need a step up, a helping hand, but they want it so they can do better for themselves" (2). Explicitly, those receiving a "handout" did not "aspire to a better life," while those getting a "step up" or a "helping hand" were worthy welfare recipients because they wanted to "do better for themselves." The simple dialectic was that a handout was evil; a step up or a helping hand was good.

All too often, the welfare recipient's rights overshadowed "the right of those who work and earn, and share the fruit of their toil to make welfare possible," claimed Reagan (3). The problem, for Reagan, boiled down to a fairness issue: working citizens could hardly afford their own medical bills, yet they provided tax dollars for unlimited free medical services to those on Medi-Cal. Implied by Reagan's appeal to fairness was that working people who paid for welfare were more worthy of government-subsidized medical payments than were the nonworking.

Reagan hinted that part of the answer to the high cost of welfare was the use of voluntary organizations: "I believe also that government, in making provision for health services for the poor, should make maximum use of the voluntary organizations," and "the answer is not the opposite extreme of no government involvement at all. It is, instead, a partnership of private effort and governmental activity—a system in which those with true need are helped and the rest of us permitted to help also" (3). The taxpayer would be "permitted" to help, not required. Volunteerism, instead of taxation, was Reagan's solution to the high cost of welfare. Reagan gave credence to this interpretation at the close of his speech: "We cannot meet the problem of part of our citizens by unduly penalizing any other group" (4).

1968

Reagan's difficult freshman year did nothing to deter his political ambitions. Though at times he professed to be campaigning for fellow Republicans, Reagan was campaigning for the Republican presidential nomination. Although he eventually lost out to Richard Nixon, the national exposure Reagan received did nothing to harm his political prospects in the long run.

As one might expect, Reagan spent much of his time during the first half of 1968 outside of California. Given this, Reagan's legislative agenda at home was minimal. Tax reform, property tax relief, tuition, and Medi-Cal all remained major economic issues, but little legislative action was taken on them by the Reagan administration.

Unlike 1967, Reagan introduced a "realistic" budget early in the legislative session, calling for spending of $5.7 billion for fiscal year 1968–69. The budget ultimately signed by Reagan in late June called for spending totaling $5.69 billion, an increase of just over $600 million from fiscal year 1967–68.[15]

California ended fiscal year 1967–68 with a surplus of $167 million. Thus in the span of a year and a half, the state had gone from a $400 million deficit to a $167 million surplus. Though the 1967 tax bill was the principal reason for the dramatic fiscal turnaround, Reagan would use this resurgence to his rhetorical advantage, attributing it to his administration's cost-saving measures.

January 6, 1968: State-of-the-State Message

Aside from calling attention to his administration's accomplishments in 1967, Reagan's 1968 *State-of-the-State Message* focused on one main economic issue: tax reform. Reagan's call for tax reform was based on the structure's antiquity as well as the demographic changes within the state:

> There has been no substantial tax reform in this state government since 1933. In that year, we were primarily an agricultural society with a population of about six million. Today we are a highly industrialized state with almost 20 million citizens. . . . [W]e have been through some of the most sweeping social, economic and political changes of any state in the nation. Yet through it all, the continued approach to taxation has been add-ons and gimmicks and gadgets and unkept promises (4).[16]

Reagan also criticized the existing tax structure as being "neither equitable nor effective," that the present tax system hurt both wealthy and poor (4).

Reagan's proposals for tax reform reflected some of his earlier Hollywood-inspired views on taxation as well as foreshadowing some of his presidential tax legislation. Specifically, on addressing the matter of tax rates, Reagan elaborated,

> Local or state taxes should not be used to redistribute the earnings of the citizenry. The federal government has pre-empted that field. The state's concern should be to see that each citizen pays the same percentage of his income in state and local taxes after payment of his federal taxes (5).

In no uncertain terms Reagan called for proportional taxation; the same proportional system of taxation that he staunchly advocated in 1958 to the House Ways and Means Committee and in 1961 to the Phoenix Chamber of Commerce, with the exception of it being implemented at the state level. However, Reagan's justification for proportional taxation had changed: from tithing to the federal government's progressive income tax structure. Implied by Reagan's justification for proportional taxation was the issue of fairness. More clearly, proportional taxation was Reagan's way of getting even with the federal government's "discriminatory" progressive income tax structure. As alluded to earlier, Reagan explicitly equated the progressive income tax with communism, thus evil. As a politician, Reagan could right this evil by implementing a proportional tax system.

Ironically, one of Reagan's major complaints about California's tax system, aside from its Methuselahen nature, was the regressivity of certain taxes. One such regressive tax was the state's sales tax: "The present retail sales tax, . . . imposes a disproportionate burden on those of lower income" (5). However, it was Reagan, acting only a few months earlier, who actually raised sales taxes by one cent as part of the state's $1 billion revenue package. Thus Reagan's guilt was confirmed by his own rhetoric.

Also of note, Reagan purposefully avoided any specifics on tax rates. Instead, Reagan transferred the responsibility for determining the specifics of his tax reform proposal onto his constituents:

> How much of his income is he willing to give—can he afford to pay—to state government? What amount of his personal resources will be spent or saved through individual decisions—and how much will he permit us to tax away and spend on his government? This must be a taxpayer's decision—not ours; we work for them, not the other way around (5).

Because the state was merely an employee, decisionmaking did not rest with elected officials, but resided with the employer: the citizen of the state. By utilizing such a strategy, Reagan tried to remove himself and the legislature from the responsibility of establishing specific tax rates. Equally significant, the citizens could avoid blame as well because the tax rates would only reflect one's willingness to pay for governmental goods and services.

Lou Cannon has noted that Ronald Reagan has always been a sucker for hero-worship.[17] Reagan was also partial to the underdog, though. Perhaps because of his own story—a rags-to-riches one—Reagan revelled in portraying certain groups as symbolic underdogs, worthy of both sympathy and admiration. Additionally, these underdogs became underdogs precisely because someone or some group had unfairly victimized them. Such was the case with the taxpayer:

> But, there is also another responsibility to which this administration will give high priority; that is to the taxpayer, the too-often forgotten man, who today is working 2 1/2 hours out of every eight-hour day just to pay his taxes. [T]his is the citizen who has no special pressure group to lobby for him. He works and sweats to make ends meet, to pay his bills and keep his family in clothes and his kids in school. . . . Before we can provide special services to others, we must first take the money from him. If he goes broke, there will be no money for Sacramento (5–6).

In this context, these characters were symbolic of a greater political conflict between Republican and Democratic leaders; Republicans were on the side of the overworked, overtaxed laborer, while Democrats stood on the side of fiscal excess, at the taxpayer's expense. Reagan spoke for and represented the underdog; Democratic leaders were content to have the taxpayers remain as underdogs.

HOUSING

February 1, 1968

In making the rounds on the speaking circuit in California, Reagan often addressed very homogeneous audiences, unified by occupation. Such audiences provided Reagan with a ready-made theme that he could relate to his fiscal agenda. Such was the case on February 1, when Reagan addressed a conference on housing and home ownership.

Home ownership was very important to Ronald Reagan. He not only viewed home ownership as a distinctly "American" activity, but also felt it encompassed an entire range of laudable values. Specifically, Reagan viewed homeowners as possessing certain Republican values. Employing a quote from Herbert Hoover, Reagan stated,

> "A husband and wife who own their own home are apt to save. They have an interest in the advancement of a social system that permits the individual to store up the fruits of his labor. As direct taxpayers, they take a more active part in local government. Above all, the love of home is one of the finest ideals of our people" (2).[18]

Home ownership had a transformative power for Reagan. Because of this power, home ownership was a savior of sorts, capable of reinvigorating the American public with Republican ideals while also providing a stimulus to the economy.

Proof of the transformative powers of home ownership was manifested by the failures of public housing. Reagan viewed public housing as a failure primary because it lacked one all-important ingredient: ownership. Reagan claimed that

> people do not develop a sense of pride in their neighborhoods when the lawns are mowed for them by public housing employees; the garbage is taken out by a public housing employee; and everything else is done for them. Despite all the efforts and fine management of many local housing authorities, they cannot overcome the fundamental weakness of most public housing: namely it fails to give a man a chance to own his own home (2).

Reagan's simple solution to the problems faced by public housing was to allow the resident to become the owner of the property. This, in turn, would precipitate the "re-establishment of law and order" (3). Significantly, Reagan understood crime as having only one basic cause: economic deprivation. And because home ownership would help alleviate this deprivation, it was viewed by Reagan as fundamental to a healthy society.

Reagan, attempting to appease those who had been critical of his business-oriented approach to government, claimed that without a healthy economy, social problems could not be tackled:

> There are those who imply that administrations which use business principles and practices as bench-marks in the operation of government are without 'compassion' and do not recognize social values. . . . They fail to recognize that it takes a healthy economy to make it possible for society to do those things which must be done for its less fortunate members (3).

A healthy economy, as Reagan freely admitted, was the only way by which the federal government could meet the needs of its citizenry. Thus social problems, as interpreted by Reagan, were contingent upon the relative "health" or "sickness" of the economy.

Reagan also interpreted the federal government's involvement with public housing as having made the problem worse, not better:

> The federal government entered the housing field in 1937 with a public housing program. . . . [T]hirty years later the streets of our cities are unsafe. Thirty years later most of that housing created under the 1937 program fails to meet the social and physical needs of the people living in it (6).

Not only had the federal government's public housing program failed to meet the needs of the people, but it had actually caused increased crime rates, and because the federal government was guilty of purposefully creating an environment that fostered lawlessness, government could not be part of the solution. Instead, Reagan proposed that the "independent sector" get involved in social problem solving. Specifically, Reagan claimed that private industry could solve the problem: "American industry has the know-how, the resources, and the motive to solve many of our problems. The motive . . . is profit, . . . A few housing units may be built out of compassion, but the major needs will be met because of improved technology utilized by our private enterprise, profit-making system" (6). Not only had Reagan shifted the responsibility, but he also claimed that technological innovation, fostered by the free hand of the market, would eventually solve the nation's housing problem.

WELFARE

March 21, 1968

Reagan outlined some of the problems with California's welfare system and offered his solutions in a speech to the state legislature. Reagan was to outline variations of these problems and solutions until passage of some of his welfare reforms was secured in 1971.

Part of the problem Reagan had with welfare and specifically welfare recipients was the attention given to them by the government:

> I have a feeling that our main objective of helping people has been lost sight of in a welter of regulations that have government prescribing allowances based on everything from how many calories and vitamins the recipient ought to have for dinner to what he should pay to have his yard kept up. [T]he average person doesn't live that way. He looks at the amount of money he has and plans his life accordingly. This is the way we all do (2).[19]

Because the "average person" didn't receive preferred treatment, stated the governor, neither should the welfare recipient. What Reagan overlooked was the fact that welfare recipients were not average persons, especially with regard to income.

Another problem Reagan had with welfare involved a responsibility issue. More clearly, Reagan believed that the family should be the provider when it came to financial hardship and not the state.

> Parents wish to be independent of their children and it has been in recognition of this that the legislature has virtually repealed responsibility of sons and daughters to contribute to the support of their parents. . . . In this anomalous situation, we still permit these relatives who have been absolved of filial responsibility to inherit the estates of the recipients (4).

Reagan believed that it was unfair for the relatives of the deceased (who had received public assistance) to inherit their estates. To address this "inequity" Reagan proposed "that where the taxpayers have assumed responsibility for the aged and disabled, then these taxpayers should share equally with relatives in settlement of the proceeds of the estates of the recipients" (4). Reagan the pragmatic politician was actually encouraging more governmental interference and bureaucracy instead of less, the very thing Reagan the ideologue abhorred.

Additionally, Reagan proposed that the "real" solution to the problem was employment: "The most efficient and effective welfare system is no substitute for employment. . . . [C]ommunity status and a personal feeling of worth are related to the extent to which an individual is a full and vigorous participant in the job market" (5). For Reagan, there existed a clear distinction between welfare and work: welfare perpetuated hopelessness while work gave the individual dignity and self-esteem. Work was a savior; welfare was self-imposed slavery.

Reagan's plan for putting welfare recipients back to work is quite paradoxical when compared to a belief he held on taxation. Reagan wanted to "remove from the Aid to Families with Dependent Children program the incentive to remain on aid by establishing a limit on family payments to coincide with the earning limit of a family breadwinner who is working at the minimum wage level" (6) Reagan was proposing nothing less than the withdrawal of funds to serve as a stimulus for work; in other words he would cut back welfare payments in order to increase employment. Paradoxically, Reagan justified cutting tax rates on the opposite assumption. That is, as the reader will recall from his speech to the House Ways and Means Committee in 1958, Reagan stated that decreasing tax rates would cause an increase in government revenues. Thus, by putting more money in people's pockets, they would save and invest more, in turn creating more sources from which government could generate tax revenue. Thus on one hand Reagan claimed that taking away money from welfare recipients would act as a stimulus to productivity while on the other hand Reagan claimed that giving more money to the taxpayer would act as a stimulus to savings and investment, hence productivity. Reagan's clear preferences lay with the taxpayer rather than the welfare recipient.

THE CAMPAIGN

Despite his wife's claims to the contrary, Ronald Reagan did, in fact, run for the presidency in 1968.[20] Though he never publicly admitted running for the Republican nomination until late in the primary season, several speeches during 1968 exemplified Reagan's presidential aspirations.

One of the problems Reagan encountered in running for the presidency was his lack of political experience. Having served only one year as governor, Reagan did not have much of a political record to run on. To overcome his inexperience, Reagan often portrayed his political innocence as a strength. Additionally, even though his record as governor was minimal at this point, Reagan emphasized, often in minute detail, the fiscally prudent nature of his administration. Typically, once Reagan had painstakingly detailed his efforts to save the California taxpayers money, he would contrast his fiscally conservative administration with the fiscally "loose" programs of Lyndon Johnson's "Great Society."

April 5, 1968

Reagan began his speech to the Women's National Press Club by discussing his fiscal achievements as governor as well as trying to develop a link between California's problems and the problems confronting the nation. Reagan noted, "We've made a start in reducing both the size and cost of government, but at the same time we've made a start on some of the most vexing programs confronting not only Californians but also, . . . all Americans in all of the fifty states" (1).[21]

This speech was shaped largely by a single controlling exigency—Martin Luther King, Jr.'s assassination on the previous day. After a brief eulogy to King, Reagan addressed the issue of civil rights. What is particularly interesting about Reagan's discourse on the issue of civil rights was how he chose to contextualize the issue: "I have a belief that jobs are the most important part of this problem. Regardless of all the social problems, . . . the ghettos' walls are economic" (8). Racism was not the primary problem, unemployment was. Furthermore, the solution to racial unrest, according to Reagan, was jobs in the free enterprise system. Employment was a panacea for Reagan, capable not only of saving human lives, but putting an end to racism as well.

Reagan's strategy for framing the civil rights issue in this manner was a purely selfish one. That is, upon detailing the cause of the racial unrest as economic, Reagan "proved" his claim by referring to his own administration: "Of the 17,800 unemployed in the Watts area who were put into jobs by the Chad McClellen program, almost immediately 30% of them moved out of that neighborhood, proving what the walls consist of in the ghettos" (8). Thus having found "the solution" to the problem in California, Reagan implied that he was capable of solving the problem on a national scale.

Additionally, not only would employment for minorities solve the nation's social problems, but Reagan saw the minority contingent as another market to be exploited: "If we can raise our minority communities to just the average level of purchasing power of the rest of the majority community, we have a potential market for our free enterprise system that is equal to or even greater than the foreign market" (10). Thus employment for minorities, claimed Reagan, would simultaneously rid the nation of racial unrest and provide positive long-run effects on the United States' economy.

May 3, 1968

In a campaign speech addressed to the American Women in Radio and Television Convention, one of Reagan's targets for criticism was the "new economics" as well as Lyndon Johnson's "guns and butter" economy.

> Today we are promised guns and butter with no down payment and easy terms. The war will be successfully terminated and the Great Society at home will be expanded. [N]ow all those who warn of a day of reckoning haven't discovered the magic brass lamp with its genie named new economics. Well, let the lamp-rubbers answer now, where is that genie? Our gold is gone, our paper money can be exchanged anytime for more paper. And our coins rattle on the counter with the flat tone of copper. . . . We are no longer in control of our currency (3).[22]

Johnson's economic policies also were a direct cause for the race riots in Detroit, claimed Reagan.

> Nowhere has government been more generous in aid to the poor than in pre-riot Detroit. . . . one of the most serious frauds one can commit upon the poor is to promise something you do not or cannot deliver. There is so little money left for the poor after salaries and fixed overhead that one can no longer refer to this fact as an irregularity. One must call it what it is: fraud (5).

What is noteworthy here is that Reagan placed culpability for the race riots on the federal government and not on the individuals involved in the riot. Reagan's usual emphasis on the individual's right for self-determination "consistent with law and order" was conspicuously absent; rather, Reagan implied that because the federal government was guilty of fraud, poverty stricken individuals had a right to express their frustrations.

July 30, 1968

The genie analogy, referring to the new economics, of May 3, had become much more serious by the end of July at a fund-raising rally held in Winston Salem, North Carolina. Specifically, Reagan likened the inflation spawned by the new economics to "radioactivity or arsenic poisoning" with its effects being "cumulative" instead of singular (1).[23] If inflation was the deadly poison Reagan claimed it was, then the Democrats who had purposefully planned it were guilty of nothing short of economic contamination.

The "paranoid" rhetoric typical of Reagan's pre-gubernatorial years would surface from time to time, largely in front of Republican gatherings. However, instead of a taxation conspiracy, the conspiracy Reagan described in this speech was one of planned inflation which ate away at workers' wages. Proof of the conspiracy to devalue workers' wages was the government's 10 percent surtax. According to Reagan's arithmetic, "when election year rolls around four years hence, . . . your salary cut is 26 percent" (1). The country could clearly not afford four more years of the new economics, implied Reagan.

In an interesting twist of irony Reagan offered a second prophesy: "The voluntary curbs on foreign investment became orders from on high; how soon will the suggestion that business and labor observe caution in price and wage increases become price and wage controls?" (1). It was Richard Nixon who, less than three years later, instituted wage and price controls.

July 31, 1968

The last speech Reagan gave prior to the Republican presidential nomination was to the Platform Committee on July 31. Reagan addressed a wide variety of topics in this speech but two economic issues were particularly noteworthy: national defense and fiscal federalism.

As alluded to in his pre-gubernatorial economic rhetoric, economic stability and national defense were inextricably linked. In this speech Reagan claimed that "the peace and security of the world depends on the fiscal and economic stability and the defense potential of the United States" (3).[24] A healthy economy was not just a prerequisite for the defense of the United States, warned Reagan, but also for the entire world's security.

Reagan's answer to problems experienced in education, housing regulations, consumer protection, health care, and employment was a simple one: returning these programs to the local level where they were "closest to the people" (4). Reagan reasoned that "local institutions are more flexible and more responsive to the needs of the people than bureaucracies thousands of miles and many years away" (4). Reagan's support for a policy of fiscal federalism was congruent with the shift in responsibility first detected in Reagan's *Inaugural Message* of 1967. That is, solutions at all levels of government should come from the people, claimed Reagan. And because people at the local level were closest to the problems being experienced, they were capable of finding the most appropriate solutions.

THE BUDGET

June 29, 1968

Reagan signed his second budget as governor on June 29. As he did shortly after signing his first budget, Reagan attempted to justify a record-setting budget while still claiming to have "cut, squeezed, and trimmed" the cost of government.

Unlike his first budget though, Reagan referred to his second budget as "a good budget, one that reflects the needs of the people of California" (1).[25] After detailing that he had blue-pencilled $16 million out of a record $5,710,315,991 budget, Reagan noted that he wished "it could be more because the cost of government in California is still too high" (1). Reagan's "good budget" had become a not-so-good budget in the span of one paragraph.

Reagan blamed the record budget on the legislature, which was "still controlled by the other party" (1). Reagan also attempted to remove himself from future record-setting budgets: "Until the Legislature, . . . approves the cost reduction programs I have submitted, the cost of government will continue to rise" (1). Reagan also continued to emphasize the lack of control he exerted over the final budget: "About two-thirds of the budget is outside of my control, and the Legislature has so far declined to give the executive branch the cost-cutting authority we need" (2).

While Reagan the ideologue emphasized his fiscal restraint that was in direct contrast to the big spenders in the legislature, Reagan the pragmatic politician noted spending increases in several areas: mental health, education, job training, and salary increases for state college and university professors. Notice that three of the four areas Reagan proudly announced would receive more funding were those that caused him political damage in 1967.

1969

In theory, 1969 should have been a productive year in the legislature for the Reagan administration. Due to gains registered by Republicans in the assembly, giving Republicans a 41–39 advantage, Reagan finally had the majority in the legislature he had sought.[26] Yet 1969 was relatively unproductive for the Reagan administration. Particularly disappointing for Reagan was that his administration's long-awaited proposal for tax reform failed to meet with legislative approval.

Despite the legislative majority, Reagan's $6.2 billion budget for fiscal year 1969–70 met with great opposition. The opposition was such that the state was without a budget for three days beginning on July 1. Additionally, the legislature's $6.36 billion budget did not meet with Reagan's approval either as the governor blue-pencilled a state record $123 million, resulting in a budget of $6.24 billion.

One of the few legislative bright spots for Reagan was the passage of his $100 million income tax rebate, effective in the election year of 1970. Interestingly, Jesse Unruh, who would challenge Reagan for the governorship in 1970, proposed a rebate of over $200 million due to the state's growing fiscal surplus.

January 7, 1969: State-of-the-State Message

Reagan addressed several economic issues in his 1969 *State-of-the-State Message* to California's legislature. Reagan spoke of California's budget for fiscal year 1969–70, taxes, government spending, welfare, unemployment, and tuition.

Reagan continued to exempt himself from responsibility, especially relative to government spending and welfare. Discussing government spending, Reagan stated, "The great bulk of our state government spending is dictated by statute; it can be changed only by statute" (2).[27] Furthermore, only the legislature could change these statutes. Also, addressing the mounting costs of welfare, Reagan claimed that "there is just so much my administration . . . can do. The bulk of these programs are locked-in by both state statutes and federal regulations" (2). While Reagan attempted to portray himself as a victim of both the California legislature and the federal government, he took credit for resisting the temptation to increase taxes and even hinted that his tough stance on taxes would soon precipitate a tax reduction: "Under *no* circumstance will I support or sign into law any tax increase. I believe the taxes we have now produce an ample income to meet our expenses, and with careful management, they permit us to offer a substantial tax reduction" (Reagan's emphasis, 2). What Reagan did not say was that his administration's 1967 revenue bill caused a surplus of state funds, which in fact was occurring. One may recall that it was Reagan who blamed the revenue bill on Pat Brown to distance himself from the political repercussions of such a tax hike. Yet Reagan, only a year and a half later, took credit for being able to cut taxes, not because of the revenue bill but because of his administration's "careful management." Brown caused the tax hike; Reagan was the reason a tax reduction was possible.

Reagan was still adamant on implementing tuition, otherwise known as his "equal education plan." Reagan called for tuition under the guise of fairness. More clearly, Reagan's equal education plan called for a series of loans and scholarships, financed by tuition, for needy students whose parents had been paying taxes to support higher education, but who could not send their children due to other related costs.[28]

Last, Reagan grounded his logic on a highly volatile, noneconomic issue by appealing to an economic entity: the California taxpayer. That is, Reagan saw the protests at Berkeley as "anarchy and insurrection" because higher education was "a privilege made available by the commitment and the sacrifice of the taxpayer" (13). Thus because the taxpaying citizen controlled the purse strings (tuition had yet to be implemented), they could justifiably demand "professional conduct from both students and teachers" (13).

POVERTY

January 30, 1969

Speaking to the Executive Symposium Luncheon on January 30, Reagan discussed two topics: his Creative Society and its accomplishments and poverty. The former was merely a reiteration of what he had said throughout much of 1967 and 1968. Reagan, however, had several "new" things to say about poverty, its causes, and its solutions.

According to Reagan, the "war on poverty" was a misguided and misunderstood battle. The reason the country had been losing the battle was "because it has been fought on the wrong fronts, with the wrong weapons, by the wrong generals" (5).[29] The enemy was not poverty, claimed Reagan, but the bureaucracy that had institutionalized it. The only general capable of winning such a battle was private enterprise: "The greatest force for winning the war on poverty comes not from the halls of Congress or the corridors of Sacramento but from the offices, and the factories and the shops of American business and industry" (5). The responsibility issue had taken on a new dimension in this speech. That is, because private enterprise had had the solutions to poverty all along, the bureaucracy was actually preventing it from implementing its solutions. Such an interpretation of this mini-drama is not at all inconsistent with Reagan's conspiratorial rhetoric. Private enterprise was the savior, capable of defeating both poverty and the villains working to perpetuate it. Furthermore, according to Reagan's logic, poverty would not have existed if the federal government had not interfered with the market mechanism. Poverty was a government creation, and the answer to it was "employment, not politics" (5).

Reagan's proof that free market capitalism could win the war on poverty was a historical one: "In 1900 . . . 90 percent of Americans were below the so-called poverty lines. By 1920, this figure had dropped to 50 percent and, by 1960, it had been reduced to 20 percent. . . . The driving force was the American capitalistic system" (6). Perhaps aware of the extreme implications of his own rhetoric, Reagan offered the following disclaimer: "No one is saying that we should cancel all government programs; but . . . it is the private sector . . . which has the great, and the only real, capacity to win the war on unemployment and poverty" (6).

Jobs, created by the market, were Reagan's simple answer to the complex problem of poverty and unemployment. Reagan did not stop here though. "A necessary companion in this immense journey is education," observed Reagan (6). Growth in the labor force as well as capital investment could not be the sole cause for economic expansion in the future. Rather, Reagan claimed that "the nations with the strongest educational system and the greatest technological innovations will be the leaders" (6). Having said this, Reagan interjected the tuition issue again. Since future jobs, and thus future prosperity, were contingent upon education, Reagan's call for tuition was somewhat more innocuous than it had been in the past. By imposing tuition, Reagan was only doing his duty to assist lower income individuals to gain access to the job market. By framing the issue in this manner, Reagan's call for tuition clearly can be seen as a "tax" on higher-income classes, with the intent of redistributing money from the wealthy to the poor. One may recall that it was Reagan the ideologue, speaking in 1961, who claimed that a progressive income tax was a manifestation of Marxist ideology, and that taxation which redistributed income was nothing short of socialism. As so often occurred as an elected official, Reagan's pragmatic persona won out over his ideological persona.

TAX REBATE

January 31, 1969

Reagan foreshadowed a tax rebate in his *State-of-the-State Message* of January 7. Over three weeks later, in a *Report to the People*, Reagan proposed a $100 million rebate to be effective in April 1970. Because of the brevity of the speech, coupled with its interesting content, we have chosen to reprint the speech in its entirety.

Two years ago we told the people of California, all of you, that we were going to try to cut government's size and cost by 10 percent across the board. This declaration was met with mixed emotions.

Now we're going to talk 10 percent again as a result of those economies, in part, and in part due to unexpected revenues as a result of inflation. We will have in the coming year a hundred million dollars over and above our budget—the budget we are presenting for this coming year.

Normally—with this kind of money left over—government finds a way to spend it. And in so doing, it usually builds up the cost of government for years to come until eventually it has to ask for more revenues.

We think we're doing something a little unprecedented, but we believe you're entitled to a rebate. You should receive that hundred million dollars back. And therefore we're asking the legislature effective April, 1970—not this coming April but in April 1970 when you compute your income tax for the state—that you subtract 10 percent—a 10 percent cut across the board in the state income tax for that year. And you deduct that amount and pay 90 percent of your computed tax.

Thus we will give the money back to the people.

We're continuing with tax reform and we hope that we'll be able to present savings that will be on a permanent basis as we achieve tax reform.

But as of now, this will be a one-time return to you of a hundred million dollars which you gave to the government—and which we, through economies, can now return to you.[30]

Two factors made his proposal for a tax rebate possible: a 10 percent across-the-board cut in administrative costs (even though Reagan, in an earlier speech, said he was able to cut only 8 percent) and a higher rate of inflation. Reagan, however, wanted his audience to believe that it was only because of the economies he had instituted that a tax rebate was possible. Proof of this claim lies in the last paragraph; inflation was curiously absent, while Reagan's economies were the sole cause for the tax rebate. What Reagan "forgot" to mention was that higher inflation coupled with a progressive income tax rate structure had caused increased government revenues (a concept known as "bracket creep"). Furthermore, it was Reagan's tax bill in 1967 which had made state income tax rates more progressive. In other words, Reagan's 1967 tax bill was the major cause of the surplus.[31]

Reagan also attempted to separate himself from the status quo by going against a tradition of spending what was left over, thereby attempting to portray himself as a truly unique member of the government establishment. Reagan was the self-proclaimed hero, whose heroism was attributable to his uniqueness and his concern for the taxpaying citizens.

Another noteworthy aspect of this speech involved the tax rebate itself. Notice that the rebate, as expressed by Reagan, was a proportional one; everyone would receive a 10 percent rebate. Clearly, such a proportional rebate would favor those who had a greater tax liability. In addition, the number, 10 percent, is also significant. After all, a 10 percent tax was consistent with the Biblical concept of tithing. By returning 10 percent of one's tax liability, Reagan was symbolically rewarding his congregation for their faithfulness.

THE BUDGET

February 4, 1969

As he had the previous two years, Reagan went public with his budget for fiscal year 1969–70. To aid him in his presentation and perhaps to supplement his ethos, Reagan had his state finance director, Caspar W. Weinberger, with him to go over the budget figures for the upcoming fiscal year. Reagan's purpose in "breaking down" the state's budget was not so much to provide the listener with a detailed account of the budget as it was an attempt to divorce himself from his administration's third straight record-setting budget.

Reagan proposed for fiscal year 1969–70 $380 million in the form of a tax rebate (of this amount $280 million was in the form of property tax relief). However, Reagan emphasized that this tax rebate would actually show up in the budget as an increase in state spending: "Here is $380 million that shows in our budget, adds to the size of the budget, looks like an expense, but actually is money that is being given back to the people" (3).[32] Thus $380 million out of Reagan's proposed budget of $6.2 billion would be going for tax reductions. As he mentioned in his January 31 *Report to the People*, Reagan reasoned that tax reductions were possible due to increased inflation and his administration's economies. Thus Reagan, while he emphasized his innocence from the record budget, stressed that he was responsible for at least part of the tax reductions.

TAX REFORM

April 8, 1969

Reagan's much anticipated proposal for major tax reforms came on April 8, when he formally presented his program to the legislature. Reagan's immediate objectives for tax reform were five-fold: (1) establishing a "simplified, equitable and balanced tax system"; (2) providing "relief from the inequitable and inelastic residential property tax"; (3) shifting "greater taxing responsibility . . . to the local level"; (4) for the state to bear "the primary responsibility for equality of educational opportunities through the public school system"; (5) and to achieve the preceding four objectives *"without increasing the aggregate total of the tax burden in California"* (Reagan's emphasis, 1).[33]

Reagan had what he termed "cardinal rules" that he would use in achieving these five objectives. The first was equity. Reagan claimed that "the burden of taxation should fall equally on all taxpayers, in proportion to their income" (2). Thus, equity, for Reagan was a tax system based on proportionality. A second cardinal rule was visibility. Reagan stated that "taxes should not be 'hidden'—the taxpayer should always know when and how he is being taxed" (2). Reagan's criterion of visibility was likely motivated by the issue of withholding. That is, Reagan felt taxpayers should always know how much of their incomes were being taken in taxes. Efficiency was Reagan's third cardinal rule. By reducing the complexities of government (bureaucracy), taxes could "go directly to the programs for which they were intended" (2). Elasticity was Reagan's final cardinal rule. Reagan desired an elastic, or flexible tax base so that the government would not have to continually rely on "the taxpayer for more money through new guises and gimmicks" (2).

The specifics of Reagan's tax reform proposal involved two parts: the first was to be enacted by the legislature in 1969, the second part would require a constitutional amendment to be voted on by the citizens of California either in 1969 or 1970.

Part One

The first part of Reagan's tax reform proposal involved three major components. First, Reagan called for an increase in the homeowner's property tax exemption from $750 to $1,000, to be financed by elimination of sales tax exemptions. Second, Reagan advocated a reduction in the business inventory tax of 23 percent. Third, Reagan advocated an additional cut in the business inventory tax, in addition to the 23 percent, of 15 percent. This was to be financed by a maintenance of the Bank and Corporation Tax in fiscal year 1970–71.

Part Two

The long range portion of Reagan's reform proposal was a call for shifting the burden of the property tax away from homeowners and landowners to the income tax. Reagan claimed that the property tax, which was used to finance California's public school system, was "inelastic and regressive" while the income tax was a more "equitable" tax (6). More specifically, Reagan proposed that "80 percent of the residential property tax, . . . would be replaced by a statewide Educational Opportunity Tax of 1 percent on adjusted gross personal income" (6). As mentioned earlier, the fulfillment of the American Dream for Ronald Reagan was owning a home. Reagan claimed that home ownership was "being discouraged by government policy, despite the fact that home ownership should be encouraged to preserve the stability and enjoyment of both urban and rural life" (7). Meanwhile, a 1 percent increase in the state income tax "offers a much better hope of achieving tax equity than continued reliance on the residential property tax" (7). Reagan claimed that the state's progressive income tax was a better indicator of one's ability to pay taxes than the state's property tax system. Reagan the pragmatic politician's claim that the state's progressive income tax was a reliable indicator of tax equity stood in direct opposition to Reagan the ideologue's belief that tax equity was represented by proportional income taxes.

In summary, Reagan's tax reform proposal had two major goals: reducing the business inventory tax and shifting some of the burden of public school financing away from property taxes to the state income tax.

May 11, 1969

Reagan, with the aid of Caspar Weinberger and Assemblyman Craig Biddle, took his proposal for tax reform to the people of California on May 11. While his address to the legislature was more of a step-by-step outline, Reagan's speech to the people contained more persuasive appeals. Because Part Two of his reforms required a constitutional amendment, and thus a vote of the people, Reagan's motivation for going public was to rally the citizen's support for his tax reform package.

With this consideration in mind, Reagan's proposals ran up against a major constraint: some taxpayers' tax share would increase. Recall that Part Two of Reagan's proposal called for a shifting of the tax burden away from property owners to those with the greatest ability to pay. Thus, aside from presenting the essentials of his proposal, this speech was designed to assuage some of the taxpayers' fears concerning where the incidence or burden of the tax would fall. Addressing this exigence, Reagan observed that "we are talking about tax reform, not tax increases, not tax reduction" (2).[34] Reagan added, "Contrary to what some have claimed, and inferred, we are not proposing a tax increase. We are proposing tax reform" (2). However, after Weinberger and Biddle had presented parts one and two respectively, Reagan equivocated on his earlier promises: "One of the problems with any tax reform program is that in spreading the base and easing the burden that has been carried too long by a given segment . . . some citizens are going to pay more than they have been paying in the past" (7). Collectively, Reagan's proposals for tax reform would not constitute an increase in the amount of taxes the state would take in. However, individually considered, Reagan's reforms would result in higher taxes for certain people.

Perhaps realizing that another tax increase for many Californians could have major repercussions on his political fortunes in a bid for reelection in 1970, Reagan attempted to de-emphasize his reforms at the state level. Reagan concluded, "There is just so much we can do about tax reform at the state level. When you get right down to it, the big part of total tax reform has to come from the federal government since that is where most of our taxes go" (10). By emphasizing that the federal government was largely responsible for tax reform, Reagan was essentially removing himself from responsibility for tax hikes that would result from his own reform proposals. In other words, Reagan viewed his tax reforms as the product of a tax system flawed at the federal level, claiming that "the only true tax reform" would come from the federal government (10). Thus Reagan was merely making the best of a bad situation, which he exerted little control over.

RECAPITULATION

September 5, 1969

As he did each year while he was governor, Reagan provided a recap of his administration's accomplishments during the year to the Sacramento Host Breakfast. Inflation, the budget, and tax reform were Reagan's main topics in this speech. Because of the conservative orientation of the audience, coupled with the ceremonial aspects of the occasion, Reagan the ideologue dominated in these speeches.

As inflation increased nationally throughout 1969, Reagan attempted to use this issue to his advantage. According to Reagan, inflation was a phenomenon that had its roots in government spending: "We know there is only one really basic, major cause of inflation—government spending, the high cost of government. Runaway inflation is the terrible companion of runaway government spending" (1).[35] Resorting to fear appeals, Reagan claimed that unless government "begins to live within the means of our taxpayers, we will, in fact, find ourselves in a very dark age" (1). Consistent with the right-wing version of "The Speech," Reagan interpreted certain economic indicators as signs of the apocalypse.

Having outlined the problem and specified its origins, Reagan was a prisoner of his own rhetoric: his own administration was responsible for record-breaking increases in state government spending. In this light, Reagan was only exacerbating the problem, not solving it. Apparently realizing the incongruity between his rhetoric and his record, Reagan attempted to redeem himself from any wrongdoing by painstakingly reviewing all of the cost-saving measures implemented by his administration. They included, among others, modernizing the statewide system of filing equipment controls, consolidating telephone switchboards, establishing a fee for state inspections, and extending the one-way toll system for government operated bridges (4–5). Significantly, Reagan did not mention that the combined savings of these four cost-saving measures was a paltry $1.53 million. Implied by Reagan's preoccupation with "symbolic savings" was the following: if he was so concerned with the small details, surely he was saving money on the large expenditures as well. Such a strategy served to reinforce Reagan's proclamation to "squeeze, cut, and trim" delivered in his *Inaugural Message*, thus adding to his image as a fiscal conservative dedicated to fighting inflation.

Even with all of the many savings Reagan had implemented, the budget of $6.2 billion was still a blemish on his record. Acknowledging the need to compensate for the third straight record budget, Reagan used a strategy similar to the one used in his budget message of February 4. That is, Reagan divided up the budget into two parts: the amount needed to finance government at the state level and the amount required to finance the cost of local governments. Detailing the latter of these two parts, Reagan stated, "Of this year's $6.2 billion budget—$3.6 billion goes back to local government. . . . What confuses almost everyone except the accountants is that the budget includes three areas of expenditures which are really not expenditures but rather are tax relief payments" (8).

Addressing the former, Reagan claimed that "in reality, the budget for operating state government is a little over $2 billion. That is the figure citizens should watch to see if government spending is getting out of line" (8). In order to avoid any lingering confusion over budget appropriations, Reagan greatly simplified the case: "We should be happy if we can report a reduction in that $2 billion cost-of-government budget and we should be happy if we can show an increase in that other part—the amount we returned to the local communities and to the taxpayers" (8). Reagan was actually claiming that budget increases in the future should be seen as a positive; in fact, the bigger the better. Given this redefinition, the $6.2 billion budget, Reagan implied, was not so bad after all.

The last issue Reagan deliberated on was tax reform. Having been introduced nearly six months earlier, Reagan's tax reform proposals had been stalled in various legislative committees. Reagan's frustration with the legislature's lack of action on his tax reform proposals was very evident in this speech. What is more significant was who Reagan targeted for blame.

> Tax reform is dependent upon politics, the process by which we govern ourselves—and politics is not a spectator sport. It is the lot of those who are spectators of politics to be mastered by those who take an active part in politics. . . . People do not always get the kind of government they deserve but they do, without fail, get the kind of government they *resemble*. . . . [W]hat it will resemble—what it will be—depends on you and your active participation in the affairs of government (Reagan's emphasis, 11–12).

Reagan's wrath was directed at the people who had failed in this instance to get involved in Reagan's call for tax reform. Reagan could only formulate policy, the people had to act on it, and this time the people had let their leader down.

1970

If 1967 was Reagan's worst year as governor, 1970 was a close second. What began as a potentially productive year for Reagan and the Republican majority in both houses of the legislature had turned dismal by the end of the year. First, the state's budget for fiscal year 1969–70 had run a deficit of over $130 million as revenues diminished due to the nation's economic downturn and welfare costs increased. Fortunately for Reagan, the surplus resulting from his 1967 tax bill was enough to cover the deficit.

Second, the budget Reagan eventually signed, four days after the fiscal year had officially started, was over $100 million higher than his original budget submitted on February 3, of $6.48 billion.[36] What made matters worse was that by late November, Reagan announced the state's $6.59 billion budget for fiscal year 1970–71 was out of balance by $150 million due to higher welfare costs and lower-than-projected revenues.

Third, what initially looked like the year's most promising legislative victory for Reagan, turned out to be his most bitter defeat in late August. After having his tax reform program passed by a two-thirds vote of the assembly in May, the program failed by one vote to pass the senate.

Fourth, Reagan's proposed Welfare Reform Act of 1970, which would have limited aid to first-year residents, cut aid to the totally dependent, placed mandatory work requirements on unemployed fathers, and increased grants to AFDC (Aid for Families with Dependent Children) families, also failed to secure passage. Coupled with this defeat, the state was threatened by a $978 million cut in federal welfare funds because California had not instituted federally mandated guidelines which stipulated cost-of-living increases in the AFDC program. Additionally, in November the Reagan administration declared that welfare and Medi-Cal were exceeding expected costs by $90 million for fiscal year 1970–71.[37]

Not surprisingly, California voters expressed their disappointment with the lack of productivity by the Republican legislative majority by electing a Democratic majority. The Republicans' two-vote majority in both houses had become a 21–19 Democratic advantage in the senate and a 43–37 Democratic lead in the assembly following November 3. Paradoxically, all but one of the statewide elections yielded a Republican victory, including Reagan's victory over former Assembly Speaker Jesse Unruh.[38] Despite outdistancing Unruh by a vote of 3,382,384 to 2,879,140, Reagan's popularity had noticeably waned as Reagan suffered close to a 500,000 vote drop between the 1966 and 1970 elections.

January 6, 1970: State-of-the-State Message

Uncharacteristically, economic issues were subordinated to environmental issues in Reagan's 1970 State-of-the-State Message. Two of the economic issues Reagan did address were welfare and government spending.

Passage of Reagan's major reforms in California's welfare system were over a year away, but according to Reagan, the situation was extremely urgent in 1970: "Even in these times of high employment, welfare costs in California continue to climb at a rate beyond the capacity of our tax structure to keep pace. *This increase each year is almost three times as great as the increase in our revenues*" (Reagan's emphasis, 8).[39] Not only were the costs increasing greatly each year, welfare was also siphoning funds from other programs. As he had in previous speeches, Reagan positioned welfare against other, more worthy programs, with the intended effect of mobilizing legislative support for welfare reform. Because welfare expenditures exceeded spending on education, and because the long term answer to welfare was education, Reagan claimed that California's funds were not being allocated "to the best possible use." According to Reagan, welfare spending increases were actually being financed by funds originally targeted for education. Education, as it had been in the past, was dialectically opposed to welfare in order to add more emphasis to an already urgent situation.

Reagan also strongly emphasized the continuing need for economy in government fiscal policy. Specifically, the nation's future was in jeopardy due to the total share of income that all levels of government combined to consume: "It is a harsh fact of life . . . that once the level of taxation reaches and remains at 35 percent of the national income for a period of time, that nation cannot remain solvent—or free. Today, . . . the level of confiscation by taxation has reached approximately 37 percent" (10). This was not some arbitrary statistic, rather it was a "fact of life," claimed Reagan, underscoring the exigency. If the nation's future was in grave danger, then Reagan was one of its saviors, as he insisted that "no area of government will receive all it asked for" (10). Thus Reagan, through his projection of fiscal prudence, was doing his part to make sure that the United States remained "solvent" and "free."

While Reagan the ideologue was decrying the need for less government spending to ensure lower taxes, Reagan the pragmatic politician was advocating "not more government, *but better government*" (Reagan's emphasis, 11). Curiously, Reagan's usual appeal for "less government" was missing, having been replaced by an appeal for "better government." The incongruity between Reagan's two personae could not have been more pronounced. Better government was oxymoronic for Reagan the ideologue. Less government spending, hence less government, went against Reagan the pragmatic politician's claims to be a humanitarian.

THE NEXT GENERATION

January 30, 1970

As governor of California, Reagan would typically address, at least once a year, a group of Young Republicans or some other youth organization on the virtues of Republicanism. On January 30, Reagan lectured to the YMCA Model Legislature on fiscal policy and the future of America's economy.

Reflecting his own philosophy on welfare spending, Reagan warned his audience on the dangers of redistribution:

> In your eagerness to build a better world you will want to do great things and to help those in distress. There is no quarrel with that; we all want to help those in need. But take care that when you recommend programs to help some, you do not cause an even greater distress among those who must foot the bill. [Y]ou are not really doing anything for anybody if all you do is take from one person to give to another. When you do this you become—at best—a *middleman*, and at worst, a *tyrant* (Reagan's emphasis, 3).[40]

Significantly, redistribution, for Reagan, was at worst a form of tyranny because of its impact on the taxpayer. In other words, welfare, financed by a progressive tax system, was nothing short of government-imposed tyranny.

Reagan's economic rhetoric would occasionally reach a fever pitch of extremism. Such was the case in this speech. More specifically, Reagan implicitly equated increased welfare spending to fascism. Reagan advised,

> We all condemn fascism. We are strongly opposed to what happened in Germany under Hitler in the thirties and forties. We must never forget what happened there; we must never allow it to happen here. [Y]ou may protest that in Germany the people were to blame; the people should have stopped it before it got started. And, you are right. It is just that the people did not see it—in the beginning. Hitler moved slowly, subtly at first, under the guise of doing good for the people. He said: "We shall banish want. We shall banish fear. The essence of National socialism is human welfare rooted in a fuller life for every German from childhood to old age." The gas ovens, the genocide, the concentration camps came later. [T]yranny always wears a disguise—until it is strong enough to show itself. In everything we do in government, and in everything the people permit the government to do for them, we must be careful to see ahead to the end results so that we can resist the beginning if the end is evil (4).

Though Reagan never explicitly stated that welfare was a manifestation of fascism, the implications were clearly in evidence from his discourse. Additionally, because welfare was predominantly a Democratic phenomenon, Reagan associated Democrats with fascism and national socialism.

TAX REFORM/BUDGET

February 7, 1970

Oddly enough, Reagan chose the California Young Republican Convention to reintroduce his proposals for tax reform. Having gone on television in a *Report to the People* to introduce his tax reform program the previous year, Reagan presented his reformed reform proposals to a much smaller, partisan gathering.

Reducing property taxes and diminishing California's business inventory tax remained Reagan's primary objectives of tax reform. However, the means to achieving these ends had changed significantly from the previous year. Several of the methods for financing property tax and business inventory tax reductions had changed. First, Reagan called for "a new rate bracket on the personal income tax for those filing joint returns of $32,000 taxable income" (4).[41] Second, and in very vague terms, Reagan advocated "an equitable adjustment in the capital gains tax" (4). Third, and in conflict with the desired goal of less taxes on business, Reagan called for "an increase of one-half of one percent on the bank and corporation tax" (4). The final source of revenue would be "a minimum income tax to close the loopholes on some, in the higher income levels, who pay no income taxes" (4). The only means of finance that had remained intact from the preceding year was an increase of 1 percent in the state sales tax.

Most significant, though, was Reagan's change of heart on tax withholding. Reagan, for the first time, expressed his support for mandatory tax withholding by the state. Acknowledging this major shift in tax policy, Reagan stated,

> Beginning about last May, our own surveys and soundings revealed a curious thing. Those who opposed withholding and who had always been in the majority had become a definite minority. I was tempted to use that as justification for my decision, and say I was simply abiding by the will of the people. [B]ut, I would have been rationalizing. The plain truth is—honest, fiscal responsibility forced me to give in. I am still philosophically opposed to withholding, as I have always been. . . . [W]ithholding would provide the same increase in revenue and at the same time solve our cash flow problem. I could not in clear conscience choose my philosophy over my clear obligation to preserve fiscal responsibility (4–6).

Reagan was not compromising his ideals, he was merely sacrificing them for the betterment of the state. One can hardly help but notice the paradox contained in the last sentence: Reagan promised that he would not let his philosophy interfere with fiscal responsibility. However, fiscal responsibility was Reagan's philosophy, or at least his stated philosophy.

Furthermore, recognizing the political consequences of such a drastic switch (the gubernatorial elections were only nine months away), Reagan attempted to distinguish among those advocating withholding: "There are two major, all-important differences between our reluctant endorsement of withholding and the intentions of those who proposed withholding in past years. They would have *kept* the windfall and *used it to increase state spending*" (Reagan's emphasis, 6). Reagan was going to give whatever savings that resulted from withholding (estimated at $450 million) back to the people; those who had proposed withholding in the past were merely interested in increasing the taxpayer's burden.

Reagan submitted his budget for fiscal year 1970–71 the same day he resubmitted his proposal for tax reform, February 3. Describing his administration's budget, Reagan noted, "We have managed to come up with a Hold-the-line budget—the tightest California budget in many years. Overall, it is about one percent less than what we expect to spend this year" (6). However, in the very next paragraph, Reagan's "Hold-the-line budget" had been replaced by a bigger budget, one that Reagan had little control over: "We have had to cut back some programs and delay others, some we would have preferred to maintain or expand. *But, we had no choice* . . . except to increase taxes and take more money from the people . . . and that's no choice at all" (Reagan's emphasis and ellipses, 6). If, as Reagan claimed, his budget for fiscal year 1970–71 was 1 percent less than California's budget for fiscal year 1969–70, then the need for a tax increase to finance the coming year's budget needs was illogical. Also, Reagan's arithmetic did not add up. His administration's $6.5 billion budget for fiscal year 1970–71 included an increase close to $300 million from the previous year. Thus Reagan's claims to 1 percent reduction in the budget for fiscal year 1970–71 were misleading, if not altogether false.

CAMPAIGN '70

April 5, 1970

Since his days at General Electric on the speaking circuit until the end of his first term as governor, the basic ideals of "The Speech" had remained intact. Even though Reagan had taken on a political persona, Reagan the ideologue still tenaciously clung to the ideals expressed in "The Speech." Lower taxes, proportional taxation, less government, decentralized government, fiscal atrocities at the federal level, apocalyptic visions, and hints of a government conspiracy were still very much in evidence in Reagan's gubernatorial economic discourse. As Reagan began to campaign for a second term, many of the themes expressed in "The Speech" reappeared. Such was the case on April 5, when Reagan spoke to the California Republican Assembly Convention.

Returning to a familiar theme, Reagan began this speech with a reference to proportional taxation: "The Judeo-Christian tradition is based on a belief in tithing—that one tenth of a man's earnings is the Lord's share. But Caesar is not satisfied with such a paltry sum" (1).[42] In fact, Reagan noted that government at all levels was taking more than one third of all income. One-third was a symbolic indicator for Reagan because "once a government takes more than a third of the producer's income, government also takes freedom, and freedom once lost is seldom, if ever, regained" (1). The nation's end was imminent, signaled by a conspiratorial system of taxation.

Archetypal metaphors associated with Heaven and Hell also reappeared in this speech. Reagan stated that

> the utopian dreams focus our eyes on pie in the sky but our feet take us ever downward. [I]f I remember correctly, four years ago we talked of digging in our heels, ending the downward slide and starting the long steep climb out of the bottomless, bureaucratic pit. We have started that climb (1).

The utopian dreamers, Democrats, were leading the nation towards a symbolic Hell. Meanwhile, Reagan, the savior, had helped dig California out of the Democratic Purgatory, and had started the climb towards a more perfect economic reality.

Reagan offered several proofs that his administration had started the climb out of the abyss. First, Reagan claimed that his administration was responsible for returning "to the citizens almost $1.3 billion—$633 million in direct property tax relief and more than $650 million in indirect relief—reimbursing local governments for expenses that would otherwise fall on the property taxpayer" (1).

Second, Reagan claimed that his administration had actually reduced the size of government despite the record-breaking budgets:

> Billions in budgets and billions in savings are hard to visualize, particularly when the budget seems to be ever increasing. Well let me point out that inflation alone adds $360 million to the cost of state government if we make no provision for growth in population at all. The budget proposed for next year actively [sic] increases less than the rate of inflation which means we have reduced the size of government (2).

Reagan dramatized events such that his budgets were a victim of inflation, yet he was, nevertheless, still able to reduce the size of government.

Third, despite the huge costs for welfare and Medi-Cal, Reagan claimed that he had saved the taxpayers $466 million dollars: "If we had raised your taxes to keep up with the increase in welfare costs . . . we would have taken another $466 million from the taxpayers. Instead, we managed to pay those increases out of the savings we have made by our cut, squeeze and trim policies in other areas of government" (2). In all three of these proofs, Reagan was clearly the hero, responsible for lower taxes and smaller government.

August 1, 1970

Instead of metaphors connoting a dialectic between Heaven and Hell, Reagan, in a speech to the GOP Platform Committee, used the metaphor of a mountain to describe the fiscal situation he inherited from Pat Brown. Taking his audience back to 1967, Reagan observed,

> In those early days, our first task was to simply stave off the fiscal chaos we inherited. Having accomplished that, we then began chipping away at a mountain of serious fiscal and social problems. . . . Eight years of neglect cannot be reversed so easily. We do not contend that the job is completed now. But we have made tremendous progress (3).[43]

More significant, Reagan emphasized, were his administration's accomplishments given that Republicans did not hold a majority "in either house for most of the past 3 1/2 years" (4).[44]

Upon detailing his heroic efforts in the areas of tax relief, economy in government, crime, education, and the environment, Reagan turned to his opponent, Jesse Unruh. Specifically, Reagan claimed that Unruh and the Democrats would run a smear campaign because "they do not want the people to see clearly the real issue because they know that the people of California are not likely to open the door again to those who created the fiscal crisis of 1966–67" (6). As he did in 1984 by associating Walter Mondale with Jimmy Carter's "malaise" economics, Reagan associated Jesse Unruh with the Pat Brown inspired fiscal chaos of 1967. Such a negative identification was one of Reagan's primary strategies in portraying Unruh as a villain of the California people.

THE NATION'S ECONOMY

September 4, 1970

As Reagan's economic rhetoric grew more national in scope with his support of Richard Nixon, he was increasingly on the defensive. The theme from this genre of discourse was Reagan's defense that "ours is not a sick society." Proof that the United States was not a sick society resided in the economic and social accomplishments of Reagan's generation.

> When we were born, two-thirds of us lived in sub-standard housing; now it is less than 10 percent. Ninety percent of all Americans lived below what is considered the poverty line; by the time it was our turn to take over that had been reduced by more than half and in our adult lifetime we have brought it down to only 10 percent. Let those who cry 'revolution now' take a second look—for,

our generation has presided over the greatest social and economic revolution the world has ever seen (3).[45]

Further proof of society's health was manifested by more jobs for minorities, billions of dollars given in foreign aid, and healthier children.

Not only was the United States "healthy," according to Reagan, it was exceedingly so, especially in comparison to the Soviet Union.

In that Marxian Utopia, the Soviet Union must force its workers to labor seven times as long as their American counterparts to earn food, 12 and one-half times as long to buy a bar of soap, and 15 times as many hours to buy a suit of clothes. By diligent effort we, too, could have their kind of Utopia—but, we would have to tear down 60 percent of our homes, 65 percent of our railroads and 90 percent of our phones (5).

Reagan's proof of the United States' health was of an economic orientation and the cause for the nation's well-being was free-enterprise: "Free men engaged in free enterprise build better nations with more and better goods and services, higher wages and higher standards of living for more people" (6). Metaphorically considered, free enterprise was the only medicine America needed in order to remain healthy. Thus free enterprise was a cure-all for Reagan, capable of healing any country that prescribed to its methods. To say that free enterprise was a "god-term" for Ronald Reagan is to understate the case. Rather, free enterprise had godly characteristics for Reagan, especially when considered in light of its healing or redemptive powers.[46]

CONCLUSION

Ronald Reagan proved to be a quick learner as he realized very early in his first term as governor that his anti-government rhetoric was much easier to formulate than its implementation. Reagan also quickly grasped which issues were politically volatile. After his initial cost-cutting barrage in early 1967, some of which generated a great deal of negative press, Reagan backed off on politically sensitive cost-cutting measures. During the four years, Reagan's economic rhetoric gradually moved away from an emphasis on cost-cutting economies to a more politically palatable emphasis on cost-saving efficiencies.

Reagan's role as governor greatly affected his economic rhetoric. Reagan recognized that he could no longer spout only his anti-government line and thus run the risk of alienating the legislature as well as the citizenry; rather, he was essentially forced to adopt a "political persona," a persona which adhered to the political realities of state government. Compromise was the very essence of this persona. This new persona not only affected Reagan's economic rhetoric, but what's more, it affected his legislative proposals, as evidenced by his tax relief bill of 1967 and his program for tax reform.

In spite of his new role, Reagan's anti-government rhetoric persisted, especially to partisan gatherings inside and outside of California. This anti-government rhetoric was not limited to predominantly Republican audiences though as Reagan's promise to "squeeze, cut, and trim" was echoed throughout his first term to audiences of varying political persuasions, including the legislature.

Audience analysis is fundamental to public speaking. To purposefully alienate one's audience, especially when the audience wields a great deal of political clout, defies the rules of common-sense public speaking. Yet this style of rhetoric typified much of Reagan's speechmaking to the legislature. Given this oftentimes confrontational discourse, Reagan's lack of legislative success comes as no great surprise. Cannon observed, "In the eight years encompassed by Brown's second term and Reagan's first, state government was long on promises and short on delivery. Reagan compounded the difficulty by persistent denigration of the Legislature. It was an attitude reflecting both his inexperience and his personal distaste for legislative processes."[47] Clearly, "the great communicator" label was not borne from Reagan's first term as governor.

Reagan kept few, if any, of his campaign promises during his first four years: California's budget swelled $2 billion, from $4.6 billion to nearly $6.6 billion; property taxes, income taxes, sales taxes, and bank and corporation taxes all increased; welfare and Medi-Cal costs continued to soar; and Reagan's budgets for fiscal years 1969–70 and 1970–71 were both out-of-balance. Reagan, however, attempted to mitigate this seeming disparity between his promises and his record through two rhetorical means.

First, Reagan consistently shifted the blame for the aforementioned "problems." Pat Brown was Reagan's scapegoat for higher budgets and higher taxes in 1967 and 1968. The legislature, specifically the big-spending Democrats, were blamed for later budgets and the "runaway" costs for welfare in addition to failed attempts to enact Reagan's tax reform programs.

Reagan also tried to avoid responsibility for any negative economic occurrences by repeatedly emphasizing the role of the citizenry. Government, as Reagan outlined in his inaugural message, would lead, but the people would have to supply the solutions to government's problems. If Reagan was not explicitly blaming Democratic legislators or implicitly indicting the citizenry, he would exempt his administration from blame by portraying himself as a victim of circumstance, unable to exert direct control over California's fiscal situation.

Second, Reagan attempted to redefine potentially damaging economic occurrences by framing them as strengths. For example, Reagan claimed that the tax rebate in 1969 was the result of his administration's economies, when in actuality most of the surplus resulted from the 1967 tax bill. Reagan also tried to redefine the circumstances which give rise to record-breaking budgets by dividing the budget into two parts: the cost of state government and the cost of local governments. In this scenario, higher budgets were not only warranted, but desirable. If this wasn't convincing enough, Reagan claimed that annual budget increases were less than the annual rate of inflation, hence he was living up to his promises.

NOTES

1. The final vote count was 3,742,913 for Reagan, 2,749,174 for Brown.

2. We are not the first to comment on Reagan's two different rhetorical personae. For example, see Lou Cannon, *Reagan* (New York: G. P. Putnam's Sons, 1982), 196.

3. The label "Creative Society" was coined by a right-wing radio evangelist, W. S. McBirnie.

4. Reagan published a book by the same name in 1968. See Ronald Reagan, *The Creative Society* (New York: Devin Adair, 1968).

5. All references to this speech are from California, Governor's Office Press Release, Ronald Reagan, *Inaugural Message* (January 5, 1967): 1–10.

6. All references to this speech are from California, Governor's Office Press Release, Ronald Reagan, *Report to the People* (February 5, 1967): 1–5.

7. Reagan mentioned in his Modified Budget Message to the state legislature on March 28, that $111.7 million of the increases was caused by Medi-Cal and the failure to implement tuition. California, Governor's Office Press Release, Ronald Reagan, *Modified Budget Message* (March 28, 1967): iv.

8. All references to this speech are from California, Governor's Office Press Release, Ronald Reagan, *Report to the People* (April 16, 1967): 1–7.

9. California, Governor's Office Press Release, Ronald Reagan, *Tax Message* (March 8, 1967): 11–12.

10. Ibid., 12.

11. Reagan, *Report to the People* (April 16, 1967): 7.

12. All references to this speech are from California, Governor's Office Press Release, Ronald Reagan, *United Republicans of California Convention* (May 6, 1967): 1–10.

13. All references to this speech are from California, Governor's Office Press Release, Ronald Reagan, *Report to the People* (July 9, 1967): 1–7.

14. All references to this speech are from California, Governor's Office Press Release, Ronald Reagan, *Governor's Conference on Medicaid* (September 20, 1967): 1–4.

15. Reagan "blue-pencilled" $16 million from the legislature's budget of $5.71 billion.

16. All references to this speech are from California, Governor's Office Press Release, Ronald Reagan, *State-of-the-State Message* (January 9, 1968): 1–12.

17. Cannon, *Reagan*, 18.

18. All references to this speech are from California, Governor's Office Press Release, Ronald Reagan, *Governor's Conference on Planning for Housing and Home Ownership* (February 1, 1968): 1–7.

19. All references to this speech are from California, Governor's Office Press Release, Ronald Reagan, *Welfare* (March 21, 1968): 1–7.

20. Cannon, *Reagan*, 163–64.

21. All references to this speech are from California, Governor's Office Press Release, Ronald Reagan, *Women's National Press Club* (April 5, 1968): 1–11.

22. All references to this speech are from California, Governor's Office Press Release, Ronald Reagan, *American Women in Radio and Television Convention* (May 3, 1968): 1–8.

23. All references to this speech are from California, Governor's Office Press Release, Ronald Reagan, *Fund Raising Rally* (July 30, 1968): 1–2.

24. All references to this speech are from California, Governor's Office Press Release, Ronald Reagan, *Republican National Convention Platform Committee Meeting* (July 31, 1968): 1–7.

25. All references to this speech are from California, Governor's Office Press Release, Ronald Reagan, *Budget Message* (June 29, 1968): 1–2.

26. The number of Republican senators fluctuated throughout the year, but Republicans never lacked a majority in at least one branch of the legislature during the 1969 session.

27. All references to this speech are from California, Governor's Office Press Release, Ronald Reagan, *State-of-the-State Message* (January 7, 1969): 1–13.

28. Reagan's equal education plan was to also finance capital construction and more teaching chairs.

29. All references to this speech are from California, Governor's Office Press Release, Ronald Reagan, *Executive Symposium Luncheon* (January 30, 1969): 1–9.

30. California, Governor's Office Press Release, Ronald Reagan, *Report to the People* (January 31, 1969): 1.

31. For a brief discussion of the increased rate of progressivity resulting from Reagan's 1967 tax bill see *The Sacramento Bee*, July 30, 1968.

32. All references to this speech are from California, Governor's Office Press Release, Ronald Reagan, *Report to the People* (February 4, 1969): 1–13.

33. All references to this speech are from California, Governor's Office Press Release, Ronald Reagan, *Tax Reform Message* (April 8, 1969): 1–13.

34. All references to this speech are from California, Governor's Office Press Release, Ronald Reagan, *Report to the People* (May 11, 1969): 1–11.

35. All references to this speech are from California, Governor's Office Press Release, Ronald Reagan, *Sacramento Host Breakfast* (September 5, 1969): 1–12.

36. This increase resulted from Democratic pressure to increase aid to California public schools. This coalition wanted an additional $300 million, but ultimately had to settle for just over $100 million.

37. In December, the Reagan administration instituted cuts that were expected to cut the deficit by $40 to 50 million. This left a projected deficit of $30 to 40 million.

38. Edmund G. Brown, Jr. (soon to be known as Jerry Brown), a Democrat, won the race for secretary of state.

39. All references to this speech are from California, Governor's Office Press Release, Ronald Reagan, *State-of-the-State Message* (January 6, 1970): 1–13.

40. All references to this speech are from California, Governor's Office Press Release, Ronald Reagan, *YMCA Model Legislature* (January 30, 1970): 1–5.

41. All references to this speech are from California, Governor's Office Press Release, Ronald Reagan, *California Young Republican Convention* (February 7, 1970): 1–9.

42. All references to this speech are from California, Governor's Office Press Release, Ronald Reagan, *California Republican Assembly Convention* (April 5, 1970): 1–7.

43. All references to this speech are from California, Governor's Office Press Release, Ronald Reagan, *GOP Platform Committee* (August 1, 1970): 1–9.

44. This statement was a blatant lie as Republicans held a majority in the legislature during most of 1969 and 1970.

45. All references to this speech are from California, Governor's Office Press Release, Ronald Reagan, *Sacramento Host Breakfast* (September 4, 1970): 1–8.

46. For a discussion of "god-terms" see Kenneth Burke, *A Rhetoric of Motives* (Berkeley and Los Angeles: University of California Press, 1969), 298–301; Richard M. Weaver, *The Ethics of Rhetoric* (Chicago: Regnery Gateway, 1953; reprint, Davis: Hermagoras, 1985), 212 (page reference is to reprint edition).

47. Lou Cannon, "The Reagan Years," *California Journal* 5 (November 1974): 363.

Chapter Three

The Creative Society: Part Two

Nineteen seventy-one was Ronald Reagan's most productive year with the legislature. Welfare reform and a "mini" tax reform package both met with legislative approval. Surprisingly, what Reagan could not accomplish in either 1969 or 1970 with a Republican majority, he achieved in 1971 with a Democratic majority in both houses.

However, welfare and tax reform were both complicated by Reagan's controversial, patchwork budget of $6.73 billion for fiscal year 1971–72, which he unveiled in early February. The budget was submitted technically in balance, as a footnote assumed that close to $400 million would be raised by legislative and administrative reforms in welfare. Reagan was essentially attempting to force the legislature to assent to his administration's welfare and Medi-Cal reforms, which were eventually introduced on March 15. If the legislature did not grant passage to these reforms, taxes would have to be raised in order to cover the huge deficit; taxes that would be raised by legislative mandate, not the governor's. Thus the Democratically controlled legislature would be responsible for higher taxes, not Reagan. Assembly Speaker Bob Moretti sensed the rhetorical and political ramifications of Reagan's contingent budget:

> As I have repeatedly said, everyone in this building knows that we need a revenue increase this year, including the Governor. [W]hat he is going to do in the next month, probably, is say to the people, 'Gosh, I really tried for you. You know I'm Ronnie good guy, and I did what I could to prevent this odious thing from happening.' But 'that damn Legislature' or 'that damn federal government' or 'the state employees,' or whatever he chooses to make the scapegoat for this issue, will be blamed for the tax increase, when everybody has known all along that it's absolutely necessary in order to avoid bankruptcy for this state.[1]

The drama was further fueled in early July as the legislature passed a budget for fiscal year 1971–72 of $7.29 billion, an increase of over $500 million to Reagan's original budget. Reagan signed the budget on July 3, minus $503 million. This outraged the legislature as Reagan rendered several months of budget negotiations null and void with several strokes of his blue-pencil.[2]

Upon signing the budget, Reagan forecasted a deficit of $230 million for fiscal year 1971–72. However, welfare reforms alone could not cover this deficit because Reagan had greatly exaggerated the savings resulting from such reforms.[3] Thus, in addition to welfare reform, Reagan advocated tax legislation that included a withholding provision to balance the budget.

Reagan's welfare and Medi-Cal reforms were eventually passed in mid-August, though having undergone some modifications. The governor did get much of what he wanted, including a work requirement for able-bodied welfare recipients, tighter eligibility standards, a ceiling on earned income exemptions, stronger family financial responsibility, and tighter administrative control over Medi-Cal services.[4]

The regular session of the legislature adjourned without having achieved a tax reform program suitable to Reagan. The legislature reconvened for a special session called by Reagan in early December. On December 7, a compromise was reached on a "mini" tax reform plan which contained very little in the way of property tax relief but contained the sought-after income tax withholding provision, which was expected to raise $650 million in fiscal year 1971–72.[5]

By all accounts, Reagan pulled off a major coup in 1971. By purposefully underfunding the state's budget, Reagan was able to exert sufficient pressure on the legislature to ensure passage of his welfare and Medi-Cal reforms as well as an income tax withholding measure.

1971

January 4, 1971: Inaugural Address

Ronald Reagan began his second term as governor by delivering his *Inaugural Address* on January 4. The theme of the Creative Society, as outlined in his first inaugural, had a central role in this speech as well. Reflecting back on his first term Reagan stated,

> On that day four years ago, I asked that we set foot on a path leading toward a Creative Society. We have travelled that road since and with all my heart I believe we should continue. It turns away from increasing reliance on government and leads toward renewed respect for . . . the collective genius and common sense of the people (2).[6]

As one might expect from a second *Inaugural Address*, Reagan mentioned several accomplishments pertaining to his first four years. Perhaps because his economic accomplishments were minimal during his first term, Reagan subordinated economic issues to the environment, declining traffic fatalities, reductions in violent crime, and the reduced prison population. Reagan did emphasize, though, that his administration was able to reduce the size of government.

The two issues that remained unsolved that concerned Reagan the most were tax reform and welfare reform. In 1971, the need for welfare reform was even more urgent, according to Reagan, due to diminished revenues caused by the nation's recession. Using the recession to his advantage, Reagan stated, "This slump in tax revenues, however, is not our greatest problem. It just aggravated a situation that has been growing worse year after year. Welfare costs have been increasing more than three times as fast as revenue and in this present year have escalated at an even faster rate" (5). The recession served as a rhetorical reinforcement for Reagan's invocation to reform welfare. Reagan claimed that "the economic downturn has brought us to the moment of truth we have avoided for too long a time" (8). Furthermore, Reagan later added, "We can be depressed by a seeming fiscal crisis, or we can recognize this as the opportunity it really is" (9). For Reagan, a tax increase would have been merely a temporary solution to a permanent problem. Additionally, the taxpayer "already pays too much for government," observed Reagan (8). Given this, the only acceptable alternative was a complete reform of welfare.

Reagan concluded his second inaugural by, ironically, chiding those whose rhetoric was based on fear: "In recent months a few in our midst have raised the haunting spectre of panic and depression. It is time we inoculated ourselves against the contagion of fear they would spread" (10). Recall that much of Reagan's gubernatorial as well as pre-gubernatorial economic rhetoric embodied fear appeals and apocalyptic visions. In this instance, Reagan was doing nothing more than indicting his own rhetoric.

January 12, 1971: State-of-the-State Message

As he iterated in 1967, Reagan emphasized that California needed to put its "fiscal house in order" (7).[7] In 1971, however, Reagan was responding to less state revenues precipitated by the nation's recession. One of the ways Reagan proposed to deal with the problem was through temporary alternatives: "Since this is a temporary dislocation, I see no reason why government should not meet it with a temporary solution" (7). Temporary spending cuts were, for Reagan, a legitimate means to balance a budget in response to less revenues; a temporary tax increase was not.

Aside from lower revenues caused by the recession, another problem, claimed Reagan, was the rising costs of Medi-Cal and welfare caused by inherent flaws in the programs. The welfare system was plagued by several deficiencies: documentation of earnings, fraud, and eligibility standards. Foreshadowing his administration's legislation on welfare reform, Reagan insisted that a distinction needed to be made between the able-bodied and the "truly needy." While the truly needy had no place left to turn, Reagan advocated "that able-bodied adult recipients work and meet their own responsibilities" (9). Another part of Reagan's reforms was to provide state-sponsored jobs for able-bodied welfare recipients. Reagan the ideologue had apparently compromised his long-held belief that only the private sector could provide meaningful, real employment. Reagan recognized that the private sector could not absorb a large influx of workers during a recession and thus called for "public jobs [that] would be financing improvements for our state and underwriting a public work force" (11). Other reforms Reagan proposed were establishing realistic eligibility standards, locating absent fathers, and removing the confidentiality of financial information from welfare recipients.

Reagan's primary problem with Medi-Cal continued to be the excessive health care coverage available to the poor. Thus he proposed to solve this inequity by limiting "health care services to the poor so they will be comparable with the health benefits provided by the various prepaid health insurance plans covering most of our citizens" (12).

The last issue Reagan addressed was the budget for fiscal year 1971–72, specifically the "gigantic deficit" predicted by many. As he often did, Reagan reduced a potentially complex issue to an either/or proposition: "We are confronted by a choice. We can reform government—reduce the cost of services, particularly in welfare and Medi-Cal, or we can increase taxes. To choose the latter without excising the cancer eating at our vitals is to face tax increases year in and year out" (13). By likening welfare and Medi-Cal to cancer, the only available choice was to save the fiscally weakened patient through major surgery of both programs.

WELFARE REFORM

January 25, 1971

Welfare and welfare reform were the major topics during Reagan's January 25 speech to the National Press Club in Washington, D.C. According to Reagan, welfare was not just a problem specific to Californians, but "welfare, our greatest single outlay of public funds at three levels of government, is adrift without rudder or compass" (3).[8] The problem with welfare spending, observed Reagan, was that it hoarded tax revenues, and thus funding for other governmental programs was problematic.

As he specified when talking on the subject of minority unemployment, Reagan identified the root cause of welfare as poverty. And, "the answer to much of poverty is employment—jobs, job development, job training and job placement" (6). In fact, Reagan claimed that the "welfare syndrome" could best be solved by expanding "the generative and derivative forces of our free competitive enterprise system" (6). Responsibility for the welfare problem lay not with government intervention, but with free enterprise, thus, the American work force. Before his non-Californian audience, government-sponsored jobs (what Reagan had advocated in California) received very little attention by Reagan. To have emphasized his program of state government sponsored jobs may have damaged Reagan's ideological persona, which he had long been cultivating, especially with regional audiences.

May 1, 1971

In a speech to the American Association of University Women, Reagan detailed many of the inequities of California's welfare system. Reagan was attempting to create a good vs. evil dichotomy between the "truly needy" and recipients who had defrauded or manipulated the existing welfare laws for their own personal gain: "Because we have to stretch the available funds to include some who should not be on welfare at all, our public assistance program is unable to provide sufficiently for those who really need hlep [*sic*] the most" (3).[9] Such an inequity served to underscore the urgent need for major welfare reforms.

In many of his speeches, Reagan simply identified the "truly needy" as persons, "who through no fault of their own," could not provide for themselves. However, in this speech Reagan explicitly identified the composition of this group: "These are the truly needy . . . the blind, the elderly, the disabled and those children from families with little or no outside income and no employed breadwinner" (Reagan's ellipses, 3). Of interest were the people omitted from the "truly needy" constituency. Specifically, single parent families and the employable but unemployed were not among this group. Thus Reagan's "truly needy" embodied one of two possible characteristics: physical impairment and/or age.

Though he strayed from the minutiae of some of his reform proposals, Reagan did mention some of the specifics of his proposals. They included, " . . . automated monthly pensions for the elderly, the blind and disabled," increased "monthly grants to those on AFDC (Aid for Families with Dependent Children) who have no other outside income or very little," imposing "a realistic limit on the amount of outside income a family may have and still qualify for welfare benefits," and abled-bodied adults "... would have to be either seeking employment, training for a job or participating in the Public Assistance Work Force to continue receiving welfare" (4–6).

Reagan had specified in his speech on January 25 that jobs were the answer to welfare. This claim is significant with respect to Reagan's claim contained in this speech, that education was one of "the positive cures for poverty" (8). Specifiying that education was a solution to welfare allowed Reagan both to emphasize the administration's spending increases on education (indicating he had been working to solve the problem all along) and to villify the current welfare system due to the funds it was usurping from education: "Our state budget for higher education is $676 million this year, the highest amount in the state's history. But welfare and Medi-Cal consume almost twice as much. . . . [W]e are providing $20 million a year for student scholarships and loans. $20 million will not pay for one week of welfare" (7). If education was a major part of the answer to welfare dependency, as he claimed it was, then Reagan had been all along acting in the best interests of welfare recipients by allocating more funds to higher education.

June 23, 1971

Welfare and welfare reform continued to dominate Reagan's speaking agenda throughout the month of May. However, during June welfare reform became increasingly intertwined with both the budget for fiscal year 1971–72 and tax reform. Reagan held that the budget would be balanced only if the legislature adopted his proposals for both welfare reform and withholding: "If the legislature will pass the $6.7 billion budget we submitted, give us the welfare reform we asked for and adopt withholding, California can still have a balanced budget and the maintenance of essential state services without a tax increase" (2).[10]

Reagan acknowledged his frustration with the legislature's inaction on welfare reform: "The governor of New York asked for our plan after we had submitted it to our own legislators. He took part of it, added his own proposals to it, submitted it to his legislators and signed it into law on April 7" (4).

Reagan went as far as to claim that his proposals for welfare reform were working by his mere talking about them:

> Tomorrow we will release the new welfare figures for May. These figures will confirm a definite decline in the total number of people on welfare in California for the second month in a row—even in the face of serious unemployment. . . . if we can cause a dent in the caseload simply by talking about the need for

reform and tightening the regulations, just think what we could do if the legislature would give us the legal authority to really reform welfare (5).

Reagan's welfare reforms, he claimed, were so effective they had even begun to work before they had been enacted into law. Given this, the legislature's inability to act was inexcusable.

TAX REFORM

June 17, 1971

Welfare reform and the budget for fiscal year 1971–72 were not the only issues on Reagan's speaking agenda during 1971. Reagan, as he did in 1969 and 1970, tried to get his proposals for tax reform through the legislature during the 1971 session as well.[11]

Reagan's tax reform plans had undergone little change. Property tax relief was still the major objective to be financed through five methods: an increase not to exceed one cent in California's sales tax, bank and corporation taxes would increase from 7 to 7½ percent in 1971 and to 8 percent by 1974, personal income tax in the highest brackets would be increased, the oil depletion allowance would be lowered, and there would be a "minimum income tax" (3).[12]

The main difference between his proposals and those favored by some in the legislature was how to use "that one time bundle of money government gets in the first year when it starts collecting state income taxes by withholding. This amounts to roughly $500 million" (3). Reagan proposed a one-time rebate whereby $250 million would go back to the taxpayers. The remaining $250 million would go to finance "essential capital construction needs" (3). The opposition, however, proposed to "use up both the ongoing and one-time revenues that will be available from withholding to finance ongoing programs" (4). In other words, the entire windfall from withholding would be allocated for spending under the opposition's proposal. The main problem Reagan had with such a proposal was that "it sets a tax time-bomb with a one year fuse because there would be a built-in future deficit. To accept that would break faith with the taxpayers" (4). Reagan's opposition to spending all of the income generated by withholding may have been only partly motivated by fiscal reasons. Reagan, because of his change of positions on withholding, may have been attempting to redeem himself to the California taxpayers by returning a significant portion of the withholding windfall to them. Such an interpretation is not too far-fetched when one considers that Reagan was facing a budget deficit if the legislature did not approve his plans for welfare reform. Politically speaking, a tax rebate offered in a time of fiscal austerity seems paradoxical at best.

Reagan concluded this speech by creating a dichotomy between the people and the legislature: "The Constitution requires us to have a balanced budget. The people want a balanced budget without a tax increase. But apparently, some in the legislature are misreading the mood of the public" (7). The legislature was out of touch with reality while Reagan, the self-proclaimed citizen-politician, knew exactly what the citizenry wanted. Also, by emphasizing that it was "the people" who wanted a balanced budget with no increases in taxes, Reagan placed himself above partisan politics. Reagan was merely representing the wants of the majority while some in the legislature were playing "politics with the future of California" (7).

September 3, 1971

Speaking on September 3, to the Sacramento Host Breakfast, Reagan took time to congratulate his administration for California's fiscal situation as well as for welfare reform. Reagan, in discussing the impact of the recession on California relative to the rest of the states, stated that Californians had "been spared some of the traumatic shock suffered by some states and even some local governments within our borders. Our past four years of cut, squeeze and trim may have been hard on the typewriter ribbon business, but they are saving us a lot of headaches now" (2).[13] In order to prove his point that Californians were indeed fortunate, Reagan resorted to a comparison: "Five years ago our state budget was second in size to the federal government's. Today, we are fourth—behind the federal government, New York State and New York City. In fact 'Fun City's' budget is $2 billion greater than the budget for this largest state in the union" (2).

Not only had Reagan's fiscal prudence saved Californians from fiscal hardships, it had also helped to finance "more than a billion dollars in direct tax relief between 1967 and 1971"; specifically $835 million for individual taxpayers and $135 million in inventory tax relief for business (4). Attempting to dispel the myth that he was only pro–big business, a label received during his pre-gubernatorial years, Reagan stressed the differences between individual and business tax relief: "Incidentally, that comes out to six times more tax relief for individual citizen-taxpayers than business received in the same period" (4).

Reagan's budget for fiscal year 1971–72, withholding of personal state income taxes, and welfare reform intermingled to create a puzzling fiscal scenario. In order to straighten out this scenario, Reagan offered a narrative of the preceding months of chaos:

> We submitted a budget technically in balance but which required adoption of our proposals for reform of welfare and Medi-Cal. [B]y May, however, the final

word was in on tax receipts and we were hit by the second half of a double whammy. We had to face a $200 million reduction in the revenues upon which we had based our budget. We had hoped that the increased revenues to be gained from a withholding system of income tax collection . . . could have been used to ease the homeowner property tax burden. But, it seemed more logical to use this to meet the new shortage. The legislature was informed that adoption of withholding plus the welfare reforms eliminated the need for a tax increase. [A] few weeks ago, an agreement was reached on welfare and Medi-Cal reforms and signed into law. It was a compromise and did not achieve all the savings we had hoped for, . . . [T]he result of not getting the total reforms we wanted leaves about $100 million which must be raised by new or increased taxes. I am hopeful . . . the legislature will adopt withholding (5–7).

Reagan initially claimed that withholding would generate revenues approaching $500 million, yet he was still calling for withholding despite the budget being out of balance by only $100 million. Based on Reagan's math, if the state adopted withholding of state income taxes, California would experience a $400 million surplus.

Aside from the year's confusing and misleading fiscal events, Reagan finally was able to reform welfare and Medi-Cal in 1971, two of the programs he had targeted for reforms since 1967. Reagan proudly declared his reforms to be a success: "Welfare caseloads had been increasing at a rate of 50,000 a month. Now for four straight months, California's welfare rolls have been declining. We ended July with 105,000 fewer people on public welfare than in March" (6). Not only were the welfare numbers rapidly declining, but "the first pilot project to place employable welfare recipients in jobs already has resulted in a savings of $105,000 in annual welfare costs" (6).

Welfare and Medi-Cal reform was to be Reagan's major legislative accomplishment during his eight years as governor. Two factors proved to play a major role in aiding the passage of these reforms: the nation's recession and the contingent nature of Reagan's budget. First, as Reagan made explicit in his *Inaugural Address*, increases in the cost of both welfare and Medi-Cal coupled with lower tax revenues combined to create the makings for a fiscal crisis. Either Reagan had to raise taxes to cover the deficits or opt for major reform in welfare and Medi-Cal. The time was right for reforms and Reagan knew it.

The second major factor encouraging passage of Reagan's reforms was of his own doing. That is, the budget Reagan submitted for fiscal year 1971–72 was a contingent one, dependent on passage of his reforms. Technically, the budget Reagan submitted was in balance, dependent on legislative approval of his reforms. If the legislature went against his reforms, they were effectively being coerced into advocating higher taxes to finance the budget deficit. Reagan could then, in turn, claim that the legislature was in favor of raising taxes during a recession, an elected official's worst nightmare. Indeed, Reagan the citizen-politician who thrived on playing the role of political naivete was learning to play hardball politics.

1972

Ronald Reagan proved that 1971 was no fluke by finally passing a significant tax reform bill in 1972. However, like the Welfare Reform Act of 1971, Reagan needed considerable help from Assembly Speaker Bob Moretti to secure passage of his tax reform bill. In fact, on June 30, Reagan and Moretti merged their two different tax reform bills into one, AB-1000, which was eventually amended into SB-90. Thus a Democrat actually carried the Reagan administration's tax reform proposal.[14]

One of the principal reasons the bill succeeded in passing the legislature involved a California Supreme Court ruling from 1971. Specifically, on August 30, 1971, the court ruled that California's school finance method was unconstitutional due to its heavy reliance on local property taxes. Furthermore, the court ruled that children in low wealth school districts were being denied equal education opportunity relative to wealthier school districts. Thus the court ordered the state to adopt a statewide property tax in place of the existing local property taxes.[15] Given the court's ruling, California had little choice but to adopt a major tax reform bill.

Following the legislature's three-month recess, the Reagan/Moretti tax reform package finally passed the senate on the last day of the legislative session.[16] After six years, a court ruling, and much assistance from Moretti, Reagan finally accomplished one of his administration's major goals.

The other significant economic news of 1972 involved the state's budget for fiscal year 1972–73. Spurred by lower rates of unemployment and shrinking welfare rolls, hence greater tax revenues, Reagan's budget was much less "austere" than the previous year. More specifically, Reagan's budget called for expenditures of $7.68 billion, an increase of more than 10 percent from the previous year. What complicated the budget proceedings was State Finance Director Verne Orr's projection on May 18 that the state would experience a $459 million surplus for fiscal year 1972–73. Given this projection, the legislature appropriated more than $250 million of the surplus into their budget package, which eventually totalled more than $7.9 billion. Reagan, in turn, blue-pencilled $257 million, declaring that the large surplus should go for tax relief. The budget Reagan ultimately signed for fiscal year 1972–73 amounted to nearly $7.7 billion, his sixth straight record-breaking budget.[17]

January 6, 1972: State-of-the-State Message

Despite the nation's economy being on what he termed an "upward curve" due to Richard Nixon's economic program, Reagan continued to emphasize the need for fiscal prudence at the state level. The economy was still very precarious, cautioned Reagan: "With the average citizen spending almost a third of his work week just earning the money to pay his taxes, there is still an urgent need to reduce the size and cost of government" (1).[18]

Reagan's *State-of-the-State Message* typically outlined the coming year's legislative agenda. This was also true in 1972, yet Reagan also reflected back to 1971 and the passage of his administration's welfare reforms. Calling it "the most significant social legislation in California's history" Reagan translated his welfare and Medi-Cal reforms into dollars and cents: "If we had not passed these reforms, welfare during these last eight months would have cost the taxpayers another $100 million" (3). Reagan added, "These reforms have reduced the cost to the taxpayers an estimated $208 million in state, local and federal funds" (4). Reagan's reforms, because they effectively reduced the number of people receiving welfare, which, in turn, reduced the cost of state government, were to become the economic signature of Reagan's governorship. All along, Reagan the ideologue had preached less government, less government spending, and lower taxes. However, up until the passage of some of his administration's reforms, Reagan had relied almost exclusively on projecting an image of a fiscal conservative based on relatively minute and largely insignificant savings. Upon passage of the Welfare Reform Act of 1971, however, Reagan had more tangible proof to undergird his claims to be a fiscal conservative.

Reagan declared that the most urgent tasks left to attend to were California's "educational system, its financing and direction and the equally important necessity of providing comprehensive property tax relief . . . [T]he issues are closely related. It is impossible to discuss property tax reform without considering the impact on educational finance" (6).

The final economic issue Reagan discussed was the budget and specifically his new method for submitting it.

> We are going to submit it in two parts as we logically should have been doing for a long time. . . . Roughly two-thirds of the state budget is money collected by the state but returned to cities, counties, school districts and local programs. The other one-third of the budget covers the actual cost of state government. [L]umping them together makes it difficult for the citizen to keep track of where the increased expenditures take place. . . . So the first part of the budget we

submit will be for those monies we return to local entities. We will follow this with a second section covering the cost of actually operating state government. In this way, the taxpayers can bette [*sic*] check on our stewardship (9).

Reagan's new policy for submitting his budget was not done so much for the citizenry as it was for purely political reasons. Reagan recognized the incongruity between the annual record-breaking budgets and the image he wished to portray as a fiscal conservative. Accordingly, his two-part budget was designed to dissociate himself from the increasing costs of California's state government. As he had mentioned in an earlier speech, Reagan implied that higher budgets should be viewed favorably, reflecting more dollars being returned to local property taxpayers. By framing his administration's budget this way, an increase was not to be viewed in a negative light.

THE NATION'S ECONOMY

January 24, 1972

As Reagan's tenure as governor entered its sixth year, regional economic issues continued to occupy much of his discourse. Increasingly though, the nation's economy crept into Reagan's rhetoric, reflecting both his own future presidential ambitions and support for Nixon's reelection bid.

In a speech to the Sacramento Chamber of Commerce on January 24, Reagan addressed, in his view, one of the most important economic problems confronting the nation: the United States' mounting trade deficit. Reagan related, "Twenty years ago, we produced 47 percent of the world's steel. Today, our share is down to 20 percent. An article . . . indicates that the Soviet Union has passed us up in steel production and is now the world's No. 1 steelmaker" (6).[19]

Reagan attributed two causes for the United States' decline in world trade: inflation and productivity. Addressing the former, Reagan stated that "the plain truth is that in some products, America is pricing itself out of world markets" (6). As he had in previous speeches, Reagan blamed inflation on proponents of the New Economics "who tell us a little inflation on a permanent annual basis is good for us" (6). Even though Lyndon Johnson's presidency had long since concluded, Reagan continued to target that administration as being responsible for inflation.

The second reason for the United States' decline in world trade was a lack of productivity:

The blunt truth is we have not been keeping up in productivity. Between 1965 and 1970, Japan's output per man-hour increased an average of 14.2 percent a year. Ours increased only 1.9 percent a year. . . . And I believe it is a major reason for the fact that our balance of payments . . . has turned from a surplus in our favor to a deficit (6).

Having identified one of the primary culprits as declining productivity, Reagan backed himself into a corner. More clearly, Reagan, by identifying productivity as a cause for the growing trade imbalance, implicitly indicted his own audience for having contributed to the problem. Perhaps recognizing this, Reagan shifted the discussion to the adversarial relationship between labor and management and the resultant strikes "that cripple whole industries," which were induced by labor leaders, not management. "I have every confidence in the American working man," stated Reagan, "but some of our national labor leaders had better acquire some statesmanship and stop thinking the calendar reads 1933" (7). According to Reagan, management was holding up their end of the bargain, and labor leaders were not.

Unrelated to his comments on the growing trade imbalance were Reagan's revealing remarks on government spending and taxation:

I do not believe the working citizens of this state are golden geese to be plucked by government. And neither is business. [O]ne cannot hold this position without dreaming of what he would like to leave as something of a permanent condition. My dream is very simple, although not easy to attain. For as long as government has existed, governments have grown in size and cost and ultimately, power. Every few years, the cry is raised that government must have new or additional taxes. . . . This does not have to be. [O]ur state tax structure grows with the economy and on the average produces about an 8 percent increase in revenues each year without increasing the rates or the percentage it claims of the workers' pay. Government spending should stay within this 8 percent growth rate. . . . [T]his dream is not impossible to attain (5).

The legacy Reagan desired to leave behind was merely a maintenance of the status quo, not a reversal of government spending patterns. Based on previous encounters with Reagan's political persona, one would not expect to see this persona exposed to a group of businessmen and entrepreneurs. In fact, one would expect to get glimpses of Reagan the ideologue in such a context. Perhaps Reagan had finally resigned himself to the fact that government spending in California would never shrink; that he could only hope to contain spending increases to the levels precipitated by inflation and population growth.

February 14, 1972

Reagan's speech to the Lincoln Club of Los Angeles on February 14 is similar in content to his January 24 speech to the Sacramento Chamber of Commerce with one glaring exception: culpability for the nation's high rate of inflation. Labor had replaced Johnson as being responsible for inflation. Reagan observed,

> Labor sets its own goals, often without regard to the inflationary and even destructive impact those goals may have on other Americans. Businessmen react by raising prices because they must to meet the demands of labor—even if doing so means surrendering more and more of their markets to lower priced foreign competition (2).[20]

According to Reagan's account, business/management was totally at the mercy of labor, having no choice but to give in to labor's demands. The growing trade imbalance, caused by both inflation and low productivity growth, was now clearly assigned to labor, effectively removing management from any wrongdoing.

TAXATION/TAX REFORM

June 27, 1972

Reagan's speech to a hospital appreciation banquet on June 27 provides some revealing insights into his evolving views on taxation. In order to make these views as palatable as possible, Reagan resorted to two brief narratives.

> There have always been those who pretended someone else could be made to bear the cost of government. A long time ago in England, someone decided there was money to be raised by taxing windows, and since the rich had bigger houses and more windows, they would pay the tax. But it was the poor who discovered they were the first to have to wall up their windows and live in darkness. [I]n France, the tax was levied on fireplaces—the rich had them in every room. Again it was the poor who suffered cold because they could no longer afford that one fireplace in their tiny homes (3–4).[21]

These two accounts reflect Reagan's beliefs on wealth generation relative to taxation. That is, given the appropriate incentives (for example, low taxes) the wealthy would, in turn, generate more wealth by creating jobs that the poor would fill. Low taxes for the wealthy were warranted based on Reagan's faith in the ability of the rich to create more wealth through investments, thus producing more tax revenues for the government. Reagan had consistently, even in his 1951 address to the Kiwanis, voiced his displeasure with the imposition of high tax rates on the wealthy. More significant, however, were the means by which Reagan expressed his dissatisfaction. Recall that in 1951 high taxes on the wealthy were criticized because they were "discriminatory." By 1972,

Reagan had turned matters of taxation on the wealthy from a fairness issue to a productivity one. Paradoxically though, state income taxes on the wealthy increased during Reagan's eight years as governor.

October 11, 1972

As he had the previous three years, Reagan offered a proposal for comprehensive tax reform in 1972. The legislature had passed some of Reagan's reform proposals during a special session late in 1971, yet according to Reagan, these reforms "did not do what needs to be done to reduce the property tax burden on the typical homeowner" (2).[22]

Reagan's tax reform proposals of 1972 were "blocked in the state Senate this time by four votes" (2). According to Reagan, his tax reforms were not flawed; rather "some elected officials" were continuing "to put partisanship ahead of responsibility" (2).

A tax reform proposal did make it to the ballot to be voted on by the citizens of California: Proposition 14, better known as the Watson Initiative. Reagan, however, stated that he had to "oppose Proposition 14 if I am to meet my responsibility to the people" (3). Reagan outlined several reasons why he could not lend his support to Proposition 14. One of the most important considerations was the "massive $1.8 billion increase in consumer and business taxes" (3). The bottom line for Reagan was that "to raise consumer taxes and business taxes—to shackle him with an unbearable fiscal burden is a solution I cannot accept" (4).

To counter Proposition 14, as well as to put his own signature on tax reform, Reagan proposed reform measures—to be formally presented to the legislature following the November elections—that he promised would "reduce homeowner taxes without increasing income taxes" (4). The reasons permitting Reagan to propose such a measure were primarily his doing: "Savings from our continuing tight state budget policy . . . by the welfare and Medi-Cal reforms we made last year . . . and by widely using the state's share of federal revenue sharing" (Reagan's ellipses, 4). Reagan "forgot" to mention another major factor that led to such a measure: withholding of state income taxes.

Reagan's tax reform proposal contained three main measures: to reduce property taxes, to increase state support for elementary and secondary school financing, and to institute a permanent reduction in the state income tax of 10 percent. The last of these three measures was to be financed by Reagan's welfare and Medi-Cal reforms and by "the improved economy of the state" (6). To finance property tax relief and increased state support for elementary and secondary education, Reagan called for just two tax increases: "a one cent increase in the sales tax and a one percent increase in bank and corporation taxes" (5). What is significant about these two means of finance is that they were the very ones Reagan condemned relative to Proposition 14. Reagan likened increased consumer taxes and business taxes to shackling the citizenry; a prospect he would not accept.

The other measure contained in Reagan's property tax reforms was of a more political nature. Specifically, Reagan proposed "that *all* increases involving major tax sources in the future require a two-thirds majority vote of the legislature" (Reagan's emphasis, 6). Such a provision would add "another safeguard to protect and make permanent the overall tax reductions possible in this program" (6). Having had his reform proposals rejected the past three years and anticipating another defeat, Reagan announced his new plans for passage of his tax reforms: "I am not unmindful of the times we have been frustrated by willful men in the legislature. That is why I am proposing this package as a referendum" (6). Reagan declared that he would "personally lead an initiative campaign . . . to place on the ballot property tax relief, a solution to the school problem and a permanent tax cut" if the legislature refused his requests (6).

Proof that his tax reform proposals would be effective were grounded in his welfare and Medi-Cal reforms. Reagan stated,

> If you recall this time last year, there were screams of outrage about our reform efforts. It was said that the welfare reforms we proposed would saddle counties with higher costs. Others said it just could not be done. [W]ell, we did it. And this year, 42 of California's 58 counties managed to reduce their basic property tax rates (7).

As he had in the past, Reagan elevated the people of California to an important position of responsibility. Reagan stated, "Only when the people are made aware of the fact that they can have tax relief will they demand the reforms necessary to achieve further tax cuts. . . . [W]orking together, the responsible citizens of this state can light a prairie fire of reform and efficiency" (8). Reagan had done his job of making citizens aware of the possibilities; it was now their duty to see that his tax reforms would be approved.

NATIONAL DEFENSE

October 12, 1972

Addressing the World Affairs Council in Los Angeles on October 12, Reagan emphasized the interrelationship between economic prosperity and peace. Reagan put the matter very succinctly: "We know that commerical contacts among nations not only help achieve prosperity for all; it also represents a contribution to peace, because political stability cannot be maintained without financial stability among the major nations of the world" (1).[23] Reagan added, "Despite the lessening of tensions and the hopeful signs of great power cooperation in the future, it is America's industrial and economic strength, translated into military potential that represents the single greatest guarantee of peace for the world" (3). Very clearly, Reagan viewed the nation's and its allies' defense as being contingent on the strength of the United States' economy. With this in mind, Reagan's frequent apocalyptic visions come into sharper focus. That is, because the future of the United States and its allies depended on United States' economic prosperity, Reagan would frequently interpret economic decline at home as a sign of imminent democratic collapse. Economic prosperity was an all or nothing proposition for Reagan: either the United States' economy would prosper and remain a world power, or the nation's economy would falter and western democracies would fall to the communist menace.

TOWARD 1976

December 8, 1972

Reagan had resigned himself to waiting until 1976 to run for the presidency. However, this did not keep Reagan from occasionally campaigning for himself. Such was the case on December 8, when Reagan delivered a speech to the 77th Congress of American Industry, National Association of Manufacturers in New York City.

Reagan tried not only to inform his audience of what he had done in California, but to foster identification between himself and the business community in this speech. To accomplish his goal, Reagan emphasized that most people did not have an understanding of how business functioned: "There is an appalling lack of understanding regarding the workings of the marketplace and the simple business of making something people want and need and getting it to them at a reasonable price" (197).[24] Reagan also attempted to create an identification between himself and the business community with such statements as the following: "Free enterprise is a rough and competitive game. It is a hell of a lot better than a government monopoly"; "[I]t is time for business to start presenting the facts, because the facts are on your side"; "None of what had been done could have been accomplished without the practice of noblesse oblige by the business and industrial community in California"; and "But realize your strength, because if you did not go to work, I am sure the country would feel it and grind to a halt in about 24 hours" (197, 200).[25]

Reagan continued to identify the growing trade imbalance as a serious economic problem. However, whereas in previous speeches Reagan blamed labor leaders for the trade imbalance, he hinted that the federal government was the real culprit. "The nations of the European Common Market average a tax burden that, in relation to the gross national product, is less than half of what yours is, and possibly this explains why our balance of trade is at the lowest point it has been since 1893" (198). In this context, business and industry were merely reacting to the dictates of the federal government, and thus were absolved by Reagan of any responsibility for raising prices, which, in turn, fueled inflation.

Reagan, in detailing the virtues of free market economics, implied that free enterprise had defeated poverty. More revealing, though, were the proofs that Reagan offered to support his claim:

> Hardly a week passes without some television program sponsored by some of you, but what portrays the horrors of poverty and hunger in the United States—and yet 99 per cent of the homes in America have electricity and the basic appliances such as refrigerator and range and 96 per cent of the homes have television and telephones; 80 per cent have automobiles (199).

Ownership of refrigerators, ranges, televisions, telephones, and automobiles signaled to Reagan that poverty and hunger had been eradicated, except in the make-believe world of television. The misleading elements of Reagan's proofs, of course, were that his statistics were based solely on homes, hence homeowners. And clearly homeowners would tend to fall outside the lattitude of the impoverished. In other words, Reagan's proofs that poverty was non-existent begged the question of poverty altogether.

Reagan concluded this speech by detailing the accomplishments of his Creative Society, which hinted strongly of his presidential aspirations. In the past, when detailing his administration's accomplishments, Reagan was usually quick to take the credit. However, on this occasion Reagan was willing to share some of the credit with his audience: "I had an abiding faith in common-sense business practices that you use every day and a belief that they would also work for government" (200). Reagan's success was business and industry's success, thus further establishing the identification between Reagan and his fellow compatriots.

1973

Less than a year after State Controller Houston Flourney's proclamation that California's fiscal crisis was over, the state was confronted with a unique situation: a projected surplus of $850 million by the end of fiscal year 1972–73.[26]

California's unparalleled fiscal prosperity played a prominent role in shaping legislation in three main areas during 1973: the budget, tax rebates, and tax reduction. First, Reagan's budget soared to $9.3 billion causing State Finance Director Verne Orr to declare it as being "loaded with fat."[27] Much of the increase was due to the Reagan/Moretti tax reform bill, yet the budget was highly uncharacteristic of the preceding six budgets submitted by Reagan. The budget he eventually signed called for expenditures of $9.38 billion as Reagan blue-pencilled some $78 million from the budget submitted by the legislature.

Second, despite the surplus, both Reagan and Moretti were castigated for the previous year's tax reform bill. Specifically, before SB–90 was eventually signed by Reagan on December 1, 1972, it was widely known that the state would experience a surplus of $700 million for fiscal year 1972–73.[28] In other words, increasing sales, bank and corporate taxes during a time of unprecedented prosperity were politically damaging to both Reagan and Moretti.

To try and remedy the problem, both sides proposed legislation to rebate the huge surplus. Reagan's initial plan called for a one-time 20 percent rebate in the state income tax and for a postponement by six months of SB–90's provision to increase the state sales tax by one cent. Opponents of Reagan's tax rebate proposal, chief among them Moretti, claimed that the proportional income tax rebate would benefit the wealthy at the expense of the poor; thus the legislature adjourned on June 30 without passing either side's tax rebate bill.

Surprisingly, when the legislature reconvened, Moretti and his fellow Democratic colleagues voted in favor of Reagan's tax rebate plan on August 16 (ironically, it too was known as SB-90).[29] Their motivation for doing so, however, was decidedly political. That is, Moretti and many of his fellow Democrats in the assembly pushed through Reagan's tax rebate plan in order to subvert Reagan's proposal for Revenue Control and Tax Reduction, which would become known as Proposition 1.

Proposition 1 was designed to effectively put a cap on state spending by limiting the amount the state could take in tax revenues each year. In other words, the state's budget was contingent on a predetermined tax percentage; ranging from a high of 8.75 percent in fiscal year 1973–74 to 7.0 percent in fiscal year 1988–89. But the passage of SB-90 decreased California's total tax take in fiscal year 1973–74 from an estimated 8.75 to 8.35 percent. Moretti and others claimed that this lower percentage would cause the state budget to be underfunded in ensuing years, which, in turn, would cause higher taxes and/or major cutbacks in spending.[30] Ultimately, Moretti's gamble paid off as Proposition 1 was defeated on November 6, with 54 percent voting against the initiative.

January 11, 1973: State-of-the-State Message

Reagan's 1973 *State-of-the-State Message* functioned more as a self-congratulatory speech than an outline for future economic legislation.

Tax reform and welfare reform together "represents the most significant legislative achievements of the past quarter century in California" (65).[31]

Reagan was not only pleased with the reforms, as he contrasted the state's fiscal condition in 1973 with the conditions he inherited in 1967: "California's financial condition is the best it has been for 15 years. . . . [I]nstead of a massive deficit requiring higher taxes or program cuts, a situation we faced six years ago, we have a surplus this year in the neighborhood of $850 million" (66).

Despite the positive economic indicators, Reagan still emphasized his administration's fiscally prudent nature: "The state recently saved 9.7 percent on a purchase of alfalfa hay for the correctional system's dairies. I only mention this unusual item to emphasize our intent to squeeze every penny of value from every tax dollar" (67). To be fiscally conservative in times of economic hardship was nothing out of the ordinary; to be a fiscal conservative, however, in a time of economic prosperity was truly extraordinary, inferred Reagan.

Perhaps the most interesting aspect of this address is its irony. More specifically, Reagan's repeated praise for himself and the legislature suggested a partnership in the affairs of state government. By the end of the year though, Reagan would be projecting the legislature as his archenemy as well as the enemy of the people.

REVENUE CONTROL AND TAX REDUCTION

February 9, 1973

Reagan spent nearly all of 1973 canvassing California to encourage voter support for his administration's comprehensive plan for revenue control and tax reduction, better known as Proposition 1. Reagan, in a February 9 speech to the California Newspaper Publishers Association, went public for the first time with his new tax proposals.

Reagan's tax reform proposals were motivated, in part, by two considerations: "We have reached a unique point in time. We have both an $850 million state budget surplus and a once-in-a-lifetime opportunity to permanently and systematically reduce the amount that government takes from the people in taxes" (3).[32] The latter of these two considerations was further elaborated by Reagan: "In 1930 it (the cost of federal, state and local government) was 15 percent of the people's earnings, by 1950 it was 30 percent, and today government takes 43.8 percent. If you continue that rate of increase in 15 years, government's share will be almost 55 percent. We think that is too much" (3). As he had in previous speeches, Reagan attempted to create an urgency by projecting into the future. These futuristic visions were typically of an apocalyptic sort, characterized by the imminent and symbolic death of the United States. Within this context, Reagan took on the role of the savior, responsible for the country's economic salvation. At this early point in his campaign for Proposition 1, however, Reagan's rhetoric lacked the apocalyptic ingredient. However, as opposition to Reagan's proposals mounted throughout the year, his rhetoric became more extreme.

The first phase of Reagan's proposals was a return of the $850 million surplus, which he declared "belongs to the people who paid it" (4). The surplus was to be rebated in three forms: a six-month deferral of the one cent sales tax increase, a one-time state income tax rebate of 20 percent, and the balance, or $65 million, would be allocated to refurbish the state capital building (4).

The second phase of Reagan's proposal, the main part, involved two major goals: imposing a ceiling or a limit on the amount the state could take in taxes; and permanently reducing by 10 percent California state income taxes, both beginning in fiscal year 1974–75. Reagan claimed that these two measures would eventually reduce the tax take of the state from 8¾ percent to 7 percent, which represented "almost a 20 percent cut in taxes" (5). Without these changes "the state's revenues will grow to $47.4 billion in 15 years. [I] do not believe our people want nor can they afford that much government 15 years from now" (4).

Attempting to assuage those who would be opposed to his proposals on the grounds that government spending would all but evaporate, Reagan stated, "At the end of 15 years it (Proposition 1) would permit a budget of more than $27 billion. Surely no one can complain about restrictions on a tax structure that will permit doubling the budget in 10 years and trebling [sic] it in 15 years" (5).

Reagan also presented several of the specific details of his proposal. First, the legislature would be responsible for which taxes to cut, but any tax increases would have to be eventually approved by a vote of the people. Second, the state's budget would be determined by projecting a percentage tax limit (somewhere between 8.75 and 7 percent). Third, Reagan's proposals included an emergency fund in order "to meet unexpected extreme emergency needs beyond the state's control and which result in costs exceeding the spending limit for any given year" (5). If this fund were exhausted, the legislature could, with a two-thirds majority coupled with approval of the governor, raise taxes. This tax, Reagan emphasized, would only be operative until the next general election "when it could be cancelled or extended by a *vote of the people*" (Reagan's emphasis, 6).

Consistent with his propensity for reducing the complex to the simple, Reagan concluded this speech by essentializing his proposals: "It is simply designed to permit the take-home pay of our people to grow faster than the taxes deducted from their paychecks" (7). Revenue control and tax reduction were innocuous enough, devoid of partisanship and political self-interest, implied Reagan.

April 27, 1973

During his April 27 speech to the Association of California Water Agencies, Reagan mentioned some of the likely effects of his revenue control and tax reduction proposals.

> Instead of constantly higher taxes that force our people to reduce *their* standard of living to finance government, the people will have that money to *raise their* standard of living. [T]hink how much this will mean in increased savings, increased investment opportunity, and how many jobs this can generate in the private sector (Reagan's emphasis, 5).[33]

Left unstated was the logical conclusion that increased government revenues would result due to the creation of more jobs in the private sector. The supply-side strain was clearly evident in Reagan's discourse.

Advocates of supply-side economics believe, among other things, that higher after-tax incomes stimulate supply due to increased savings and investment. In other words, supply creates its own demand that would eventually result in more jobs, hence a greater base from which to draw tax revenues. In 1973, Reagan may have been a bit skeptical of a tax cut resulting in greater tax revenues, hence the omission of it. However, by claiming that a tax cut would stimulate more jobs, Reagan was implicitly acknowledging that tax reductions would result in greater tax revenues. Ironically, though, one of the purposes of Proposition 1 was to put a "ceiling" on the amount California state government could take in taxes. Thus on one hand Reagan was implying that increased tax revenues would result from Proposition 1. Yet on the other, it was specifically designed to decrease California's tax take.

Proposition 1 also contained a significant addition by the time Reagan delivered this speech. That is, responding to charges that his proposals favored the rich, Reagan went on the counteroffensive: "Another charge is that this program favors the rich. But our proposal *totally eliminates* state income taxes for every family with an income of $8,000 or less—this year! And for every single person with an income of $4,000 or less" (Reagan's emphasis, 6). Exempting these two groups from paying income taxes was an open acknowledgment that his original proposal had been skewed to favor the wealthy.

As he had in his speech introducing Proposition 1, Reagan was careful to create a balance between tax cuts and budget growth. That is, Reagan tempered his fiscally conservative rhetoric with assurances that the budget "in ten years, . . . can double to $18 billion and in 15 years, it can triple to $27 billion" (5). Directly countering these efforts to placate his skeptics was Reagan's claim that "this plan does not accept the idea that government costs should always go up" (6). The rhetoric of Reagan the ideologue and the rhetoric of Reagan the pragmatic politician were clearly at odds with one another.

In outlining the virtues of Proposition 1, Reagan resorted to some misleading statements: "We think the people should decide how much they can afford to pay for government and government should establish the proper priorities so as to fit within that amount" (6). Reagan implied that Californians would be directly determining the state's tax take. In reality, the only instance in which the citizenry would exert any influence on tax policy would be in the case of legislatively imposed tax increases or a deferral in the annual decrease in the revenue limit. The voting populace would not play an active and direct role in determining their collective tax liabilities; they could only vote to overturn decisions made by the legislature.

Reagan concluded this speech by recontextualizing his proposals to embody a cherished American ideal: "We believe the people of California want lower taxes. And apparently the only way we will have them is by allowing the people to vote for them . . . [M]ore than money is at stake—we are actually voting for freedom" (6). To vote against Proposition 1 was to be anti-American; to vote in favor of it was to confirm one's Americanism.

May 22, 1973

Addressing the California Federation of Women's Clubs on May 22, Reagan defended his proposal of rebating the huge surplus of state revenues (phase one): "Spending proposals for that one-time surplus total more than a billion dollars already. And some of these would be for ongoing programs which means that for the second year of the program you would have to have a tax increase" (3).[34]

Furthermore, some in the legislature were, by Reagan's definition, stealing the taxpayer's money: "But the surplus is the same as an overpayment you might have made on your utility bill. . . . We took more from you in taxes last year and this year than we needed to pay the ongoing costs of government. This overpayment should be returned to those who paid it" (4). By likening the surplus to an overpaid bill, the only lawful thing to do was to return the money to the taxpayers: precisely what Reagan had proposed. The alternative, spending the surplus, what several Democrats had proposed, would have been akin to breaking the law.

As his campaign for Proposition 1 wore on, Reagan's discourse became increasingly urgent. Urgency was exhibited in this speech as Reagan played the dual role of historian and prophet:

> History reveals that no society has long survived a tax burden that reached one-third of the people's earnings. Looking back on the fallen empires of the past one sees the first warning signs appear. As the burden grows heavier, there is a growing lack of respect for government and the law. Fraud becomes widespread and crime increases. Are we to say none of those things are taking place here? (5).

According to Reagan, the manifestations of the apocalypse were at hand. Tax reductions were necessary in order to save the United States from imminent doom.[35]

Reagan's rhetoric also exhibited a defensive posture as criticism of Proposition 1 mounted. For example, Reagan stated, "The truth about the nit picking and carping criticism is that many of those who are talking the loudest in the legislative chambers do not even believe their own words. . . . they really cannot find anything wrong with our proposal" (6).

In addition, Reagan attempted to create a negative identification of those opposed to Proposition 1: "Those who say the Tax Control and Tax Limitation Plan will not work or that it will raise your local taxes are the same ones who said the welfare reforms would not work. . . . Well, the reforms have worked better than we predicted they would" (7). The logic in this statement is quite simplistic; yet, underlying it was a deeper revelation. That is, Reagan saw Proposition 1 as an extension of the Welfare Reform Act of 1971. Both were measures designed to provide tax relief. In this sense, Proposition 1 was merely a continuation of welfare reform. And because his welfare reforms were achieving their desired ends, so too would Proposition 1, implied Reagan.

Continuing the assault on his opponents, Reagan claimed that by blocking the citizens' right to vote on Proposition 1, several in the legislature were anti-constitutional. "It is an arrogant denial of the democratic process for a few legislators to say the people must not even be allowed to vote on something as fundamental as their right to their own earnings" (7). Those opposed to Proposition 1 were doubly villainous: first, by being opposed to it they favored higher taxes; and second, by not permitting the populace to vote on it, these same people were subverting the democratic process that they pretended to uphold.

May 30, 1973

Some of Reagan's rhetorical strategies on Proposition 1 had changed by May 30. Instead of appealing solely to the interests of the taxpaying public, Reagan's appeals had expanded to include the preservation of government. Reagan noted, "If taxation becomes a drag on the private sector, we do not have a healthy economy, and if we do not have that, we will not have a healthy balance in the state's accounts, and we will not be able to properly fund essential programs" (6).[36] Not only was tax reduction vital for the private sector, it was also imperative for the maintenance of government's essential programs. In his April 27 speech to the Association of California Water Agencies, Reagan did not explicitly make the connection between tax reductions and tax revenues. In this speech, however, Reagan made it clear that tax reductions had the potential to stimulate tax revenues. Thus at this point the supply-side equation was complete. At some as yet unspecified point, a tax cut would stimulate tax revenues.[37]

The completion of the supply-side equation is especially significant in relation to Reagan's two personae—the ideological and the political. Supply-side economic theory permitted and even encouraged flaunting both personae. First, supply-side appealed to Reagan the ideologue insofar as it purported to stimulate savings and investment, hence productivity in the private sector, by cutting tax rates. Supply-side tax cuts resonated with Reagan's long-held beliefs on the virtues of lower taxes, especially on the wealthy. Second, Reagan's political persona was equally at home with the supply-side equation. Specifically, supply-side holds that tax revenues can actually be augmented by means of a tax cut. Given this, Reagan the politician could appeal to the potential revenue enhancement available to governments at all levels via tax cuts. Tax cuts appealed to Reagan the ideologue; increasing government revenues appealed to Reagan the pragmatic politician. The fusion of the two personae was perhaps best exhibited in the final paragraph of this speech. "If we are to have stable government and stable career employment opportunities in government, we must have a stable private economy. If the private economy falters or collapses under its tax burden, the entire structure of government can fall with it" (7).

September 21, 1973

As the November 6 deadline approached, Reagan repeatedly launched counterattacks on those opposed to Proposition 1. Not surprising, Reagan's rhetoric was of a highly partisan nature. Whereas Proposition 1 was purported to have been apolitical shortly after its inception, Reagan had made it decidedly political in the final months leading up to November 6. In fact, many of the speeches Reagan delivered during this two-month period did not even address the specifics of Proposition 1. A case in point was Reagan's September 21 speech to the California Real Estate Association. Villifying the opposition, Reagan urged his auditors to recall "their" malicious acts: "I would like to ask everyone here to recall, if you will, the situation we faced earlier this year before our long-range tax initiative qualified for the ballot. . . . they were not talking about returning the surplus. [T]hey were talking about spending it" (2).[38]

One of the problems Reagan faced was identifying who the culprits really were. Not all the members of the legislature, or even all Democrats, attempted to block Reagan's efforts to put Proposition 1 on the ballot or were advocating spending the surplus.[39] Reagan tried to overcome this anonymity factor by juxtaposing several of his most cherished political successes with those who had opposed them.

> You will be hearing this chorus of criticism in the next couple of months. When you do, I would like you to remember one thing: when have these critics ever advocated reducing the overall tax burden? . . . Some of them were against our welfare reforms, against the property tax reform, efficiency in government. . . . [I]f we had listened to them, there would have been no rebates in the past, no welfare reform, and no budget surplus to rebate to the people this year (5).

Reagan also attempted to identify himself with the nation's Founding Fathers. Such a strategy was an effort to transcend the specifics of Proposition 1 in order to situate it into a much larger historical narrative.

> In the original 10 amendments to the Constitution, the Founding Fathers said government could not seize your property without due process of law. And that protection against excessive government was "locked" into the Constitution. [T]he money you earn by your own labor or through investments is your property. The people have a right to say how much of it they can afford for government. If they do not have that right, then freedom as we know it will not survive very long (5–6).

Proposition 1 merely corroborated what the nation's Founding Fathers had advocated during the nation's formative years. The specifics of the measure were no longer at issue, nor were they important. Rather, Reagan transcended the specifics in order to emphasize the constitutional validity of Proposition 1. In this sense, freedom was the issue on November 6, not tax policy.

October 15, 1973

Desperation had set in by October 15. Sensing a major defeat on an issue he had campaigned for for the better part of 22 years, Reagan the extremist surfaced in a speech given to the California Order of the Eastern Star.

> Government in the United States at every level has been on a long financial drunk. . . . [F]or a look at where we will be if we do not sober up in a hurry,

> hark back to Germany of the 1920s. Workers were given time off every two hours to spend their earnings before the value of their money dropped. Germans carried 50,000 mark notes for lunch money. And that wild inflation bought them finally, an Adolph Hitler (2).[40]

As he had in a speech on welfare reform in 1971, Reagan used the facism analogy to signal the need for tax reductions. More significant than the analogy itself were the implications for those opposing Proposition 1. That is, those opposed were not only giving assent to rampant inflation, but implicitly they were abetting in creating a situation whereby a maniacal dictator such as Hitler could come to power. The hero/villain dichotomy had never been more emphatic in Reagan's discourse.

The villain became even more insidious as Reagan addressed the reason that people opposed Proposition 1: "Do not be taken in by the consortium of lobbyists, politicians and big spenders who have mobilized to defeat this plan . . . They are not opposing Proposition 1 because they fear it will not work. They know it *will* work. That is why they are against it" (Reagan's emphasis, 5). The opposition was guilty of not only aiding in creating conditions ripe for a dictatorship, they were doing so knowingly and purposefully. The enemy had changed political affiliations, but the overthrow of the United States remained its goal.

To say that the political stakes for passage of Proposition 1 were high for Ronald Reagan is an understatement. In fact, it is clear from his discourse that Reagan had put all of his political eggs into one basket. For example, in a startling reversal of six and one-half years of rhetoric, Reagan humbly noted,

> We are proposing Proposition 1 because the total income of the people of California has been going up an average of 7 ½ percent a year for the last 20 years, while the state's spending has increased 10 percent a year. [M]ore than a year ago, I appointed a task force to find a solution to this, since six years of cut, squeeze and trim was obviously not an answer (5).

In one brief utterance, Reagan dismissed a major aim of the Creative Society. The only way to restore financial balance to state government, Reagan admitted, was through passage of Proposition 1.

October 19, 1973

In what was to be one of his last speeches prior to the November 6 election, Reagan reaffirmed the "all or nothing" nature Proposition 1 had come to embody in an October 19 speech: "This is the single most important election ever held in California, perhaps in the nation" (2).[41]

Not only had Reagan upped the political consequences of Proposition

1, but some of the statistics he had been using throughout the eight-month campaign moved upward as well. Specifically, throughout 1973 Reagan had repeatedly claimed that in 15 years, government's tax take would grow to 55 percent. By late October though, Reagan claimed that "government will be taking 67 percent" in 15 years (3).

One of the last strategical adaptations Reagan made was to acknowledge that Moretti's willingness to "concede" SB-90 to Reagan had taken away some of the attractiveness of Proposition 1.

> Only *after* the people claimed the right to vote on it and the special election was called, did the leaders of the legislative majority decide they would return the surplus to the people after all. They were very frank about the reason for their change of hearts. They wanted to take some of the attractiveness away from Proposition 1. Giving back the rebate was, in their eyes, the lesser of two evils. So you can thank Proposition 1 for having already given you a six months suspension of 1 cent of sales tax and about a $400 million rebate in this year's income tax (Reagan's emphasis, 5).

The Moretti-led Democrats in the legislature were guilty of a mini-conspiracy, designed to subvert Proposition 1 by taking away one of its most attractive features. Reagan declined to mention the real reason for the rebate and the delay in the imposition of the state sales tax, which was to lower the projected tax ceiling for fiscal year 1973–74.

1974

Many predicted that California's fiscal prosperity would be short-lived, due to the nation's energy shortage. However, thanks largely to higher inflation, Reagan was able to leave office with an estimated surplus of $400 million by the end of fiscal year 1974–75.

Nineteen seventy-four was more reminiscent of Reagan's first term than his second. With Proposition 1 having gone down to defeat, Reagan's legislative agenda was minimal. Even the year's budget proceedings were described with such adjectives as "pedestrian" and "non-controversial."[42] The only major significance of the state's budget was that it exceeded the $10 billion mark.

Events on the national political scene greatly influenced California politics during Reagan's final year as governor. The Watergate fallout was nowhere more pronounced than in Nixon's home state of California. Democrats captured five out of the six statewide positions, including the governorship as Jerry Brown defeated State Controller Houston Flourney. In addition, Democrats captured 17 out of the 20 state senate seats as well as accumulating 55 assembly seats compared to 25 for Republicans. What was initially supposed to be Reagan's last hurrah on his way to the Republican presidential nomination turned out to be little more than a whimper as Watergate and its aftermath left Reagan and his entourage uncertain of his political future.

January 9, 1974: State-of-the-State Message

Reagan's final *State-of-the-State Message* was reflective of his administration's past seven years. Detailing his administration's accomplishments, Reagan noted, "We can be proud of what we have already achieved. We have reordered priorities to control costs and assure funds for essential services. We have cut, squeezed and trimmed, and, at every opportunity, returned the benefit of those savings to the people" (64).[43] Reagan's cut, squeeze, and trim philosophy was responsible for tax rebates, property tax reductions, increased support for education, a well financed teacher's retirement system, completion of the California Water Project, mental health care, and welfare reform.

Recognizing that a comprehensive plan for tax reduction was out of the question for 1974, Reagan called for a different type of constitutional amendment. Specifically, Reagan proposed legislation requiring passage of an amendment whereby "the Legislature must return to the governor a balanced budget or propose additional taxes necessary to bring it into balance" (66). Reagan's legislative proposal was at once an admission of defeat and an attempt to get back at the Democratic-controlled legislature for its role in subverting Proposition 1. The mounting cost of government programs, transferred to the people in the form of higher taxes, was not a relevant concern for Reagan at this time. Instead, the proposed legislation was designed to single out those advocating the spending and how it would be financed. Two months after the defeat of Proposition 1, tax cuts had become subsidiary to methods of government finance. If Reagan could not have his tax cuts, he was going to try and make it such that the legislature could no longer ignore finance concerns.

Aside from Reagan's finance proposal, the major issue Reagan addressed was the nation's energy crisis: "The issue demanding our attention this year is the energy crisis . . . We know it will affect almost every part of the economy and every citizen, and we must all join in meeting this challenge" (65). In response to the energy crisis Reagan asked Californians "to *reduce their own personal gasoline consumption by a minimum of 10 percent*" (Reagan's emphasis, 65). Reagan also urged "every family and every business to *reduce energy use 10 percent by taking similar steps in their homes, offices, and other places of business*" (Reagan's emphasis, 65). However, Reagan exempted industry from having to cut back fuel usage. In fact, Reagan all but encouraged additional fuel consumption by industry. Reagan advocated such a posture by contrasting environmental goals with energy needs:

> Industry and utilities have been inhibited or prevented from using available fuel because of requirements necessary to meet stricter environmental standards. . . . I do not believe we need abandon this environmental progress. But *where energy needs conflict with environmental goals, we must strike a reasonable balance*. It will do little good for someone to have all the gasoline he can use, if he has no job to drive to because the industry for which he worked is shut down by an energy or fuel shortage (Reagan's emphasis, 65).

Reagan's "reasonable balance" was tipped strongly to the side of industry. Productivity concerns clearly outweighed any of Reagan's environmental concerns.

Reagan concluded his final *State-of-the-State Message* by underscoring the responsibilities of the people:

> Those nations and states which have secured man's highest aspirations for freedom, opportunity and justice, have always been those willing to trust their people, confident that their skills and their talents are equal to any challenge. Those societies which falter or merely survive are those which lack this faith, . . . No crisis is beyond the capacity of our people to solve; no challenge too great (67).

What is significant about this statement is its element of self-revelation. On the surface, Reagan was the living embodiment of his own rhetoric; his faith was in the people, not government. However, in the context of his rhetoric on Proposition 1, Reagan by his own definition, was faithless. Reagan's frequent references to the symbolic death of the United States illustrated his lack of faith in the people.

FREE ENTERPRISE

June 15, 1974

Occasionally, Reagan used the forum of a commencement address to espouse the virtues of free enterprise.[44] On very rare occasions Reagan would offer his own philosophy on human nature and the economic ideology most appropriate to this view.[45] Midway through his June 15 speech to the California Polytechnic State University graduating class of 1974, Reagan unveiled his simple philosophy. "Generations are not as they have been pictured, structured horizontally with all of mankind stretched out like a sausage divided into separate slices by age groups. Mankind is structured vertically with each succeeding generation finally standing on the shoulders of those who have gone before" (9).[46] Verticality, or the ability to progress upward through the social order, represented Reagan's somewhat Darwinian notion of economic determinism.[47] A stratified social order was consistent with Reagan the ideologue's vision of an economic hierarchy typified by free market economic principles. Also, within this hierarchy, the market forces of supply and demand were the determining factors in the formation of the social order. Equality was not in the lexicon of this social order. Within this notion of a vertically layered society, government's role was minimized to compensate for the occasional shortcomings of the market. A vertical social order emphasized work, thrift, productivity, and minimal government interference, staples of Reagan the ideologue's economic rhetoric.

Reagan also discussed the redemptive features of free enterprise. "A socialist country would give their copies of Karl Marx for our standardization and our assembly lines. For standardization means products for the masses and the assembly lines have freed the worker from back-breaking drudgery which for centuries had kept him at an almost animal-like existence" (12). Because of free enterprise's cathartic effects on all its workers, the merits of a vertically arranged social order far outweighed the inferior horizontal social order manifested by socialism.

Reagan used signs indicating material wealth to prove that in a vertically structured society, poverty was nonexistent. In this instance, however, some of Reagan's "indicators" had changed.

> As for the poverty that we haven't totally eliminated, 95 percent of the families in this country have an adequate minimum daily intake of nutrients, and I think part of the 5 percent who don't are on a diet. . . . [T]here's an automobile for every two people, . . . [N]inety-eight percent of American women have their babies in hospitals with a doctor in attendance, and in most countries, they have them at home with only a midwife (13).

Food, automobiles, and medical availability were Reagan's material signs that poverty had been eliminated by his generation. In addition, these materialistic luxuries had been spawned solely by free enterprise, whereby "the genius of the individual man was freed to perform such miracles of invention, construction, and production as the world had never seen" (12). Free enterprise for Reagan was not just a name to describe the economic way of life in the United States; rather, free enterprise was a redeemer in the strongest sense of the word, as it had singlehandedly wiped out poverty, improved technology, and had emancipated human kind from "back-breaking" labor. Though he often thought of himself as the savior of California, the United States' savior was free enterprise.

FOOD STAMP REFORM

August 10, 1974

As his governorship drew to a close, Reagan attempted to parlay his successful welfare reforms in California into welfare reform at the national level. Instead of taking on the entire welfare system, Reagan targeted the nation's food stamp program as being in need of major reforms during his August 10 speech to the Young Republican's National Convention.[48]

As one might expect, Reagan used his 1971 welfare reforms in order to warrant his claim "that the cost of government can be brought under control" (2).[49] However, likening the situation to an epic battle, Reagan remarked, "we have also discovered that it (welfare) is a never-ending battle. . . . [W]e intend to continue the battle, and tonight I am taking advantage of your hospitality to fire the first shot" (2). The battle he was about to initiate was part of a much larger war against welfare, one that he had partially waged and won in 1971. Reagan's use of war metaphors in this context is particularly significant when situated in the much larger context of Reagan's two terms as governor. Specifically, the only major "battle" Reagan had won as governor involved welfare. And by "taking the first shot" Reagan was symbolically projecting the image of a confident and courageous warrior, having encountered the enemy before and emerging victorious. To have declared "war" on some other enemy (that is, taxes) Reagan would have had to surrender his leadership to a more battle-proven warrior.

Reagan likened the food stamp program to "a multi-billion dollar administrative nightmare," as well as "the newest nesting place for welfare abuse and fraud" (3). The problem, however, was not confined to financial considerations alone; rather, the abuses in the program had moral implications: "When people who really should not be receiving this aid get food stamps . . . they are—in a moral sense—literally taking bread out of the mouths of the hungry" (3). Reagan was quick to point out that he would have corrected these inequities sooner had they fallen under his jurisdiction: "When we instituted our welfare reforms in California in 1971, we did not include the food stamp program because it is totally a federal program" (4).

Besides the abuses and fraud prevalent in the program, another problem involved labor's enhanced bargaining position precipitated by food stamp availability. Reagan noted, "Strikers are exempt from the work requirements imposed on the truly needy and thus qualify for food stamps. [I]n fact, food stamps and other forms of welfare have become a major part of the resources available to striking workers and undoubtedly have prolonged labor disputes" (6). Just as he had blamed labor leaders for declining productivity and inflation, labor was guilty of using food stamps as a bargaining chip in its negotiations with management.

Not surprisingly, Reagan's solutions to the problems were simple ones: "The abuses and the outright fraud in the food stamp program can be eliminated by tightening up the eligibility requirements, by establishing reasonable regulations that will make certain that food stamps are legally available only to those who really need them" (6). Reagan also proposed "closer supervision to prevent counterfeiting or theft of the stamps while they are in transit"; and streamlining "the administration of this program" (6).

In an awkward transition at the conclusion of his speech, Reagan equated the abuses in the food stamp program with inflation. "Government—alone—is the cause of inflation. We must, therefore, eliminate every area of waste and duplication" (7). Implicitly, Reagan was claiming that reforming the nation's food stamp program would have strong residual effects on the rate of inflation. Hence, Reagan saw his food stamp reforms as solving two problems at once.

THE NATION'S ECONOMY

October 16, 1974

As Reagan's tenure as governor neared its completion, his economic discourse turned more national in scope. In a speech to the American Trucking Association Board of Directors on October 16, Reagan addressed the topic of inflation, its causes, and its cures.

Even more significant than Reagan's rhetoric on inflation was his violation of his long-revered 11th commandment: "Thou shalt not speak ill of a fellow Republican." For the first time in his eight years as governor, Reagan was publicly critical of a Republican president, Gerald Ford. Even during the months and days leading up to his resignation stemming from Watergate, Reagan had been highly supportive of Richard Nixon. Recognizing that if he decided to run for the Republican presidential nomination he would likely be running against an incumbent president, Reagan was openly critical of Ford's pro-inflationary policies: "I must voice opposition to the proposed income tax surcharge, however temporary that tax may be. [T]o combat inflation, we should be reducing excessive government spending, especially at the federal level and I submit it is counter productive to increase government's revenues" (1).[50]

The primary economic problem confronting the nation, according to Reagan, was inflation. In fact, Reagan viewed inflation as the foundation upon which all other issues rested: "Unless we bring inflation under control, we can never expect to deal with any of the other problems we face as a nation or as individuals" (1).

The primary cause for inflation resided in government fiscal policies. "The truth is: there is one reason for inflation in America and that is simply that government for too long has been spending too much money" (2). Furthermore, Reagan specified that inflation was a Democratic phenomenon, having its inception in the New Deal policies of Franklin Roosevelt. Attempting to pinpoint the historical birth of inflation, Reagan noted, "Fostered first by the economic dislocation of the Depression and later by the pressure of World War II, our country went into a decade-long period in which government vastly increased its spending, its size and its power" (2). The inflationary villain was not so much Roosevelt as it was John Maynard Keynes, who was responsible for persuading Roosevelt that "a little inflation is good for us" (2).

The dialectical opposite of Keynesian economic principles was free enterprise: "The tragedy is that our inflation problems are not the fault of the free market system. We stumbled into inflation because we strayed too far away from the free market concept" (3). Reagan's reference to government "stumbling" into inflation is significant largely because of its negation later in the speech. That is, governmental clumsiness had been replaced by a government conspiracy: "Make no mistake about it: inflation is a tax and not by accident. Lenin once said, 'Through inflation government can quietly and unobservedly confiscate the prosperity of its citizens' " (6). By using the quote from Lenin, Reagan implied that the federal government had knowingly and purposefully debauched the currency. However, Reagan stopped short of explicitly stating the ends of such a conspiracy; only declaring that "there is only a very little time to make the right decisions, to free the productive capacity of America, to loosen government's stranglehold on our economy and on our pocketbooks" (7). Whatever the political motives of the conspirators, inflation had imperiled the future of the United States.

FAREWELL ADDRESS

September 6, 1974

Reagan never delivered an "official" farewell address as governor. However, Reagan's September 6 speech to the Sacramento Host Breakfast functioned as his unofficial goodbye to California.

As one would expect from a farewell address, Reagan spent the majority of the speech reiterating his accomplishments over the past eight years. More significantly, Reagan purported to have fulfilled the objectives he had initially set out to accomplish. In essence, Reagan's discourse was self-confirming. That is, by naming the objectives at the outset of the speech, and by confirming the attainment of these objectives, Reagan defined his governorship as a success.

Reagan's objectives as governor were three-fold: to meet government's "legitimate functions without allowing new programs to proliferate"; "to cut out all waste and duplication"; and "to streamline government in every way we could so that the taxpayers would get a dollar's worth of services for every dollar spent" (2).[51] What is somewhat misleading about these three objectives is that, in a simplified form, they all constituted the same objective: less government.

Having defined his objective in this manner, proving that he accomplished this objective was very simple. This was done by his references to tax rebates, property tax relief, balanced budgets, and welfare reform. Reagan even explicitly confirmed the success of his eight-year tenure: "We did not succeed in doing all the things we tried to do or wanted to do, but I believe we demonstrated that government can be controlled; it can be efficient; it can meet the legitimate needs of the people without bankrupting them with higher and higher taxes" (8). In his own words, Reagan's first political venture was a categorical success, in the process reconfirming his belief that government could be brought under control.

CONCLUSION

Ronald Reagan's second term bore little resemblance to his first, either in legislative accomplishments or rhetoric, thanks largely to Assembly Speaker Bob Moretti. Reflecting on this "strange alliance," Lou Cannon noted, "He (Reagan) was saved from a second four-year cycle of frustration by a Democrat who recognized that the Legislature's record was in many ways as sorry as Reagan's."[52] Reagan, with the aid of the legislature, enacted welfare reform, income tax withholding, tax reform, a tax rebate, and left the state with a large surplus during his administration's second term. Reflecting these successes, Reagan's rhetoric relied less on emphasizing minute, "symbolic" economies and more on his legislative successes translated into dollars and cents.

Similarly, scapegoats appeared relatively infrequently during Reagan's second term, illustrating the successful partnership he had forged with Moretti. The major exception though was the bitter battle waged between the two on Proposition 1, a battle which Moretti eventually won due in large part to his political maneuverings on Reagan's tax rebate proposal.

Reagan learned the art of effective governance during his second term, as many political triumphs were achieved in spite of his ideology.[53] For example, the adoption of a withholding provision of state income taxes in 1971 and the tax revenue bill of 1972 both were antithetical to Reagan the ideologue. Additionally, the state's budget rose over $3 billion during

Reagan's final four years, hardly representative of a "squeeze, cut, and trim" economic philosophy. More important, though, was the perception Reagan projected through his discourse. As one columnist insightfully observed, "During his eight years as governor of California, Reagan was unable to do most of what he tried to do. But he has managed to create and convey an image of success."[54]

NOTES

1. *California Journal* 2 (May 1971): 128.

2. Major cuts included $115.5 million in increased salaries for state employees, $108 million from public school funds, $137.8 million from Medi-Cal, $78 million from the Teacher's Retirement Fund, and $57.2 million from higher education. *California Journal* 2 (June 1971): 176.

3. A. Alan Post, the state's financial expert, claimed that Reagan's welfare reforms passed in August would account for an annual savings of $35.2 million compared to Reagan's claim of $220 million. *California Journal* 2 (July–August 1971): 195.

4. For a listing of the major provisions of both welfare and Medi-Cal reforms see the *California Journal* 2 (July–August 1971): 194.

5. For other provisions of the bill see the *California Journal* 2 (December 1971): 340.

6. All references to this speech are from California, Governor's Office Press Release, Ronald Reagan, *Inaugural Address* (January 4, 1971): 1–12.

7. All references to this speech are from California, Governor's Office Press Release, Ronald Reagan, *State-of-the-State Message* (January 12, 1971): 1–14.

8. All references to this speech are from California, Governor's Office Press Release, Ronald Reagan, *National Press Club* (January 25, 1971): 1–9.

9. All references to this speech are from California, Governor's Office Press Release, Ronald Reagan, *American Association of University Women* (May 5, 1971): 1–8.

10. All references to this speech are from California, Governor's Office Press Release, Ronald Reagan, *Town Hall Meeting* (June 23, 1971): 1–10.

11. Reagan reintroduced his proposals only after assembly Democrats introduced their own reform measures.

12. All references to this speech are from California, Governor's Office Press Release, Ronald Reagan, *California Livestock Symposium* (June 17, 1971): 1–7.

13. All references to this speech are from California, Governor's Office Press Release, Ronald Reagan, *Sacramento Host Breakfast* (September 3, 1971): 1–8.

14. The bill called for a $1.2 billion tax shift, of which $530 million was to go for additional school aid, $410 million in homeowner property tax relief, $125 million in tax breaks for renters, $103 million for local governments, and $45 million for business inventory tax reductions. This was to be financed by an increase of one cent in the sales tax, a 1.4 percent increase in both bank and corporate taxes, an increase in vehicle-in-lieu fees of .85 percent, $181 million from the state's general fund surplus, and an increase of .35 percent to every

state income tax rate bracket only if the federal government did not adopt a revenue sharing plan in 1972. *California Journal* 3 (June–July 1972): 200.

15. *California Journal* 2 (July–August 1971): 216.

16. The bill that ultimately passed the legislature and signed by Reagan was similar to the Reagan/Moretti compromise bill of June 30, the main difference being the means of finance. Specifically, the bill called for a 1 percent increase in the state sales tax, a 1.4 percent increase in both bank and corporate taxes, federal revenue sharing funds, and the surplus resulting from the implementation of withholding of state income taxes enacted the previous year.

17. For a discussion of the budget proceedings see the *California Journal* 3 (May 1972): 146–48; *California Journal* 3 (June–July 1972): 178.

18. All references to this speech are from California, Governor's Office Press Release, Ronald Reagan, *State-of-the-State-Message* (January 6, 1972): 1–12.

19. All references to this speech are from California, Governor's Office Press Release, Ronald Reagan, *Sacramento Metropolitan Chamber of Commerce* (January 24, 1972): 1–8.

20. All references to this speech are from California, Governor's Office Press Release, Ronald Reagan, *Lincoln Club of Los Angeles* (February 14, 1972): 1–3.

21. All references to this speech are from California, Governor's Office Press Release, Ronald Reagan, *Stanislaus Memorial Hospitals Appreciation Banquet* (June 27, 1972): 1–7.

22. All references to this speech are from California, Governor's Office Press Release, Ronald Reagan, *California Real Estate Association* (October 11, 1972): 1–8.

23. All references to this speech are from California, Governor's Office Press Release, Ronald Reagan, *World Affairs Council* (October 12, 1972): 1–5.

24. All references to this speech are from Ronald Reagan, "Free Enterprise," *Vital Speeches of the Day* 39 (October 15-April 1972–73): 196–201.

25. For a discussion of identification as a form of persuasion see Kenneth Burke, *A Rhetoric of Motives* (Berkeley: University of California Press, 1969), 19–29.

26. Some of main reasons for the state's dramatic fiscal turnaround were the result of the Reagan/Moretti tax reform bill of 1972 (SB–90), the upturn of the nation's economy, less than anticipated expenditures in the state's budget for fiscal year 1972–73, and federal revenue sharing. *California Journal* 4 (February 1973): 46.

27. Ed Salzman, "1972's Tax Reform is 1973's Fiscal Fiasco," *California Journal* 4 (August 1973): 261.

28. *California Journal* 4 (February 1973): 46.

29. The bill had been amended to make the income tax rebate more progressive as lower income individuals and families received a higher percentage of the rebate. For other provisions of the bill see the *California Journal* 4 (September 1973): 296.

30. Ibid.

31. All references to this speech are from Ronald Reagan, "State-of-the-State Message," *California Journal* 4 (February 1973): 65–68.

32. All references to this speech are from California, Governor's Office Press

Release, Ronald Reagan, *California Newspaper Publishers Association* (February 9, 1973): 1–7.

33. All references to this speech are from California, Governor's Office Press Release, Ronald Reagan, *Association of California Water Agencies Luncheon* (April 27, 1973): 1–6.

34. All references to this speech are from California, Governor's Office Press Release, Ronald Reagan, *California Federation of Women's Clubs* (May 22, 1973): 1–7.

35. Reagan's reductions called for a decrease of only 1.75 percent over a 15-year period in California's tax take. Effectively this would have reduced the state's tax burden from 44 percent to 42.25 percent. Thus, according to Reagan's "signs" of the apocalypse, a tax take of 33.3 percent, the United States was still in grave danger.

36. All references to this speech are from California, Governor's Office Press Release, Ronald Reagan, *State Women's and Men's Club Luncheon* (May 30, 1973): 1–7.

37. This "unspecified point" is known as the critical rate of taxation. See David N. Hyman, *Public Finance: A Contemporary Application of Theory to Policy*, 2d edition (New York: Holt, Rinehart & Winston, 1987), 425–28.

38. All references to this speech are from California, Governor's Office Press Release, Ronald Reagan, *California Real Estate Association* (September 21, 1973): 1–6.

39. In fact, by the time Reagan delivered this speech, the legislature had passed Reagan's tax rebate bill, SB-90.

40. All references to this speech are from California, Governor's Office Press Release, Ronald Reagan, *California Order of the Eastern Star* (October 15, 1973): 1–6.

41. All references to this speech are from California, Governor's Office Press Release, Ronald Reagan, *Commonwealth Club of California* (October 19, 1973): 1–8.

42. *California Journal* 5 (August 1974): 274.

43. All references to this speech are from Ronald Reagan, "State-of-the-State Message," *California Journal* 5 (February 1974): 64–67.

44. Reagan had done so at William Woods College in 1952 and at Eureka College in 1957.

45. In all the speeches we examined, the notion of a vertically structured society appeared in only two speeches: a speech dedicating the Eureka College library in September of 1967 and this speech.

46. All references to this speech are from California, Governor's Office Press Release, Ronald Reagan, *68th Annual Commencement Address* (June 15, 1974): 1–18.

47. Reagan's notion of verticality is not at all dissimilar from Kenneth Burke's definition of humans, particularly Burke's observation that humans are "rotten with perfection" and "goaded by hierarchy." Kenneth Burke, *The Rhetoric of Religion* (Berkeley: University of California Press, 1970), 40.

48. Also included in "California's blueprint for national welfare reform" was the Aid to Families with Dependent Children program.

49. All references to this speech are from California, Governor's Office Press Release, Ronald Reagan, *National Young Republicans* (August 10, 1974): 1–7.

50. All references to this speech are from California, Governor's Office Press Release, Ronald Reagan, *American Trucking Association Board of Directors* (October 16, 1974): 1–7.

51. All references to this speech are from California, Governor's Office Press Release, Ronald Reagan, *Sacramento Host Breakfast* (September 6, 1974): 1–9.

52. Lou Cannon, "The Reagan Years," *California Journal* 5 (November 1974): 363.

53. Ibid., 366.

54. Steve Slade, "Ronald Reagan's Simple Answers," *Progressive* 40 (March 1976): 19.

Chapter Four

From Federalism to Supply Side

Ronald Reagan departed from the stage of California politics in January 1975 uncertain of his political future; his presidential aspirations having been thrown a curve with Watergate and the appointment of Gerald Ford. Reagan ruled out a third term as governor and dismissed the possibility that he would run against incumbent Democrat Alan Cranston for the U.S. Senate. Uncertainty pervaded Reagan and his entourage well into 1975. Lou Cannon noted that "all of the grand plans for a 1976 Reagan presidential campaign now seemed worthless, and Reagan himself had no idea of what to do. He was running in place, waiting for something to happen."[1]

Two factors influenced Reagan to run for the presidency in 1976: John Sears's persuasiveness and Ford's selection of Nelson Rockefeller as his vice president.[2] Sears, soon to be Reagan's campaign manager, had talked Reagan into believing "that Ford would not be able to lead the country after he (Nixon) was gone."[3] In addition, conservative Republicans had not forgotten how, in their view, Nelson Rockefeller had upstaged their leader Barry Goldwater in 1964. Thus when Ford selected Rockefeller as his vice president in 1974, conservative Republicans "were infuriated at the prospect that Rockefeller might inherit the presidency."[4] Cannon claimed, "More than any other single act of Ford's, . . . it was the selection of Rockefeller which fueled national interest among conservatives in a Reagan candidacy."[5]

1975–1976

September 26, 1975

Before Reagan even declared his intentions to seek the presidency, he gave a speech that prevented him "from winning the Republican presidential nomination of 1976."[6] The official title of the speech, "Let The People Rule," was to be remembered simply as "The $90 Billion Speech."[7]

The speech was written by Jeffrey Bell, a member of Reagan's campaign staff in Washington, D.C. The theme of the speech was one of fiscal federalism, something which Reagan had frequently advocated during his governorship. Even though Reagan did not draft the speech, "Bell's idea dovetailed neatly with what Reagan had said for years in California speeches."[8] Interestingly, the Ford entourage did not pick up on "The $90 Billion Speech" until nearly a month and a half after it was delivered. According to Cannon's account, the speech "seemed like an answer to a prayer" for Ford and his campaign staff.[9] Furthermore, Stuart Spencer, Ford's political strategist, knew that for Ford to defeat Reagan "depended on discrediting Reagan."[10] In other words, Gerald Ford needed some political ammunition in order to discredit and ultimately defeat Reagan. Reagan, with this speech, gave Ford the powder and the fuse. All that remained was for Ford and his campaign staffers to light the match.

In hindsight, it should have come as no surprise that Reagan's national economic program was initially one of federalism. Granting more autonomy to both state and local governments was highly congruent with Reagan's emphasis on allowing the citizenry to participate in governmental decision-making. In addition, "letting the people rule" had major rhetorical implications, foremost among these was a responsibility shift, which had existed from the first day of Reagan's "official" political career.

Until the election of Richard Nixon in 1968, the federal government was the conspiratorial villain in much of Reagan's economic discourse. With the election of Nixon though, the Democratic-controlled Congress as well as the federal bureaucracy assumed the role of the villain in Reagan's economic discourse. This rhetorical formula changed with the resignation of Nixon and Ford's elevation to the presidency. The villain of Reagan's economic rhetoric once again became the federal government:

> This absorption of revenue by all levels of government, the alarming rate of inflation, and the rising toll of unemployment all stem from a single source: The belief that government, particularly the Federal Government, has the answer to our ills, and that the proper method of dealing with social problems is to transfer

power from the private to the public sector, and within the public sector from state and local governments to the ultimate power center in Washington. [T]his collectivist, centralizing approach, whatever name or party label it wears, has created our economic problems (2).[11]

The villain remained the federal government, but whereas in the past the federal government had many character flaws, in this instance the villain had a single defect: a collectivist nature. The obvious reason Reagan chose to define the villain in this manner involved his program of fiscal federalism. Only through such a program could "the problem . . . be attacked at its source" (3).

The problems Reagan and his campaign staff would later encounter stemmed from the overly optimistic consequences Reagan claimed would result from his federalism program.

What I propose is nothing less than a systematic transfer of authority and resources to the states—a program of creative federalism for America's third century. . . . The sums involved and the potential savings to the taxpayer are large. Transfer of authority in whole or part in all these areas would reduce the outlay of the Federal Government by more than $90 billion, . . . [W]ith such a savings, it would be possible to balance the Federal budget, make an initial five-billion-dollar payment on the national debt, and cut the Federal personal income tax burden of every American by an average of 23 percent (4).

It is not difficult to understand why this statement was an answer to Ford's prayers. Analogous to proponents of the New Economics, Reagan's magic genie was federalism. With this soon-to-be-regretted statement, Reagan's bid for the presidency was off to an inauspicious start.

November 20, 1975

Because he was running against an incumbent president, and because he had staunchly advocated Republicans adhering to the 11th commandment, Reagan and his staffers initially ran a campaign of "quiet subversion" in which "Reagan presented himself as a superior alternative to Ford without openly knocking the President."[12] Reagan had not forgotten the 1964 Goldwater debacle that caused serious damage within the Republican ranks, and thus Reagan's criticisms of Ford were initially muted. This campaign of "quiet subversion" officially got underway on November 20, 1975, when Reagan formally announced his candidacy.

Reagan's stated motive for running for the presidency was one of concern: "I am running because I have grown increasingly concerned about the course of events in the United States and in the world" (1).[13] Not surprising, the first "event" Reagan mentioned was an economic one: "Three vital measures of economic decay—inflation, unemployment, and interest rates—have more than doubled, . . . [G]overnment at all levels now absorbs more than 44 per cent of our personal income" (1). The other two "events" that instigated Reagan's candidacy were foreign dependency on oil and the nation's defense.

Not known for his complex analysis of problems, Reagan identified "the root of these problems lies right here—in Washington, D.C. Our nation's capital has become the seat of a 'buddy' system that functions for its own benefit—increasingly insensitive to the needs of the American worker who supports it with his taxes" (1). Rekindling the spirit of John Kennedy, Reagan's solution was a "toned-down" version of federalism: "This (the buddy system) must change. It will only change when the American people vote for a leadership that listens to them, relies on them, and seeks to return government to them. We need a government that is confident not of what *it* can do, but of what the people can do" (Reagan's emphasis, 1).

As the press had gotten wind of "The $90 Billion Speech" in early November, Reagan avoided specifics in this speech and in later speeches on the amount of money his program of federalism would entail. In fact, the word "federalism" never even appeared in this speech, signalling the political damage already done by Reagan's September 26 faux pas.

December 13, 1975

As the campaign for the Republican nomination got underway in earnest, Reagan's economic rhetoric was subordinated to national defense and foreign policy. The Panama Canal, Angola, Cuba, and Laos all figured prominantly in Reagan's December 13 speech to the Southern Republican Conference Banquet in Houston.

Though they received second billing, economic issues also received Reagan's attention. The first economic issue broached by Reagan was the federal government's budget. In California, Reagan had frequently attempted to separate himself from the state's budget by claiming that two-thirds of the budget was off limits, fixed by constitutional mandate. By late 1975 though, Reagan had changed his tune: "Our goal must be a balanced budget. Oh, but we are told three-quarters of the budget is uncontrollable—fixed by statutes passed by Congress. Well, statutes passed by Congress can be repealed by Congress" (6).[14] Governor Reagan had taken solace in California's "uncontrollable budget." Presidential candidate Reagan sought the removal of congressional statutes so as to gain more control of the budget proceedings. A presidential candidate seeking less control of the nation's budget would be perceived largely as weak and ineffectual, qualities antithetical to the presidential ethos. Thus Reagan attempted to bolster his presidential character by advocating the need for greater budgetary control.

Upon defending the principles of free enterprise by comparing it with Soviet socialism (a contest free enterprise always won), Reagan turned to the touchy subject of federalism. The essentials of Reagan's federalism proposals of September 26 were still intact. However, the effects of such a program had undergone considerable revision: "These programs (welfare, medicaid, food stamps, education and community and regional development) can be better and more cheaply administered at the state level" (11). Dismantling the federal bureaucracy via federalism would result in greater savings to the taxpayers, claimed Reagan. What Reagan did not mention were the 50 "mini-bureaucracies" that would have arisen under his federalism program. In all likelihood, Reagan, because he had managed to keep the growth of California's bureaucracy to a minimum, believed that governments at the state level could take on more responsibility without the resultant growth in bureaucracy. With his Creative Society as living proof, Reagan assured his listeners that "these programs can be administered at lower cost by the states" (11).

Ever since his inaugural address in 1967, Reagan publicly declared his faith in the people. This optimism was never more apparent than in Reagan's concluding remarks: "All we need to do to turn this country around and point it in the direction in which we believe it should be going is to offer it a banner around which to rally—the banner of Responsible Republicanism" (14). Reagan truly believed that the people, presented with the alternatives, would rally to his cause.

February 21, 1976

Social Security and federalism were Reagan's main topics when he spoke in New Hampshire on February 21, just four days before the primary season got underway. Reagan's objectives in this speech were fairly clear: assuage the fears of senior citizens that he would not dismantle the Social Security system, and mitigate the damage done by "The $90 Billion Speech."

Reagan's proposals to make Social Security voluntary, advanced in his pre-gubernatorial days, would periodically come back to haunt him. To compensate for his earlier remarks on Social Security and the extremist connotations it wrought, Reagan defended the necessity for the program: "One thing must be made unmistakably certain—any reform must have as first priority the guarantee that all those counting on Social Security for their livelihood will continue to receive their monthly check" (4).[15]

Reagan also alluded to several "inequities" in Social Security needing to be corrected. Appealing to the female constituency, Reagan made mention of how Social Security discriminated against women.

> A woman must be married to her husband for 20 years before she gains any rights to his Social Security benefits. If she is a homemaker for 18 years, bears and raises children, but for some reason she and her husband are divorced after, say, 18 years, she doesn't get a nickel of his benefits when he retires (4).

Social Security also discriminated against the working class, in favor of the wealthy, claimed Reagan:

> Take the case of two men reaching age 65. One of them is the president of a company. He has made good money and invested it. He retires with enough to live on from his investments. He is also entitled to his Social Security benefits. But what about the other man, a plumber, same age, but he wants to work for two or three more years. If he does, and earns his normal income, he won't get his Social Security benefits. . . . There is something wrong with a system that won't allow people who want to work, and can, do it after age 65 without forsaking their benefits (5).

As evidenced, Reagan not only defended the virtues of Social Security, but he actually went on the offensive, claiming discrimination. More significant were the two voting blocs Reagan claimed were being discriminated against: women and the working class, typically Democratic strongholds.

Just as Reagan tried to compensate for some of his earlier remarks on Social Security, so too did he attempt to compensate for his September 26 remarks on federalism. On several occasions (welfare reform, property tax relif, Proposition 1) when he was confronted with political opposition, Reagan would often defend his proposals by insisting that the people firmly backed them. In such instances, Reagan claimed that he was not speaking for himself but merely speaking for the majority of the people. Such a tactic effectively removed Reagan from the matter at hand, instead pitting the people against his opposition. Facing political opposition to his program of federalism, Reagan emphasized that the people strongly favored such a program.

> The politicians in Washington seem to be slow in catching on to something that those in the states can feel every day. That is the reawakening of the American spirit of independence and self-reliance. . . . [T]hey don't want any more New Deal or Great Society nostrums. . . . And, they want a bigger share in deciding which programs and which ideas work and which don't. . . . [Y]es, and they want government closer at hand, not in the hands of a self-annointed elite in the nation's capital (6).

Reagan's second tactic was to deny that his September 26 statements were motivated by dollars and cents. "Last fall I proposed that we take a good, hard look at programs run from Washington . . . I suggested we consider them prime candidates for an orderly, phased transfer to state and local governments. This was not a budgetary proposal but one of transfer of control" (7). Allowing the people to have more control was the essence of Reagan's proposal for federalism, not budget numbers. The principle of federalism was what ultimately mattered, inferred Reagan; money was of secondary importance.

A third tactic Reagan used to strengthen his federalism proposal was to identify it with past popular presidents: "It (federalism) isn't a new idea. Franklin Delano Roosevelt said the federal government should get out of the business of welfare and John F. Kennedy protested against centralizing all authority in Washington. And, . . . Dwight Eisenhower set up a commission . . . to study the whole matter of inter-governmental relations" (7). Not only did federalism have a tradition, but it was widely supported by three of the most popular presidents of the 20th century, implied Reagan.

Reagan concluded this speech by reducing the complex to the simple: "I make no promise of having instant solutions to all the problems besetting us. But I know those problems can be solved—solved if government will trust in the people and have faith in their capacity for greatness" (10). Hoping to have his listeners reciprocate, Reagan avowed his faith and trust in the people. Governance was their duty; Reagan's was one of believing.

March 31, 1976

Ronald Reagan was being urged by many Republicans by mid-March to call it quits for the sake of party unity. After having narrowly lost to Ford in the New Hampshire primary (54,824 to 53,507), Reagan proceeded to lose primaries in Massachusetts, Vermont (both uncontested), Florida, and Illinois. In fact, by the time of the Illinois primary, Reagan was said to be "happy" with 40 percent of the vote in his favor.[16]

Reagan's defeats, coupled with his campaign's lack of funds reached a crisis stage by March 20, as Reagan's campaign manager, John Sears, secretly negotiated the conditions under which Reagan could withdraw from the race. However, the March 23 primary in North Carolina proved to be the turning point for Reagan in 1976: "Without his performance in North Carolina, both in person and on television, Reagan would have faded from contention before Kansas City, and it is unlikely that he would have won the presidential nomination four years later."[17]

Aside from his resurgence in North Carolina, Reagan experienced two lucky breaks. First, Ford's campaign manager, Bo Callaway, was "eased out" of his duties by Richard B. Cheney due to charges that Callaway had improperly influenced a U.S. Forest Service decision. Second, Ford became the victim of his own rhetoric after giving a speech on March 20, which Cannon called "one of the silliest in the annals of presidential campaigning."[18]

Eight days after Reagan's first major victory of the primary season, Reagan went on national television with the same political themes he had so successfully extrapolated in North Carolina. Unquestionably, the speech was a success for "it raised $1.5 million and enabled Reagan to stay in the race."[19]

Economics, defense, and foreign policy dominated this speech to the nation. Reagan did not focus on only one economic issue, but rather discussed inflation, the federal budget, taxation, unemployment, and various government fiscal policies. Significantly, Reagan's proposal for federalism was ignored as his economic rhetoric took on a more offensive posture.

One of Reagan's first attacks on Gerald Ford was on the latter's spending policies: "It took this nation 166 years . . . to finally accumulate a debt of $95 billion. It took this administration just the last 12 months to add $95 billion to the debt. And this administration has run up almost one-fourth of our *total* national debt in just these short nineteen months" (Reagan's emphasis, 2).[20] What made matters worse, claimed Reagan, was that Ford's extravagant spending was triggering a host of other economic maladies. Not only had Ford's spending programs resulted in inflation, hence unemployment and recession, but he was also guilty of defrauding the American people. "Mr. Ford, . . . promised he absolutely would not allow the Federal deficit to exceed $60 billion . . . Later he told us it might be as much as $70 billion. Now we learn it's $80 billion or more" (3). Ford had made sure, though, that his pro-inflationary policies would not be felt by his political colleagues in the Congress: "Washington doesn't feel the same pain from inflation that you and I do. . . . last July Congress vaccinated itself against that pain. It very quietly passed legislation (which the President signed into law) which automatically now gives a pay increase to every Congressman every time the cost of living goes up" (3).

Watergate had not endeared politicians to the American public, particularly Washington politicians. Reagan attempted to capitalize on this pervasive sentiment by repeatedly referring to Gerald Ford as "one of them"—a lifelong member of what Reagan called "the puzzle palace on the Potomac."

> An effort has been made in this campaign to suggest that there aren't any real differences between Mr. Ford and myself. I believe there are, and these differences are fundamental. One of them has to do with our approach to government.

Before Richard Nixon appointed him Vice-President, Mr. Ford was a Congressman for 25 years. His concern was the welfare of his congressional district. For most of his adult life he has been a part of the Washington Establishment (6).

Reagan countered his caricature of Ford as a professional politician by emphasizing his own political virginity:

Most of my adult life has been spent outside of government. My experience in government was the eight years I served as Governor of California. . . . I had never in my life though [sic] of seeking or holding public office and I'm still not quite sure how it all happened. In my own mind, I was a citizen representing my fellow citizens against the institution of government (7).

To put it mildly, politicians were not in vogue in 1976. Thus, Reagan, as he had done in 1968, chose not to define his former job as a political one; rather, Reagan was merely a "citizen" representing other citizens. Not surprisingly, another outsider, Jimmy Carter, used the same strategy in much of his campaign rhetoric.

Reagan, though, could not hope to win his party's nomination over an incumbent president without some sort of "political" record to run on. Recognizing this, Reagan mentioned such accomplishments as his Creative Society task forces, leaving office with a balanced budget and a $500 million surplus, tax relief, and welfare reform. Reagan, however, tempered these political achievements by naming their source: "I turned to the people, not to politicians for help" (8). Thus, Reagan's political achievements were defined by him as the people's achievements. In this context, Reagan's distrust of politicians was not a new pronouncement provoked by public sentiment following Watergate. Rather, Reagan had known this all along and his gubernatorial record underscored this belief.

July 6, 1976

Reagan's all-out offensive on Ford had waned by July. Sensing that he was going to fall short of the 1,130 delegates needed for the nomination, Reagan's nationwide speech of July 6 was much less critical of Ford.[21]

Reagan shaped this speech around American values, specifically those central to family and work. Reagan's major claim was that by working against these basic values the federal government had not only lost the faith of the people, but it had also lost faith in the people: "But there seems to be a discontent in the land today. Government, which once did those things which strengthened family and traditional values, now seems to have lost faith in us" (2).[22] Government, according to Reagan, was guilty of a most reprehensible sin: losing faith in its most valuable resource, the people. This sin was particularly damning to Reagan, who had remained adamant throughout the campaign that all government must do to solve its problems was to "have faith in the people."

Government's lack of faith in the people was a categorical sin. However, the people's loss of faith in its government was a natural outgrowth of government's subversion of basic American values. The people, declared Reagan, could not expect to have faith in the very institution that threatened not only their values but also their survival. Inflation was a perfect example:

> But now the dollars we earn don't increase in number as fast as they *decrease* in value. The savings we counted on to see us through our non-earning years melts away like ice in a summer sun. And we're told that's due to inflation, as if inflation were some kind of plague or natural disaster for which no one is to blame. Well, it is a killer, it kills jobs, it kills savings. It kills hopes and dreams, but someone *is* to blame. . . . Every time the buying power of a paycheck is reduced because the government is pursuing inflationary policies, government is acting against the values of thrift, of honesty, of savings—the values that our people brought with them to this country, the values they instilled in their children. . . . And there is no group in this country which has been more viciously savaged by anti-family governmental action than America's elderly. Inflation can quite literally kill someone who is living on a fixed income (Reagan's emphasis, 3–4).

By legitimatizing his auditors' lack of faith in government, Reagan was attempting to create an identification with them. Analogous to a clergyman soothing his guilt-laden parishoners, Reagan warranted the people's lack of faith in government.

Reagan had not yet conceded the nomination, for he reminded his listeners, "I believe I can do the job that has to be done" (11). However, whereas Ford and his pro-inflationary policies had been the object of Reagan's scorn in late March, by July the blame for inflation had shifted to Congress. Thus the 11th commandment that Reagan had so fervently preached in California, and had so blatantly violated in the spring of 1976, exerted a strong pull on Reagan's rhetoric as the inevitability of Ford's victory drew near.

Conclusion

Three discernible rhetorics emerged during Reagan's campaign for the presidency in 1976: defensive rhetoric that attempted to mitigate damage done by "The $90 Billion Speech"; offensive rhetoric typified by attacks on Gerald Ford; and conciliatory rhetoric aimed at unifying the party as Reagan's defeat grew imminent.

Reagan and his speechwriters were quick to learn that his new role as a presidential candidate did not require specific numbers to back up his proposals, as evidenced by the shift away from federalism to a more innocuous emphasis on faith and values. Whatever the consequences of "The $90 Billion Speech," Reagan had gained some much needed political and rhetorical seasoning, which proved invaluable in 1980.

1980

Before Jimmy Carter had defeated Gerald Ford, Reagan had already decided to run for the presidency in 1980.[23] In 1968, Reagan was still a little known commodity, representing the far right-wing of the Republican party. In 1976, Reagan nearly pulled off a major upset against an incumbent president. By 1980 Reagan had become the standard by which all Republican candidates were measured.[24]

After a scare in the Iowa caucus in 1980 (George Bush defeated Reagan by 2,182 votes), Reagan dominated the Republican primaries. The primary season was to be remembered for two incidents: George Bush's labeling of supply-side economics as "voodoo economics" and Reagan's theatrics prior to the Nashua, New Hampshire, debate, where responding to the threat of his microphone being turned off, he declared, "I paid for this microphone, Mr. Green."

Having easily outdistanced his Republican competitors, Reagan had only Jimmy Carter standing between himself and the presidency. Reagan was to win in an electoral landslide by the count of 489 to 44.[25] In accounting for his victory, many concluded that the nation's recessed economy helped elect Reagan. No doubt Carter's failed domestic economic policies helped to precipitate the election of Ronald Reagan. This explanation, though, does not tell the whole story. Equally important as the nation's recession was Reagan's prophetic rhetoric. Jimmy Carter's "malaise" economy was the material embodiment of much of Reagan's economic discourse. Most of Reagan's "Republican" life had been spent preaching against the ills of Big Government and its negative effects on the economy. By 1980, Reagan's warnings had finally been actualized. Even more important, they had been actualized under Democratic leadership.

Additionally, the prophetic discourse gave Reagan's ethos a boost. Reagan could no longer be justifiably dismissed as a paranoid right winger of the Goldwater ilk. Prophets whose prophecies had materialized could not be rightly viewed as radicals, but had to be acknowledged as carriers of "The Message." Carter may have provided the nation with the impetus for a conservative conversion, but Reagan had successfully transformed this impetus into a renewed national faith.

Much of this faith was placed on the healing powers of supply-side economics. Reagan was never a "convert" to the basic principals of supply-side theology; he had been one of its spokespersons long before Kemp-Roth was conceived in 1978. Reagan's commitment to enacting legislation based on supply-side logic was manifested in 1973 under the auspices of Propostion 1. Speculatively, the rejection of Proposition 1 in 1973 may inform Reagan's economic program of federalism in the 1976 campaign. Having endured defeat on tax reduction less than two years earlier may have deterred Reagan from re-introducing tax cuts during a presidential election.[26] By 1978, though, Reagan's Proposition 1 wounds had healed to the extent that he was a supporter of the Kemp-Roth tax cut bill. In addition, retroactive assent was given to Proposition 1 in 1978 when California voters passed Proposition 13, which went far beyond Proposition 1 in scope, thus inaugurating the "Tax Revolution."[27] Tax cuts had become more politically palatable by 1980.

July 17, 1980

Reagan officially accepted the Republican nomination in his acceptance speech at the Republican National Convention.[28] Echoing the theme of shared values he had elaborated in 1976, Reagan stated that Republicans were building "a new consensus with all those across the land who share a community of values embodied in these words: family, work, neighborhood, peace and freedom" (63).[29] At first glance, these five values appear largely unrelated. However, at closer inspection these five values are all contingent upon, and connected by, economics. First, Reagan saw the family as an economic entity in which the family's mental and physical well-being were dependent on "meaningful" employment, hence work, the second value. Neighborhood was closely linked with work insofar as employment made home ownership a reality. Peace, as Reagan had expressed before, was tied to economic prosperity. Last, freedom for Reagan was based on minimal government interference and the right of the individual to pursue his/her dreams in the free enterprise system. Thus the "community of values" of which Reagan spoke were dependent on shared economic values.

The conspiracy theme resurfaced in this speech as a Carter-led economic conspiracy was implied by Reagan in his metaphorical usage:

> We must overcome something the present Administration has cooked up: a new and altogether indigestable economic stew, one part inflation, one part high unemployment, one part recession, one part runaway taxes, one part deficit spending, and seasoned by an energy crisis. It's an economic stew that has turned the national stomach (66).

Carter, implicated Reagan, was the chef responsible for purposefully poisoning the economic stew. The conspiracy, though masked in the metaphor of stew, was clearly implied. Carter's stew, after all, had followed a recipe, hence he was guilty of engaging in a conspiracy against the American people. Unlike the right-wing version of "The Speech," Reagan did not explicitly indict the president and his administration of engaging in a conspiracy. However, the conspiratorial theme lay only slightly removed from the surface of Reagan's discourse.

Supply-side logic also appeared in this speech as Reagan claimed that such tax cuts would preserve the family unit and the workers' self-esteem. "When we deprive people of what they have earned, or take away their jobs, we destroy their dignity and undermine their families. We cannot support our families unless there are jobs, and we cannot have jobs unless people have both money to invest and the faith to invest it" (70). By emphasizing the relationship between work and family, Reagan was claiming that tax cuts were motivated by a pro-family bias, not purely a pro–big business bias, or a bias that favored the wealthy. One of the major assumptions of supply-side theory was manifested in Reagan's pro-family statement. Specifically, supply-siders assumed that, given greater after-tax incomes, people would save and invest more, which, in turn, would stimulate supply. This supply side stimulus would then result in greater demand for various goods and services.[30]

The success of his supply-side tax cuts were all but a given, concluded Reagan: "When I talk of tax cuts, I am reminded that every major tax cut in this century has strengthened the economy, generated renewed productivity, and ended up yielding new revenues for the government" (71). Supply-side was not "voodoo economics" but a tried and true economic theory, according to Reagan.

Surprisingly, Reagan concluded his acceptance speech at the Republican National Convention by quoting from Franklin Roosevelt. Reagan had employed Roosevelt's famous "rendezvous with destiny" phrase since 1964.[31] In this speech, however, Reagan borrowed generously from Roosevelt, eliciting his statements at the 1932 Democratic National Convention.

> "For three long years I have been going up and down this country preaching that government—federal, state, and local—costs too much. I shall not stop that preaching. As an immediate program of action, we must abolish useless offices. We must eliminate unnecessary functions of government. . . . [W]e must consolidate subdivisions of government and, like the private citizen, give up luxuries which we can no longer afford" (Reagan's ellipses, 77).

Reagan's listeners likely assumed that such a statement was excerpted from a conservative's discourse. Only after Reagan's recitation did he reveal the author as Roosevelt. Such a tactic was significant for two reasons. First, this statement was intended to have some degree of shock value, especially given Reagan's immediate audience. Second, Reagan was cleary attempting to identify himself with one of the most popular presidents in U.S. history so as to broaden his constituency. Reagan's stated fiscal agenda mirrored Roosevelt's, hence Reagan was speaking over the heads of his Republican listeners, appealing directly to Democrats. Ironically, Reagan would attempt to dismantle many of Roosevelt's New Deal programs in his first year as president.

September 25, 1980

Following the Republican National Convention, Reagan went out on the stump, often delivering half a dozen speeches in a single day. Much of Reagan's campaigning took place in the "Rust Belt," where the effects of the nation's recession had crippled the steel industry, and in the South, a potential Carter stronghold. Reagan, however, did campaign in the West. One such occasion took place on September 25 in Sunnyvale, California, the site where Reagan had made his first campaign stop in 1966.

The lack of American productivity under the Carter administration was Reagan's major theme to his Sunnyvale audience. When the nation's productivity levels had waned during his governorship, Reagan blamed labor and labor leaders, not Richard Nixon, for this declining productivity. However, Reagan blamed Carter for this economic circumstance in 1980. More specifically, decreasing levels of production were traceable "to the failure of imagination and vision of the Carter Administration" (2).[32] Carter, claimed Reagan, was merely "content with the status quo" (2).

The conspiracy theme also reappeared in Reagan's economic discourse. This time, however, Reagan did not couch the conspiracy in metaphorical language. "He has managed, through diligent effort, to give us the worst of all possible economic worlds. His unemployment, high inflation, high interest rates and high taxes" (2). Carter had actually worked to create the economic environment, claimed Reagan. Reagan's extremism had been muted in front of a nationally televised audience in July. On the stump, partially removed from the nation's ears, Reagan's conspiratorial rhetoric came across loud and clear.

Reagan differentiated himself from the opposition, in this case Jimmy Carter, by creating a simple dialectic of good and evil. For example, Reagan stated, "In place of imagination, Jimmy Carter says we must have regulation. In place of ingenuity he says we must have conformity to federal guidelines. In place of expansion, he says we must have restriction. In place of growth he says we must be content with the status quo" (2). Such a dialectic not only highlighted the differences between him and Carter; it also greatly simplified the issues of the campaign for Reagan's audience.

Reagan's response to the Carter-induced productivity stagnation was to "improve business confidence by having consistent economic policies" (4). These policies included improving patent procedures, reducing tax rates on business and industry, accelerating depreciation schedules, and reducing government regulation of private industries (4). Reagan only promised to make the conditions conducive to increased productivity. Industry alone was ultimately responsible for increasing productivity. Reagan was careful not to overpromise the results of his economic program. The contingent nature of this program was highlighted by Reagan at the conclusion of his speech. "I believe that with the economic program that I have proposed, with an American people committed to restoring the health of our economy, we can increase our productivity" (5). Reagan's economic program did not promise success at all; rather, the success or failure of his economic program depended upon the "commitment" of the American people. The outcome of the soon-to-be Teflon president's supply-side program, whether his audience knew it or not, was in the hands of the American people.

September 30, 1980

Reagan mounted an all-out attack on Carter's economic policies in a September 30 speech delivered in Iowa. After concluding that Carter's farm policy was a "national disgrace," Reagan turned to inflation, specifically what he termed "Carter inflation" (6).[33] Significantly, Reagan claimed that "Carter inflation" was not just an economic affliction, but also a spiritual one: "Inflation is a spiritual as well as an economic evil and Jimmy Carter has stood by while this evil has chipped away at the very heart and soul of Americans" (6). By making inflation a spiritual matter, Reagan was perhaps questioning Carter's self-proclaimed Christianity; a true born-again Christian would not sit idle while a spiritual evil worked in his midst, implied Reagan. Reagan's discourse suggests a more extreme interpretation: that Carter was guilty of creating the evil force since his economic policies had caused inflation. Thus Reagan projected Carter as a material embodiment of evil, perhaps not the Anti-Christ but surely anti-Christianity.

What bothered Reagan the most about "Carter inflation" was that Carter would not take responsibility for it: "There's nothing that makes me more angry than the smugness of this Administration in the face of the disasters it has caused. There are no apologies, no admissions of error, no attempt to *do* something substantive about these tragedies" (Reagan's emphasis, 6). Paradoxically, this statement was spoken from the man, who only five short paragraphs later emphasized that "we have to break the hold of inflation and we can do it, with the help of the American people" (7).

October 7, 1980

Reagan maintained the attacks on Jimmy Carter's economic policies during an October 7 speech delivered in Philadelphia. Inflation, and its debilitating effects on the nation's standard of living, was Reagan's major theme. Reagan continued to emphasize Carter's unwillingness to accept responsibility for high inflation, that he had repeatedly "blamed high inflation . . . rates on the American worker, the American people in general, the Federal Reserve, and the OPEC nations. He's put the blame on everyone except right where it belongs—on the policies of his own administration" (1).[34] What was even worse than Carter's scapegoating tactics was his distortion of statistics, stated Reagan. Specifically, Reagan informed his audience that a Carter campaign brochure had wrongly asserted that real income had actually increased 8 percent during his four years as president. Reagan, the one usually under question for his statistical "facts," corrected Carter, stating "that average weekly earnings, including all cost of living raises, now buy 8-½% less than they did when Mr. Carter took office" (2–3).

The portrait Reagan was painting of Carter was clear: when things were bad, the blame was not his; and when he wasn't blaming someone else for the problems his administration had created, he would manipulate statistics to his own political advantage. Knowingly or not, Reagan's portrait of Jimmy Carter bore distinct resemblance to its creator.

Following his attacks on Carter, Reagan defended his economic program. Specifically, Reagan promised that decreases in federal spending, taxes, and government regulation combined with tight monetary policies would restore "predictability and stability to economic policy" (3). Additionally, Reagan promised that his economic plan would "gradually reduce inflation and unemployment at the same time" (4). Reaganomics, as it would soon be referred to, exhibited strong biases for the wealthy, particularly for the wealthy to generate additional wealth that would trickle down to those lowest on the economic ladder. With this bias in mind, Reagan pointed out that his economic program would greatly aid the "less fortunate—for the poor, for minority Americans, and for the elderly" (4). The less fortunate, stressed Reagan, had "the most to gain when we establish economic policies which preserve the value of the dollars they earn" (4). Thus because his economic program sought to reduce inflation, thereby increasing the living standards of the less fortunate, it was not exclusively a pro-wealthy program.

October 9, 1980

Two days after defending his economic program in Philadelphia, Reagan was on the defensive again, this time in Birmingham, Alabama. Reducing inflation, though, was not at issue. Instead, Reagan claimed that his plan for tax rate cuts, 10 percent a year for three years, would benefit middle-income Americans the most: "Mr. Carter has tried to imply that only the rich would benefit from tax rate reductions. . . . [A]ccording to a study recently released by the IRS, middle-income Americans make up only 38% of the taxpaying population, but they pay more than 60% of all taxes. Thus, any proposal to reduce tax rates for everyone is bound to help working men and women the most" (3).[35] At first glance, Reagan's logic appears sound; because middle-income Americans pay the lion's share of all taxes, tax rate reductions would benefit them the most. A closer look though, finds Reagan's argument wanting. Reagan was addressing two very different entities: total tax percentages and tax rates. In other words, an across-the-board tax rate reduction would not alter, in the aggregate, the total tax share paid by the middle-class. Individually, one's total tax burden would be reduced, but collectively the middle-class would still be paying, according to Reagan's numbers, 60 percent of the nation's tax burden. Viewed in this light, tax rate reductions, on an individual basis, would favor the wealthy taxpayers the most. For while the wealthy's collective share of the nation's tax burden would not have changed either, their individual tax liabilities would decrease much more than the taxpayer in a lower income tax bracket.[36] By confusing taxes with tax rates, Reagan's defense of his supply-side tax cuts was grossly inadequate. This inadequacy, however, would manifest itself only after Reagan's election on November 4.

Conclusion

Two situations influenced Reagan's economic rhetoric during the 1980 presidential campaign: the nation's recession and the tax revolution. By 1980, Reagan was an expert at scapegoating, and the recession provided him with a readily identifiable scapegoat: Jimmy Carter. However, as illustrated, Reagan did not rely solely on an anti-Carter rhetoric; he offered his solution to the recession in the form of supply-side tax cuts, tax cuts, Reagan emphasized, that would benefit the lower- and middle-income classes the most. The public would only find out in early 1981 that supply-side tax cuts were only part of the solution; the others being major cuts in social welfare programs and large increases in defense spending.

Reagan likely could have defeated Carter without a specific economic program designed to stimulate the economy. However, with the tax revolution underway, large tax cuts made a great deal of sense from a political as well as rhetorical standpoint. Reagan had learned his lesson from the 1976 campaign though, as he avoided specifics as to how much the tax cuts would generate in additional revenues.

Typically, American voters do not elect candidates with extreme views, particularly presidential candidates. Yet Reagan, at several points during the campaign, openly flaunted his extreme interpretation of the nation's recession, specifically Carter's purposeful poisoning of the economy, a conspiracy, in other words. Perhaps by this time, extremist rhetoric had become wholly permissible at the level of campaign discourse, but certainly not presidential discourse.

NOTES

1. Lou Cannon, *Reagan* (New York: G. P. Putnam's Sons, 1982), 193.
2. Ibid.
3. Ibid., 192.
4. Ibid., 193.
5. Ibid.
6. Ibid., 202.
7. Ibid.
8. Ibid.
9. Ibid., 204.
10. Ibid.
11. All references to this speech are from Ronald Reagan, "Let The People Rule" (September 26, 1975): 1–13.
12. Cannon, *Reagan*, 200.
13. All references to this speech are from Ronald Reagan, *Candidacy Announcement* (November 20, 1975): 1.
14. All references to this speech are from Ronald Reagan, *Remarks to the Southern Republican Conference Banquet* (December 13, 1975): 1–14.
15. All references to this speech are from Ronald Reagan, *Excerpts of Remarks Made in Manchester, New Hampshire* (February 21, 1976): 1–10.
16. Cannon, *Reagan*, 214.
17. Ibid., 217.
18. Ibid., 215, (The remarks referred to the merits of homemakers).
19. Ibid., 219.
20. All references to this speech are from Ronald Reagan, *National Television Address* (March 31, 1976): 1–19.
21. Cannon notes that by mid-July it was clear that Reagan would fall short of the needed votes. Cannon, *Reagan*, 220.
22. All references to this speech are from Ronald Reagan, *National Television Address* (July 6, 1976): 1–16.
23. Cannon, *Reagan*, 229.
24. Ibid., 234.
25. The popular vote measured 50.7 percent for Reagan and 41 percent for Carter.

26. Reagan did in fact advocate lower taxes during the 1976 presidential election, but only as a consequence of less government spending.

27. Cannon, *Reagan*, 235.

28. We have begun our critique of Reagan's economic discourse with this speech due to the lack of surviving speech texts from the Republican primary season. In fact, according to the universe of extant Reagan speeches compiled by Stuckey, not a single speech text exists from the primary season. Mary E. Stuckey, *Getting Into the Game: The Pre-Presidential Rhetoric of Ronald Reagan* (New York: Praeger, 1989), 174.

29. All references to this speech are from Ronald Reagan, *Ronald Reagan Talks to America*, introduction by Richard M. Scaife (Old Greenwich: Devin Adair, 1983), 63–78.

30. The opposite, however, was to occur. That is, people saved less after their purchasing power had been increased, thereby stimulating demand. See Lester C. Thurow, *The Zero-Sum Solution: Building a World-Class American Economy* (New York: Simon & Schuster, 1985), 30.

31. Our first encounter with the phrase was in Reagan's speech for Goldwater on October 27, 1964.

32. All references to this speech are from Ronald Reagan, *Sunnyvale, California, Campaign Speech* (September 25, 1980): 1–5.

33. All references to this speech are from Ronald Reagan, *Iowa Campaign Speech* (September 30, 1980): 1–12.

34. All references to this speech are from Ronald Reagan, *Philadelphia Campaign Speech* (October 7, 1980): 1–6.

35. All references to this speech are from Ronald Reagan, *Birmingham Campaign Speech* (October 9, 1980): 1–5.

36. This is especially true given that Reagan's tax cuts greatly diminished the progressivity of the income tax rate structure.

Chapter Five

A New Beginning

Neither the Reagan campaign speeches nor his gubernatorial or earlier speeches assumed the symbolic importance of a presidential speech. The presidential persona requisits a different rhetorical form though not necessarily a new ideology. The style of presidential speech and the role of the modern president calls for a speaking president who is frequently in public view and whose message is uplifting and hopeful. Presidential speaking is epideictic in nature—occasional or ceremonial. This genre is prone to thematic development with commonplaces that include praise, blame, and advice. Amplification is the preferred argumentative mode whereas proof of facts are not always present. The subject matter of epideictic speaking incorporates several virtues and acts of nobleness.[1]

Presidential audiences tend to support a president's lead based on oratorical skills displayed and the confidence and credibility attributed. Given the stakes of the rhetorical presidency, presidents must attune carefully to their audiences in ways not familiar to many earlier presidents.[2] In appealing to the largest segments of the nation, modern presidents must structure their messages to a "universal audience," the kind that adheres to abstract, universal values such as justice and truth.[3] To accomplish this rhetorical objective, "*memoria* or recollection of a shared past is an exceptionally important resource for epideictic speeches."[4] Though epideictic speeches, in this context, have been discussed primarily in reference to inaugural addresses, Reagan extended the inauguration genre to most of his national speeches.

In analyzing Reagan's presidential economic discourse, we opted to provide an analysis of most major addresses, including inaugural addresses, State of the Union addresses, and selected speeches. What unifies the speeches selected for analysis is their address to the national audience. We have taken a topical approach in numerous cases to sharpen the focus to specific issues while also reducing unnecessary repetition. The rationale for this approach was given to us, in part, by Reagan himself whose major national and ceremonial addresses were often reduced to a single or a few major topics. Additionally, Reagan's rhetoric was often structured around a dominant metaphor, theme, or argument, subordinating several political and social concerns. This topical approach to selected speeches enables us to discern more accurately Reagan's rhetorical consistencies, shifts, and progressions.

Reagan entered the White House having a clear economic course to follow. His aversion for taxes and government's irresponsible spending spree conditioned an agenda that sought to reduce government spending as well as limit the role of the government in guiding the nation's economy. Allowing people to keep more of their income was, in Reagan's view, the key to a vibrant and consumer-oriented economy. Government's primary responsibility was to ensure the safety and security of the nation, thus the need to invest in the nation's defense. The context of the Carter presidency with its negative economic indicators of high inflation, high interest rates, high taxes, unemployment, and the perception of an economic decline, made Reagan's economic principles appear simple and attractive. Reagan was the right person at the right time, translating complex issues into populist sentiments.

"THE RHETORICAL PACKAGE"—THE FIRST 100 DAYS

Like 1967, Ronald Reagan inherited a fiscal mess from a Democratic administration. A prime lending rate exceeding 20 percent, an annual inflation rate of 12 percent, an unemployment rate of 7.4 percent, and a national debt hovering around $1 trillion were hardly hopeful signs for a "new beginning."

According to most accounts, the Reagan administration got nearly all it asked for in 1981, thanks in part to the Republican majority in the Senate and a more conservative House of Representatives, and Reagan's own persuasive rhetoric. Together, the unprecedented tax cuts, major cuts in social welfare programs, and the increases in defense spending combined to make Reagan's first year as president truly extraordinary.

Shortly after his election, the Reagan team of advisors outlined a "rhetorical agenda" for the first 100 days. Advising the president to concentrate solely on economic issues, the team designed a thematic approach to speeches incorporated as a "rhetorical package" comprised initially of three major addresses. This approach, intended to control the agenda by defining the issues, gave coherence and direction to the president's economic policy, and caught Congress by surprise.[5]

Inaugural Address: January 20, 1981

Reagan's first rhetorical act was shaped by situational variables within the context of a highly symbolic setting but also conditioned by ideological underpinnings that guided his economic views over his political life. In this address, Reagan outlined the formula for a "new beginning" in contrast to Carter's farewell to American greatness.[6]

Unlike many speaking occasions, the inaugural address has a relatively strong rhetorical precedent embedded in tradition.[7] A presidential inaugural address typically contains notes for an optimistic future, discusses traditional values and ideals cherished by the nation, serves as a launching pad for the president's political agenda, and affords the president the opportunity to appear "presidential" before the constituents. "The presidential inaugural address is part of the process by which the President is invested in office."[8]

Several situational variables other than the preceding tradition helped shape Reagan's rhetoric. Most prominent of these situational factors was a new administration and a new agenda. Reagan chose to shape his message around the "present (economic) crisis" to indicate its severity and how it could be overcome. In the opening paragraphs of the address, Reagan set an urgent tone by informing his audience of the high rate of inflation that punished the young and old alike and threatened to "shatter" their lives. What is of interest in this introduction was the way in which Reagan personified the economy, depicting a symbolic death.

> These United States are confronted with an economic affliction of great proportions. We suffer from the longest and one of the worst sustained inflations in our national history. It distorts our economic decisions, penalizes thrift, and crushes the struggling young and the fixed-incomed elderly alike. . . . Idle industries have cast workers into unemployment, human misery, and personal indignity. Those who do work are denied a fair return for their labor by a tax system which penalizes successful achievement and keeps us from maintaining full productivity (1).[9]

Affliction, distortion, penalty, struggle, misery, and lack of dignity were the negative terms Reagan used to label the inherited economic situation. Reagan identified the villains by attributing the nation's economic crisis to the intrusion of Big Government as well as a tax system that did not offer a fair return to the American work force. Reagan went as far as using the term "robbed" in describing previous administrations' tax policies. By implication, the American taxpayers were victims of these economic felonies.

To counter, Reagan introduced the discourse of rebellion by quoting from Thomas Paine: "We have it in our power to begin the world over again."[10] Repeating a line from his governorship, Reagan noted that government was not the solution to the problem; government was the problem. Government was thus articulated as a victimizer at the outset of the Reagan presidency, reducing a complex economic problem to a simple one.[11]

However, Reagan projected two kinds of government: the villainous one which preceded him, and the one he was part of. "Government can and must provide opportunity, not smother it; foster productivity, not stifle it" (2). Government was villainous or virtuous based on what it did to the economy. Until his presidency, the federal government was largely incapable of positive actions. As president, Reagan carved out a role for himself, that of a restorer of economic soundness. The solution to the "villainous" government, declared Reagan, lay in the simple words "We the people." Reagan continued the theme he introduced during his governorship of transferring responsibility to the people through the use of constitutional phraseology.

Reagan also called for sacrifice since, "It (the economic crisis) does require, . . . our best effort and our willingness to believe in ourselves and to believe in our capacity to perform great deeds, to believe that together with God's help we can and will resolve the problems which now confront us. And after all, why shouldn't we believe that? We are Americans" (4). Reagan's substantive claims were grounded on tradition and faith while his style was anecdotal. Stated Reagan, "I did not take the oath I've just taken with the intention of presiding over the dissolution of the world's strongest economy" (3). Reagan, in an effort to overcome present obstacles, proposed to "remove the roadblocks" that slowed the economy, "restoring the balance" between various levels of government, "reawakening the industrial giant," and "lightening" the tax burden. These metaphors meant to project quick and simple economic recovery.

To relieve the despair, Reagan frequently alluded to a vision as the only way to induce optimism in an otherwise unoptimistic time: "I believe we, . . . are ready to act worthy of ourselves, . . . to ensure happiness and liberty for ourselves, our children, and our children's children" (3). His vision depicted a strong economy that provided equal opportunity for all and created a rhetorical prescription for an "era of national renewal" (2). The vision of prosperity was augmented by projecting "average citizens" as heroic in their daily economic endeavors.

> Those who say that we're in a time when there are no heroes, they just don't know where to look. You can see heroes every day going in and out of factory gates. . . . You meet heroes across a counter, and they're on both sides of that counter. There are entrepreneurs with faith in themselves and faith in an idea who create new jobs, new wealth and opportunity. They're individuals and

families whose taxes support the government and whose voluntary gifts support church, charity, culture, art, and education (2).

Interestingly, Reagan's heroes were exclusively economic beings, both producers and consumers. This was the first time in Reagan's economic discourse that heroes were explicitly described.

Reagan's initial rhetorical strategy was to blame previous administrations for the nation's economic performance and to praise working citizens for their efforts to help revive the economy. Short of specifics, Reagan's inaugural sought to uplift the people's mood by projecting a vision everyone could identify with. This rhetorical plot-line established a model for many of Reagan's later speeches on the economy, with restoration, renewal, and optimism as the recurrent themes. These themes countered Carter's "malaise" rhetoric and the admission of inability to cope with the economic situation.[12]

The Reagan administration was quick to come out with a supply-side program that would capitalize on the momentum established by Republican victories in the 1980 election. In February 1981, the President's advisers produced a document calling for a savings of $41.4 billion for fiscal year 1982. Two basic assumptions guided the administration: improving economic welfare could be achieved only by reducing the scope and power of the federal government, and all objectives were achievable simultaneously (inflation could be reduced without recession and without slowing economic growth, and that economic growth would generate greater tax revenues).[13]

A Televised Address to the Nation: February 5, 1981

In a televised address to the nation, Reagan outlined his economic plan and built momentum and support for his program. The president avoided specifics, appeared conciliatory to Democrats, depicted a dire economic situation, and promised a rosy and optimistic future, provided that his economic plan was accepted.[14] With this so-called "Reaganomics" speech, Reagan chose an anecdotal approach over charts and figures, analogizing the economic situation to parents who could lecture their children against extravagance or simply cut their allowance. The message intended for Congress was simple: the president could lecture Congress against waste or simply refuse to authorize its budget. The threat was meant to send early on Reagan's serious intentions regarding the economy.

Reagan limited this address to three major topics: the effect of the economic mess, its causes, and solution.[15] Reagan described the economic situation as the worst since the Great Depression, stating that "the Federal budget is out of control," the value of the dollar having dropped from the value of 1.00 in 1960 to only 0.36 in 1981, and many could not accomplish the dream of buying a house (93–94).[16] Furthermore, Reagan observed that, "We can't even hold our own market here in America against foreign automobiles, . . . Japanese production of automobiles is almost twice as great per worker as it is in America," and, "We once produced about 40 percent of the world's steel. We now produce 19 percent . . . Your standard of living is going down" (95). Emphasizing the crisis-like condition, Reagan noted, "We've come to a turning point. We're threatened with an economic calamity of tremendous proportions" (96). This "turning point" strategy or "the only path" solution implied that the Reagan solution was the only possible one.[17]

Reagan also observed that, "We're victims of language," noting that the very word inflation leads many to think just of high prices but forget it also means a reduction in the value of the currency (94). Reagan further added "that language, . . . can get in the way of a clear understanding of what our program is intended to do. Budget cuts can sound as if we're going to reduce total Government spending . . . Well, this is not the case" (96). Reagan's observation about the nature of language is intriguing, as it suggests that Reagan sought to inoculate the American people against critics of his program, or was simply attempting to justify his departure from technical language on economic issues in favor of simple and generalized discourse, the kind he considered more persuasive. The president was quick to point out that taxes could not be the solution to economic problems since they put businesses out of the market. Reagan presented the practice of taxing as morally wrong, thus portraying the opposition to tax reduction as immoral (94–95).

The economic recovery plan had a four-fold solution: cutting taxes, reducing government spending, deregulation of various federal government agencies, and a stable monetary policy. In order to placate those in need of government's support, Reagan offered comfort: "We can, with compassion, continue to meet our responsibility to those who, through no fault of their own, need our help" (97).

It is noteworthy that the person who earlier stated that language was a problem himself produced persuasive language as a means to implementing his program. By associating taxes with morality and expressing compassion while proposing to cut the very programs that benefitted the socially disadvantaged, Reagan sought to circumvent the perception of implementing economic measures detrimental to the poor.

Address to a Joint Session of Congress: February 18, 1981

Two weeks later, in his third major address on the economy, Reagan reaffirmed his pledge before a joint session of Congress, to restore "the promise that is offered to every citizen by this, the last, best hope of man on Earth" (130).[18] The themes of restoration, hope, and the myth of America's destiny intertwined to create a message expressing confidence, vision, direction, and urgency.

With high inflation and interest rates reaching levels of more than 20 percent, newly built homes, claimed Reagan, were standing vacant and unsold and about eight million were out of work. Despair dominated people's lives, lamented the president, as many were threatened by layoff, declining earnings, and a national debt that stood at $1 trillion. Metaphorically, Reagan depicted the nation as a ship out of control, portraying an economy that, in his words, was "a pretty grim picture" (130). If the economy was an out-of-control ship, then Reagan was the captain who would navigate it to calmer waters.

Reagan warned that "unless we act forcefully—and now—the economy will get worse" (130). In contrast, Reagan claimed that there was nothing wrong with our internal strength and that "we can act with hope" (130). Reagan's recovery program was grounded on a quasi-religious faith whereby an improvement in the nation's economy was possible provided the American people had faith in the wisdom of the president and his program.[19]

At the core of the recovery program was Reagan's request from Congress to reduce federal spending by $41.4 billion in fiscal year 1982 and a 30 percent across-the-board tax cut.[20] (The program also called for $467 billion of federal spending cuts and $709 billion of federal personal and corporate tax cuts over the next five years.)[21]

The economic plan publicly discussed earlier in the month resulted in heightened levels of rumors and fears concerning future economic difficulties. To counter, Reagan argued that stories spread about people losing their benefits (social welfare programs) were exaggerated and the fear unfounded. Using a fairness strategy, Reagan assured that the poverty-stricken, the disabled, and the elderly would not be harmed by his economic program, stating that the "social safety net" of programs they depended on were exempt from any cuts.

Reagan's political thinking was grounded on the principle that federal money should not be used to bring about social change. A return to basic American values was the ideal espoused.[22] However, on the issue of defense spending Reagan made clear no cuts would be introduced, and that it was his duty to increase defense spending and restore America's strength. Reagan rationalized this increase claiming it would be cheaper in the long run to invest now and correct the power imbalance with the Soviets than at a later stage. Reagan implied that his economic program was not tailored exclusively for the wealthy nor was it contradictory. Rather, he was merely acting in the best interests of the nation.

Reagan proposed that $85 million in federal subsidies for the arts and the humanities be replaced by private contributions. Attempting to paint this cut in a positive light, Reagan recalled the historical generosity of the American people whose support for artistic and cultural activities superseded that of all other countries combined. Unnecessary subsidies to business, stated the president, would be cut as well. Positioning the business community after the arts and humanities was, no doubt, designed to defend the president's program from potential criticism.

Proposing to restore the Food Stamp program to its original purpose (helping only the truly needy) and calling for tighter welfare regulations allowed Reagan flexibility in targeting further saving and reform without being perceived as hurting the needy. The proposed savings in several areas, consistent with his criticism of ineffective and wasteful administrative overhead, thus permitted Reagan to suggest either their elimination or the shifting of resources and decisionmaking authority to local and state governments.

Reagan confidently stated that there was nothing wrong with America that could not be fixed together. With an economic program largely outlined in a framework that avoided specifics, Reagan delivered a speech that identified the problems by describing the level of despair and frustration resulting from economic malaise. This speech, in particular, blamed the economic problems on the New Deal–Great Society excessive spending and challenged the Democrats to come up with a better program if they had one. Reagan outlined the proposal for a recovery and restoration, dispelled any notion of more difficulties, called for action, and concluded with a strong projection of confidence, opportunities, and a better future. The solution to economic ills was based on the claim that no action would be disastrous and that enacting the recovery program would save the economy.

On April 9, 1981, as the president ended his first 100 days in office and despite the enthusiasm built by his rhetorical package, the Republican-controlled Senate Budget Committee did not approve the final draft of the budget for fiscal year 1982. With this setback, the administration was concerned it had lost its momentum.[23] The assassination attempt on Reagan's life added further concern for the White House's mighty public posturing. In attempting to regain control of the economic agenda, Reagan "went public," repeating the message he delivered in February and hoping to rekindle the spirit of hope and gain support for the Gramm-Latta budget "compromise" bill.[24]

Address to a Joint Session of Congress: April 28, 1981

The president addressed a joint session of Congress, asking that the economic package be approved in order to "lift the crushing burden of inflation off of our citizens and restore the vitality to our economy and our industrial machine" (478).[25] The situation was described as urgent and thus in need for a "joint mission" (479). The "mission" metaphor transformed the economic recovery program to an inspirational crusade, of which Reagan was the leader.

Reagan claimed he had reasons to be hopeful and optimistic. In three months, "we've come a long distance," referring to the quick presentation of a recovery program (479). Reagan, once again, outlined the essential parts of his economic recovery. The need to repeat this message was the likely result of the White House concern over a loss of momentum.

Continuing the theme of fighting against the governmental system, Reagan stated that when he took office he pledged loyalty to only one special interest group—"We the people." Reagan identified the American people as distinct from the many selfish interest groups that helped foster the nation's economic problems. Though he positioned himself as the champion of the common people and against the government, Reagan also resorted to identification with Congress in order to build an atmosphere of trust and compromise. Though a paradoxical strategy, Reagan seemed not to mind arguing both against and with the government. With frequent "you" and "I" references, Reagan pointed to the spirit of candor, openness, and mutual respect with Congress.

Reagan outlined two possible measures to be taken relative to the economy. One measure, offered by the House Budget Committee, Reagan opposed. The other measure, sponsored by the Phil Gramm–Delbert Latta duo and favored by the administration, aimed at achieving all the essential objectives of the Reagan economic program. The unfavored measure, stated Reagan, "adheres to the failed policy of trying to balance the budget on the tax payer's back," and "reflects an echo of the past rather than a benchmark for the future" (480). Reagan opposed the House Budget Committee's projected spending of $141 billion more than the bipartisan substitute. By contrasting the failed past with a vision of recovery, coupled with the House proposal of more spending, Reagan simplified his economic principles to a formula whereby less was better and waste unacceptable.

This address concluded with a vision of the bold and courageous American spirit. Quoting from the poet Carl Sandburg, Reagan noted, "The republic is a dream. Nothing happens unless first a dream" (481). Reagan made dreams a national symbol. His restoration theme presented an epic-like theme that seemingly asked nothing from the people but complete faith in the administration's economic recovery program. Dreams and faith were the ultimate conditioning factors. Any failure would be the result of people's faithlessness and lack of vision, not of Reagan's doing.

The "rhetorical package" of the first 100 days depicted the economy in dire need of an overhaul. Reagan used urgency to present a dramatic portrayal of a gloomy situation, hoping the alarmist approach would get quick approval of his recovery program by Congress. Reagan balanced the exigency in the situation with his confidence in the people's ability to turn the economy around, thus his request to the people to have faith in him. The recovery program was limited to a few general principles, incorporated in a reductionist approach to solving complex economic problems. The themes of restoration, rebirth, and renewal were extensively employed, indicating a return to traditional American values. Implied in this formula was the equation of the recovery program with past historical events of paramount national importance. To complement this approach, Reagan fashioned himself as the savior, healer, and rescuer from disaster.

THE RECESSION

With the rhetorical package complete, Reagan introduced a new alternative to the relationship between government and the people—that of a partnership whereby free enterprise was not considered a selfish pursuit but a healthy cooperation between supplier and customer.[26] With the less-government archetype, Reagan sought to implement a radical departure from years of an accepted conceptualization of political and economic thought. The economic recovery program offered seemingly sensible and relatively simple solutions to the stagnant economy. However, as the nation plummeted into a deep recession, Reagan's rhetorical approach attempted to overcome the perception that his recovery program was not working.

During this period Reagan signed into law the single largest tax reduction in the nation's history, known as the Economic Recovery and Tax Act of 1981 (ERTA). Reagan initially proposed a 30 percent across-the-board income tax rate reduction to be phased in incremental units of 10 percent over the course of three years and accelerated depreciation schedules for business. By the time the measure had passed Congress and was signed in mid-August, the tax rate reduction had been lowered to 23 percent, while tax breaks to businesses and investors were actually higher than the administration proposed.[27]

The budget submitted by Reagan and eventually approved by Congress called for large increases in defense spending as well as reductions of $30 billion in social welfare programs. Some programs were largely "off limits" to cuts, programs Reagan referred to as the "social safety net," which included Social Security, Medicaid, food stamps, AFDC, and child nutrition programs.

Federal Tax Reduction Legislation: July 27, 1981

The enthusiasm of earlier months, especially the potential for an accommodating relationship between the executive and the legislative branches, waned as Reagan's economic program experienced difficulties in Congress and public concern mounted as the economy continued its downturn. Central to Reagan was a federal tax reduction proposal that required congressional support. Yet,this proposed legislation with cuts in several programs met with strong opposition.

Reagan did not spell out the administration's proposal at the outset of the speech. Instead he chose to begin by reducing unnecessary concerns over some parts of the program as well as to rationalize the need for a reform. Plans to cut Social Security benefits were quickly denied as public protest was strong and potentially damaging. Consequently, Reagan was both apologetic and reassuring in this address, claiming that those who depended on Social Security had been needlessly frightened, pledging not to deprive those in need of benefits. Reagan acknowledged that the Social Security system had experienced financial problems, but he also pointed out that these problems had been building for more than 20 years (814).[28] With this strategy of affirmation by denial, Reagan refuted any plans to cut Social Security, dismissing such talk as rumors. In fact, the administration's reform of May 1981 (attempting to reduce Social Security expenditures, which accounted for 30 percent of federal spending), was so strongly opposed that the Senate voted 96–0 against the proposed reform, leaving the administration no choice but to back off.[29] Yet, Reagan's discourse revealed no admission of a failed policy or inconsistency with previous stands on the issue.

Next, Reagan announced that on the economic front the news was promising: "It's been nearly 6 months since I first reported to you on the state of the Nation's economy. I'm afraid my message that night was grim and disturbing" (814). In contrast to his earlier grim discourse, progress had been made, claimed Reagan, pointing to the reduced inflation rate.

Complementing the American people, Reagan told his audience that all the interest groups opposed to the federal tax reduction were no match for the voice of the people supportive of the administration. Despite many who said it could not be done, his objective, Reagan stated, was to change "control by government" to "control of government" (815). The guilty party was Big Government, which in the past had not listened to the people. Erosion of income, claimed Reagan, was due to the invisible tax called inflation, an automatic tax increase which benefited the government but which required no vote. In one stroke, Reagan attacked two of the causes for the economic mess: Big Government and inflation. Consistent with this viewpoint, Reagan stated he would put a stop to such practices, proposing drastic cuts in government spending in the fiscal year 1982 budget and cutting the budgets for fiscal years 1983 and 1984, primarily by eliminating unnecessary regulations and implementing across-the-board tax cuts. Such a solution, with the emphasis on putting a stop to unwarranted practices, positioned Reagan as the lone hero doing battle for the people. In so stating, Reagan sought to minimize the damage of cutting programs many were dependent on.

Despite the growing disagreement with Congress, Reagan resorted to identification in order to project a positive working relationship between Democrats and Republicans and between his administration and Congress. Accordingly, the negotiation conference for a bipartisan tax bill, stated Reagan, was called to reconcile differences as well as proving the strength of the political system and the optimism in the land. Yet Reagan balanced political expediency that called for a compromise by blaming Democrats for years of neglect and bad policies, and now, for resisting to accept his recovery plan. In like manner, he accused the congressional committee's proposal for holding people's tax reduction hostage to future economic events thus eliminating the ability to plan ahead. With the Iran hostage crisis still fresh in people's mind, Reagan's metaphor is significant as it situated people's honestly earned money to be unlawfully held (through taxing) by an unscrupulous government. "There's also a little sleight of hand in that trigger mechanism," complained the president, adding "we have some people around here who never met a tax they didn't hike" (817–18). Reagan's dual approach pointed to positive aspects of the negotiation as well as attacking those opposing the administration's plan, thus projecting both toughness and willingness for accommodation. Reagan praised the bipartisan tax bill stating that tax cuts would give the economy and the future of the nation *back* to the people.

Reagan's proposal for a reduction in tax rates called for a 5 percent reduction in the income tax rates by October 1, a 10 percent reduction starting July 1, 1982, and another 10 percent cut a year later, a total of 25 percent reduction in tax rates over three years (816). The bipartisan tax bill, contended Reagan, was so clearly drawn and broadly based, that it provided predictability and certainty for stimulating productivity. The money people would get back through tax cuts would be theirs, promised the president, and would not be available for Congress to spend. This, in Reagan's view, was what the entire controversy was all about; were people entitled to the fruits of their labor "or does government have some presumptive right to spend and spend and spend?" (819). Reagan challenged government's presumption regarding what was best for the people. His Robin Hood–like philosophy sought to restore justice to the land.

Tangible proof of a better future was limited to a discussion of inflation, which had dropped below double-digit figures, allowing the president to contrast his "lasting commitment to the future of working Americans" with Congress's "empty promise" (818–19). With this hopeful indicator, Reagan challenged America to believe in his administration's economic recovery program. Using the road metaphor, Reagan stated: "One road is timid and fearful; the other bold and hopeful" (820). Reagan called for a new beginning asking Congress to join him "in this dramatic but responsible plan to reduce the enormous burden of Federal taxation" in order to make America great again (819). Reducing the severity of the economic situation by projecting confidence in a better future was the formulaic line Reagan used extensively during the recession.

This speech was considered an overwhelming success. Donald Regan called it "a homerun with the bases loaded"; "devastating," declared Tip O'Neill; "The dam broke . . . It fell apart," lamented Richard Gephardt. Fifteen million letters were sent to House representatives in support of Reagan's program.[30]

Program for Economic Recovery: September 24, 1981

Though the economy began to show some signs of improvement, relative to inflation and declining fuel prices, the rise in unemployment rates found Reagan frustrated and defensive. Emphasizing that the recovery would take time and unable to promise too much, Reagan asked people to have faith in him urging them "to hold to a firm, steady course" (1025).[31] The use of the ship metaphor portrayed the economy as a vessel in a storm and whose fate was dependent on the wisdom of its captain, who, against all odds, decided to stay the course.[32] Instead of the Carter malaise, the ship metaphor underscored Reagan's heroism, faith, determination, and courage, the implied qualities of such a captain and the rhetorical strategy of the anecdotal president.

After Congress passed in August the Omnibus Budget and Reconciliation Act of 1981, progress, stated Reagan, had been made on all four points of his economic plan.[33] Especially pleasing to the president was a bipartisan coalition over the biggest tax cuts and the greatest reduction in federal spending in the nation's history (1024).[34] Reagan gave the greatest tribute to the American people whose voices made those in Washington realize what needed to be done. Reminiscent of Franklin Roosevelt's successful argument that the New Deal needed time to work, Reagan stated, "Our problems won't suddenly disappear next week, next month, or next year. We're just starting down a road that I believe will lead us out of the economic swamp we've been in for so long." (1024). The road metaphor depicted a solid path unlike the swamp, unstable and unpredictable.[35]

The specific purpose of this address was to spell out the next steps that had to be taken, including additional reductions in federal spending to further stimulate growth and reduce inflation. Serious problems remained over balancing the budget, which, according to the president, had "hemorrhaged badly and wound up in a sea of red ink" (1025). The health and sea metaphors depicted an unexpected occurrence that resulted in further confusion. The sea metaphor usually portrayed a negative experience whereas Captain Reagan was the one to make safe harbor just like the physician whose mission is to heal the patient. Painting a dire picture of the nation being economically ill and bleeding was an attempt to garner support and secure public opinion for deeper cuts in government programs ($16 billion more were needed to balance the budget by 1984) while continuing the anti-government, anti-bureaucracy theme.

Juxtaposing threats and challenges was another strategy Reagan used in this speech. The threat to the economy appeared in the form of driving the deficit upward unless failing to act, while the challenge was to hold down the deficit in the upcoming fiscal year. The challenge was the conditioning factor in averting the threat, however, a failure, and any ensuing consequences, if materialized, would not fall on the president. Reagan's rhetoric absolved the administration of any blame and projected success on congressional compliance with his economic plan.

Throughout this address, Reagan stated there was no choice but to accept the plan with its hardship. "We can try to run from it but we can't hide. We have to face up to it" (1025). What the nation could not run from, stated Reagan, was the massive explosion in federal spending that had grown to about $100 billion by 1962, doubled the following eight years and tripled five years later, reaching $300 billion. Big Government, the kind that spent more on interest payments than on education, nutrition, and medical programs combined, justified Reagan's severe budget cuts. By implication, it was bad government that invested less on education and social programs. Reagan's solution to the crisis was straightforward: "Our government must return to the tradition of living within our means" (1026).

Sacrifices were needed, declared the president, yet the "truly needy," he promised, would not be victimized. By using phrases such as the "truly needy," Reagan projected empathy for the poor, the unemployed, and the elderly without appearing to divert from his conservative stand.[36] The president, who earlier in the speech blamed previous administrations for cutting defense spending thus weakening the nation's security, stated reluctantly that cuts would even be made in defense spending. In fact, only the increase requested was to be cut by $13 billion (1026). The compromise also proposed that the Departments of Energy and Education be dismantled. Further cuts were promised through savings in areas such as federal loan guarantees and welfare reform measures. The last area, a touchy issue, brought Reagan to say that many of the programs came from a good heart but not from a clear head. Kindness was one thing, but common sense was an entirely different issue. Reasoning by analogy, Reagan stated that despite screams and protests, his welfare reforms as governor saved money while needy welfare recipients had seen increases in grants by as much as 40 percent.

Reagan portrayed the recovery program as a crusade, asking the nation to join him in *saving* the economy. By calling his program a crusade Reagan could justifiably ask for sacrifices from virtually all Americans. Those opposed to his plan, Reagan reminded, had participated in the extravagances that brought inflation, unemployment, high interest rates, and an intolerable debt (1028). Reagan pointed out the selfishness of the opposition and the guilt they carried with them, further justifying the urgent need for a drastic economic plan.

Social Security and the assurances given to its recipients resulted from a serious exigency. After indicating in earlier speeches the short- and long-range fiscal problems, apprehension over the future of the Social Security system remained. Despite pledges to keep the "integrity" of Social Security, the administration's solution, which Reagan presented, included cuts to those who were *adequately* provided for by pensions or other income (as distinct from the *truly* needy). Reagan also asked that early retirees (aged 62) receive only 55 percent of the total benefits but that 20 months later the benefits would increase to 80 percent, rationalizing this policy on the assumption that few retire early. In addition, Reagan requested a one-time delay of three months in the cost-of-living adjustment. In a marked deviation from his campaign promises, but consistent with his long-held philosophy, Reagan spelled out some cuts in Social Security.

The administration's economic plan was based on reducing the role of the government and its financial assistance to many social programs, calling on private enterprise to fill the gap. Private generosity was to replace government help. To make this argument palatable, Reagan recalled Alexis de Tocqueville's observation that when an American citizen saw a problem, he would cross the street and talk to a neighbor about it, and the first thing you knew, a committee would be created. Problems were solved without the need for a single bureaucrat, claimed Reagan. With this brief narrative, Reagan sought to convince the people of the merits of volunteerism while at the same time advancing his argument against a big government and its bureaucratic tangle.

The ideological strain in Reagan's rhetoric clearly appeared at the end of the speech when the president called for government to give *back* to the people what was *theirs* to begin with (1031). Behind the idea of giving people what was originally theirs stood many of Reagan's cherished economic principles: less government, less government spending, individual enterprise, less regulation, and above all, less taxes.

The momentum of 1981 had slowed by early 1982 as Congress approved only half of the president's spending cuts spelled out in the budget negotiation. When the election of 1982 yielded 26 additional House seats for the Democrats, the administration found it increasingly difficult to implement its economic plan. The president also did not enjoy the earlier Republican solidarity, as the Republican-dominated Senate Budget Committee rejected his budget proposal, accusing the administration of being overly optimistic.[37] The administration had no choice but to compromise around the Gramm-Latta II proposal. Though the battle against inflation was successful, it also resulted in causing a deep recession and an increased unemployment rate of 11.5 percent.

Regardless of some legislative setbacks, 1981 was a successful year for Reagan as he was able to pass in August the massive Omnibus Budget and Reconciliation Act and the Economic Recovery Tax Act (ERTA), including an income tax reduction of 23 percent over three years.[38] These successes were largely the result of a Republican solidarity and the support of disenchanted Democrats.[39] With Congress acceding to the administration's proposed cuts of $35 billion for fiscal year 1982, Reagan began to slow down a 50-year trend of larger and more intrusive domestic government. Yet, the notion that a supply-side tax cut coupled with tight monetary policy would quickly reduce inflation and increase employment simultaneously was erroneous. Though the tax cuts boosted the economy at a later stage, it had no immediate effect on employment, savings, and productivity.[40] On the contrary, a restrictive monetary policy was a primary cause for the recession.[41]

During 1982, ERTA gave way to the Tax Equity and Fiscal Reform Act (TEFRA) and the Omnibus Reconciliation Act of 1982 as the recession caused a larger-than-predicted budget deficit. TEFRA was designed to increase tax revenues by $98.3 billion and cut federal spending by $17.5 billion for fiscal years 1983–85. In addition, the Omnibus Reconciliation Act cut $13 billion from government spending programs for the same period. Thus, a year after passing the largest tax cuts in the nation's history, the administration supported legislation to increase tax revenues by nearly $100 billion.

Both TEFRA and the Omnibus Reconciliation Act resulted from a congressional budget resolution that sought to limit federal deficits to $103.9 billion for fiscal year 1983. Though initially he proposed a much more modest deficit reduction package, Reagan ultimately supported both measures. Despite the new tax increases, Reagan was successful in keeping intact the 10 percent tax rate cut effective July 1, 1982.

The State of the Union Address: January 26, 1982

As the nation was in the middle of a major economic recession that would be remembered as one of the worst since the Great Depression of 1929, Reagan delivered his first *State of the Union Address* highlighting an optimistic future and dwelling less on the painful realities of the present economic situation. The general purpose of a state of the union address is to detail the successes of the past year as well as outline the coming year's agenda. Reagan, however, used this ceremonial occasion not just as a platform for recommending legislation, but also as a bully pulpit.[42]

Reagan presented several rhetorical visions precipitated by his New Federalism.[43] Prior to addressing the vision, Reagan apologetically stated, "Yes, we have our problems; yes, we're in a time of recession. And it's true, there's no quick fix, as I said, to instantly end the tragic pain of unemployment" (78).[44] Due to the hardships of the recession, Reagan could not, in good judgment, simply overlook the present crisis, thus he explicitly addressed the situation, hoping to maintain credibility in the eyes of his audience.

Recalling his newcomer message a year earlier, Reagan reiterated how critical he was of past policies and how his administration countered with a new spirit of partnership with Congress. The promise then and now, declared the president, was prosperity, peace, and the blessing of individual liberty (72). The guiding force, stated Reagan, lay in making the government *again* the servant of the people. With the culprit (the government) clearly identified, Reagan attributed past recessions, increased unemployment, high interest rates, and runaway inflation to an unacceptable relationship between the people and their government. Reagan's rhetorical line for the recession was to blame past policies for the present economic situation and project a better future. Yet, in fairness to the president's 1981 economic plan, economic improvements could not be expected overnight. Reagan stated, "Our current problems are not the product of the recovery program that's only just now getting underway, as some would have you believe; they are the inheritance of decades of tax and tax and spend and spend" (73).

Reagan spoke of the present using an argument by *sign*: "Already interest rates are down to 15 ¾ percent . . . Inflation is down from 12.4 percent to 8.9 . . . If we had not acted as we did, things would be far worse for all Americans than they are today. Inflation, taxes, and interest rates would all be higher" (72–73). Though the economic policies were yet to fully take hold, Reagan attributed partial success to favorable signs of economic progress.

The reference to a better future based primarily on identification between the president and his audience was quite evident in the anaphora of "together, we" appearing at the beginning of seven paragraphs. "Together," described the President, "we" cut taxes, "we" cut the growth of government, "we" reduced inflation, mobilized the private sector, and restored the nation's security.

Reagan's visions overlapped in that they collectively pointed to a prosperous economy. For example, Reagan stated that

> the program for economic recovery that is in place will pull the economy out of its slump and put us on the road to prosperity and stable growth by the latter half of this year . . . I can report to you tonight that in the near future the state of the Union and the economy will be better (73).

A better future was promised upon accepting the administration's economic plan despite criticism and the continuing recession. Reagan's visions coincided with a prophetic genre whereby the people were asked to have faith in their leader, his conviction, and his prophecies.

Arguing against raising taxes as the solution to budget deficits, Reagan indicated that higher taxes would not mean lower deficits, otherwise, pointing to the doubling of tax revenues since 1976, how could one explain the increase rather than a decrease in deficits. Neither would higher taxes balance the budget, but rather they would slow down economic growth. With such a paradox, the average citizen could easily rationalize which was the better direction to take. Behind this argument was the concern over a rejection of the administration's solutions and the potential perception that the administration was part of the problem.[45] Though Reagan envisioned the economy would be a mighty engine of freedom, hope, and prosperity again, in the meantime, he argued, the budget deficit would exceed earlier expectations, due partially to the success of bringing inflation down faster than predicted, resulting in revenue reduction (74). Reagan had found a silver lining in the recessed economy. In order not to contradict himself Reagan attributed revenue loss to curbing inflation; not to reducing taxes.

Regan also reiterated earlier promises not to hurt the elderly and the poor, yet emphasized his administration's intentions at reforming the welfare system and saving $63 billion in entitlement programs over a four-year period (75). At the same time, Reagan stated that by 1984 the federal government would assume full responsibility for the cost of the rapidly growing Medicaid and continue the responsibility over Medicare (76).

The theme of renewal was intertwined in this address with the themes of faith and the saving of America. Against despair, Reagan sought to create a consensus, stating the people did not believe that America's best days were behind her. Reasoning from analogy, Reagan stated that just as President Lincoln and Congress did not fail the American people and together they weathered the storm and preserved the Union, "Let it be said of us that we, too, did not fail; that we, too, worked together to bring America through difficult times" (79).

Reagan's primary problem during the recession was to convince both Congress and the people that his recovery program would work. Reagan understood the human craving during difficult times to believe and hope for a better future, and thus extensively projected appealing visions. Reagan presented himself as confident and optimistic, reassuring the people and asking them to continue to have faith in him. He also asked for sacrifices during the difficult economic phase. Extensively blaming Congress was Reagan's strategy of keeping the pressure on the legislative branch, minimizing Congress' ability to either propose counter-policies or counter the administration's claim to a better future.

"THESE ARE DIFFICULT TIMES"

With his initial economic legislation behind him, Reagan reduced the frequency of addresses to both Congress and the nation. Economics continued to dominate Reagan's public agenda as he found the Saturday radio addresses to the nation good fillers between major speeches. The specific concerns occupying Reagan's economic discourse were the budget for fiscal year 1983, inflation, unemployment, and the budget deficit.

The Budget: April 29, 1982

The goal, stated the president in his April 29, 1982, address to the nation, just days before Congress was to vote on a bipartisan budget, was the enactment of a federal budget that would bring the deficits and interest rates down (545).[46] However, declared Reagan, the "other party" did not agree with the goal, blaming several Democratic-controlled committees that called for increases in spending and taxes.

The solution Reagan called for remained simple and general: less spending, less taxes, and more prosperity. However, admitted the president, the administration's budget proposal for fiscal year 1983 was rejected by Congress where screams of protest and an insistent drumbeat charged that the proposal would deprive the needy, the handicapped, and the elderly. After months of negotiations, narrated Reagan, a new budget proposal was offered. In a series of "we" against "they" statements, Reagan ridiculed the Democrats for pursuing a philosophy of more spending and more taxes while "we" support less spending, less taxes, and more prosperity. In the last forty years, joked the president, there has not been much opportunity to see what the Republican philosophy could do while Democrats have shown much and it was not very impressive (547). To increase the pressure on "they," Reagan described recent budget negotiations. The original cuts of $101 billion, stated Reagan, were rejected by Congress. A second proposal, cutting $60 billion, was also rejected only to be countered by a $35 billion cut: ". . . I swallowed hard and volunteered to split the difference between our 60 and their 35 and settle for 48, and that was rejected. The meeting was over" (548). Reagan presented himself as a willing and compromising president challenged by an unyielding and selfish Congress controlled by Democrats.

Faith and optimism drew this address to a close as Reagan stated he was convinced a recovery would take place in the second half of 1982. The choice, stated Reagan, attacking big spenders, was clear: turning the presses to print money and feeling good about everything for about five minutes or enacting a responsible budget. By stating "this is no time for 'politics as usual,' " Reagan sought to dramatize the situation in an attempt to ensure that Congress would not reverse his program for economic recovery (548).

This address was not meant only to emphasize the difficult negotiations with Congress over the budget talks but also to align public support against Congress. Reagan was confident that grassroots support for a balanced budget amendment existed and would carry the day against congressional pressure. To get the support he needed (in the form of spending cuts), Reagan's narrative turned inspirational: "So often in history great causes have been won or lost at the last moment, because one side or the other lacked that last reserve of character and stamina, of faith and fortitude" (548). Reagan positioned himself and his administration on the side of stamina, faith, and fortitude, implying the opposition lacked such qualities. Prior to the crucial budget legislation, in an attempt to persuade the people of the needed spending cuts, Reagan rhetoric turned to Puritan and secular values, such as hard work, thrift, sacrifice, love of God, and free enterprise, depicting the nation as chosen and driven by a special mission.[47]

Deficit Spending: May 1982

In early May, a budget agreement with Congress resulted in a three-year package of $416 billion in deficit reduction. Of this amount, announced Reagan, only 23 percent would come from revenue increases while the rest would come from spending cuts. According to this package, the projected budget deficit was $106 billion in 1982, $69 billion in 1983, and $39 billion in 1984.[48] The cuts in various programs were sure to result in congressional outcry.

On May 22, 1982, Reagan stated that Washington, D.C. was a town that loved to spend the people's money. Advocating a policy that would stop such spending, the president warned that to continue the wasteful road would mean disaster.[49] Unlike the Senate, the House, declared the president, was trying to spend more, eliminate $150 billion of the tax rate reductions, and hurt the country's defense. Only with the help of *responsible* Republicans and Democrats, stated Reagan, would a better plan be proposed, implying irresponsible individuals in Congress were to be blamed for not cutting enough in budget spending.

A week later, in a significant shift from the recent addresses, Reagan stated that "nothing in our Federal Government is more in need of an overhaul than the ridiculous procedure we have misnamed 'the budget process.' "[50] Due to the recession and mounting pressure from both Democrats and Republicans identifying the budget deficit as the primary cause of economic problems, Reagan shifted the focus to the budget process itself as inadequate and in need of correction. This shift is noteworthy in that it allowed the president to accuse the legislative process as the cause for the deficit, not the lack of revenues.

Deficit Reductions: August 16, 1982

Reagan went on prime-time television to defend himself against charges that he would propose the biggest tax increase in history. Setting the record straight, Reagan stated that his administration was not planning a significant tax increase, nor had the economic recovery program been abandoned (1035).[51] The president justified his recent proposal as fair since it had cut government spending, reduced interest rates, and put more people back to work. To ease the severity of the economic program, Reagan attributed part of the problem to interest rates, asserting the problem was a psychological one—a pessimism in the money markets borne out of the perception that his administration would not stay the course. By blaming a psychological state, Reagan indicted pessimists for lacking faith and commitment, whereas all economic prosperity required was faith and confidence.

Next, Reagan claimed as untrue reports that indicated he planned to have withholding taxes due on interest and dividends but admitted taxes would be withheld only at certain income levels, repeating his earlier explanation of having "to swallow hard to agree to any revenue increase" (1038). Against his own economic philosophy, Reagan agreed to a compromise, yet, made no secret of the dislike he had for raising taxes. Implied in the quote was Reagan's way of going along with unfavorable policies but not without indicating his reluctance and blaming others for pressuring him. This way, Reagan absolved himself of any accusation of inconsistency either with his administration's policies or with his long-held economic philosophy. Reagan sought to maintain the image of an outsider trying to correct Washington's wasteful ways even when pragmatics conditioned a different approach.

In fact, Reagan agreed to $99 billion in revenue increases over a three-year period as part of a package to cut spending by $380 billion. In defending the accusation of imposing the biggest tax increase in history, Reagan stated that of the $99 billion, $32 billion represented collection of presently owned taxes, and that $48 billion represented closing of special-interest loopholes. The remaining $19 billion were excise taxes on cigarettes and telephones (1037). With this explanation, Reagan sought to minimize the extent to which he agreed to a tax bill. Economic and political reality brought Reagan to pursue a course he opposed. Though principled and dogmatic, Reagan was also adaptable. To minimize the perception he had retreated from his charted course, Reagan's rhetoric continued its familiar anti-government and anti-waste message.

The choice, expressed Reagan, was between reducing deficits and interest rates by raising revenues from those who were not paying their fair share, or accepting bigger budget deficits, higher interest rates, and higher unemployment (1037). By pointing the finger at those not paying their share, Reagan implied that if only everyone would pay their share, the economic situation would improve. Raising taxes, then, was not Reagan's fault but the fault of unscrupulous individuals. Though Reagan's discourse only slightly revealed the extent to which his administration initiated new taxes, taxes were put on Social Security payrolls, telephone, cigarette, airport and airway taxes, and a five-cent-per-gallon increase in gasoline taxes, effective 1983.[52]

The address to the nation ended with a familiar hopeful note. Economic indicators regarding inflation encouraged the president to declare that "the present recession is bottoming out without resorting to quick fixes" (1038). Reagan dispelled any notion of losing hope or that the economy was like a ship dead in the water because those entrusted with manning that ship could not agree on which sail to raise. On the contrary, declared the president: the nation was within sight of the safe port of economic recovery. The choice was now between making port or going aground on the shoals of selfishness, partisanship, and just plain bullheadedness (1039). Facing a deep recession and unable to defend much, the improvement in one area—inflation—brought Reagan to extensively "prove" his other parts of the recovery program would work as well. All that was required was confidence, faith, and optimism.

Radio Addresses: September–October 1982

By September 1982, the political climate changed dramatically as Reagan's popularity rating fell sharply. The recession was severe and the budget deficit threatened to double (the budget deficit increased from

$63.8 billion in 1981 to $145.9 billion in 1982).[53] Since unemployment and the budget deficit became the focal point in criticizing the administration, Reagan countered by "proving" that Democrats caused the recession.

Since the word unemployment alone became symbolic of the recessed economy, Reagan lamented in his Labor Day radio address of September 4, 1982, how terrible was the experience of being unemployed. Reagan blamed previous administrations' level of intervention in the marketplace as the cause for the economic ills. Specifically, Reagan identified tax policies that took a greater percentage of overall earnings as causing decline in economic growth, resulting, among other things, in unemployment. Reagan envisioned an improved economy but conditioned such a vision on a strong will and determination to hold the course.[54]

Later in the month, Reagan possessed more good news, informing the nation that the number one enemy—inflation—was being defeated, attempting to deflect the enormity of the unemployment rate. Yet blaming Democrats for past policies gained persistency as they, claimed Reagan, had taken the nation to the edge of economic Armageddon and thus could not consider themselves qualified to lecture others on what was the most fair and effective way to end the economic crisis.[55] It was tragic, added Reagan, that those who had controlled Congress for so long and who took the nation to the brink of bankruptcy were still playing politics. What seemed to have angered Reagan was the *liberals'* intention to take away the third year of the 1981 tax cuts. The resolved president rhetored, "We're not going to let them do it" (1213). The extreme language coupled with the conspiratorial theme was reminiscent of Reagan's early discourse. The year-long frustration, the need to compromise with Congress, and Reagan's unwillingness to accept less than his entire economic agenda, all resulted in more vindictive rhetoric. The perception, wrote Hugh Sidney in *Time* magazine, was that "Reagan is going to cure us even if he kills us."[56]

Unemployment: October 13, 1982

By fall of 1982 interest rates were down by 40 percent; stocks and bonds surged upward, and inflation was down 59 percent. Only unemployment remained high. Growing public concern over unemployment brought Reagan to change strategies in favor of facing unemployment squarely, abandoning the stress on others' past failures.[57] In an address to the nation, Reagan turned emphatic, using patriotic appeals to the struggling young and old alike, and giving tribute to their love of country and for their bravery (1305).[58] Reagan said he understood the people's confusion with regard to all the statistics, slogans, and political jargon surrounding the economy. His task, he stated, was to explain what stood behind the various statistics, and specifically identify the causes of unemployment.

Behind the numbers and the statistics, stated Reagan, stood brave people who loved their country, but who struggled to make ends meet, had difficulties finding work, and who were threatened by inflation. Attributes of courage, national pride, and hard work identified simple people as heroic in their respective endeavors, and whose sacrifice justified the cause of aiding them in improving their lives. Identification with the economically disadvantaged and the unemployed heightened when Reagan recalled his father announcing on Christmas Eve of 1932 that he had lost his job (1306). By describing his own family's experience with unemployment, Reagan sought to empathize with those still suffering. Reagan personified the unemployment issue in an attempt to indicate to struggling Americans that unemployment was not foreign to him and that his own family had struggled through difficult times. By using patriotic and emphatic appeals, deflecting facts, and pointing to the causes of unemployment, Reagan sought to expand his discourse on a troubling topic without implicating his administration.

Unemployment could only be cured if its causes were addressed, hastened Reagan, pointing to out-of-control government spending, high interest rates, and above all, skyrocketing inflation as the main culprits. Reagan also addressed inflation among the causes of unemployment. Inflation, described as the single most pressing long-term problem, was metaphorically equated with a virus in the economic bloodstream that was sometimes dormant and sometimes active, but which left the patient weaker after every attack. The responsibility, according to Reagan, fell on "big spenders" and a "stubborn minority" in the House of Representatives who, 12 days earlier, denied the president's request for a constitutional amendment to balance the budget. Stated Reagan: "We've got to stop these trendlines to disaster" (1307). To add credibility to this assertion, Reagan quoted Thomas Jefferson's warning that public debt was "the greatest of dangers to be feared" (1307).

To summarize his address, Reagan pointed out two major responsibilities he was entrusted with: to protect the people from enemies, foreign and domestic, and to protect the people from the worst enemy at home—the economic situation. Economy and security were Reagan's most cherished causes and rhetorically they were presented at the top of his poltical hierarchy. Equating national security with economic viability transformed a fairly mundane economic problem to the highest level of importance, that of survivability, whereby the presidency possessed a unique ethos and responsibility.[59]

The populist theme of proposing practical solutions to complex problems brought the president to declare, "I didn't come to Washington to play politics as usual. . . . I came to Washington to try to solve problems, not to sweep them under the rug" (1308). With a dramatic epilogue to his address to the nation, Reagan spoke of his economic plan as the better road, asking others for the courage to see it through. A vision of a better future was conditioned by the heroic nature of the people. Not to be overlooked, the notion of heroism put responsibility for economic progress on the people.

Radio Addresses: October–December 1982

In an October 23, 1982, radio address, Reagan mounted another attack to counter accusations on the economic front. Reagan chose to dispel various accusations as "myths." The first "myth," that an increase in defense spending was the main cause for the federal deficit, was countered by stating that defense spending's share of the federal budget had sharply declined in the last 20 years. The second "myth," that tax cuts had also contributed to the deficit, was countered by stating that holding tax rates even was meant to keep hard-pressed Americans from "being bled even drier through further hikes and the bracket creep caused by inflation" (1383).[60] The real culprits, added Reagan, were the congressional big spenders who voted down the balanced budget amendment. For the third "myth," that government slashed federal social spending, Reagan gave a simple "not true" answer, indicating the government was spending three times as much on nondefense items as the Kennedy administration did in 1963. The "myth" of high unemployment (standing at 11 million) was modified by the president who stated that as bad as the situation was, it was only a temporary problem. The "fifth" myth, that America's best days were behind her, was dismissed with a denial, affirming that, "the good old U.S.A. is still the most productive of the world's major industrial countries" (1384). (Recall that on February 5, 1981, Reagan lamented the fact that other countries, especially Japan, had become more productive than the United States.) The final "myth" was the cruelest of all, declared the president—that there was no end in sight to the recession. The reality, he replied, was that things were improving. For each myth, Reagan used a denial as his rhetorical approach.

Overall, none of the answers were very accurate. Labeling them as myths was Reagan's way of disproving accusations difficult to refute without having to advance well-developed counter arguments. The most troublesome accusation—unemployment—was buried in the middle of this myth-dispelling refutational line. What Reagan did advance was his own archetypal myth—that of the "good old USA" and its long-standing prominence—to diffuse any doubt about the strength of the nation's economy. A careful look at the answers Reagan gave reveals inconsistency with previous statements and an attempt to mask any causal relationship between tax cuts, increased defense spending, and the budget deficit.

On December 18, 1982, the president, in a celebratory tone, declared: "Together, we've launched a great national effort to correct the dangerous, neglected problems that were leading our country toward disaster" (1639).[61] Reagan added that for many, "Economic recovery is still a faceless stranger in some cold, distant future, not a warm friend who's come to grace our family hearth" (1639). This imperfect situation was countered by Reagan forecasting 1983 as a good year; America was on the mend, promising to lead the world out of the longest, deepest recession in postwar history. Reagan's redemptive rhetoric sought to overcome what was difficult to accept on the economic front.

Overall, the recession caused the president much anxiety. Reagan resorted to attacking Democrats while also courting their legislative efforts, shifted his discourse from emphatic to defensive to outright denials there was anything wrong. Envisioning a better future was the most consistent rhetorical approach in the president's economic discourse.

"THE NATION IS ON THE MEND"

The nation's recession ended in early 1983 as the gross national product (GNP) rose dramatically and inflation, unemployment, and prime lending rates all declined. With the recession behind him, Reagan capitalized on the inactivity of the 98th Congress regarding its own budget resolution.

After both Houses had again rejected the president's budget upon arrival, Congress eventually agreed on a budget resolution for fiscal year 1984 in late June, appropriating $850 billion in outlays with a projected deficit of $179.3 billion. The deficit prediction was contingent on spending reductions totalling $85.3 billion over a three-year period. Such legislation never materialized as Congress could not agree on a compatible deficit reduction plan.

Though Congress was unable to meet the specifics of their budget resolution, three significant economic-related laws were signed by the president. First, Social Security underwent major changes as cost of living adjustments (COLA) were delayed for six months and payroll taxes were increased for both employees and employers. Second, the federal government extended revenue sharing through fiscal 1986 to local governments at an annual cost of $4.6 billion. Ironically, Reagan vetoed over $400 million in additional aid, a move that went against much of his gubernatorial rhetoric. Third, legislation that repealed a withholding provision on interest and dividend income was signed into law due to public outcry over the provisions.

After a difficult first two years, Ronald Reagan emerged victorious in

1983, claiming that his unorthodox economic program had singlehandedly rescued the nation from its worst recession in nearly 50 years. Expectedly, Reagan's economic rhetoric had undergone some distinct changes. Reagan sounded more assured, regaining the confidence of his first year in the White House.

The State of the Union Address: January 25, 1983

The critical situational event that shaped Reagan's second *State of the Union Address* continued to be the nation's economy, specifically the deep recession the country was only beginning to emerge from. At the outset of the speech, Reagan lamented that, "the state of our Union is strong, but our economy is troubled," pointing to the high unemployment among the working class and the growing federal budget deficit (103).[62] Reagan did not detail why the state of the Union was strong, only that it was strong.

This address, extensively descriptive of the economic ills, advocated a consistent solution. The problems the administration inherited, claimed Reagan, were far worse than expected, and the recession deeper than predicted. Curing the problem had taken more time and with a higher toll. More profound was Reagan's challenge to the American people: "It has fallen to us, in our time, to undo damage that was a long time in the making," and, "We must all do everything in our power to bring their (fellow citizens) ordeal to an end" (103). Inherent in this mission was Reagan's requested sacrifice by all; but with courage, patience, and strength, a better future was at hand.

Even though the Reagan administration had been in office for more than two years, Reagan was still reluctant to accept blame for the recession. He continued to reject accusations that defense spending and the tax cuts caused the recession, alluding to their insignificant percentage of the GNP. The deficit problem, stated Reagan, was a clear and present danger to the basic health of the republic (105). Of special concern to Reagan was the state of the Social Security system, which, in his words, faced disaster. For 30 years, stated the president, he had warned of the problems with Social Security and now, in 1983, the system was on the brink of bankruptcy and a victim of the nation's economic ills. Reagan was quick to promise that no one's payment would be reduced. Reagan pointed out that since becoming president his compromise on Social Security was politically necessary but that his views had not changed.

Quick fixes, like those applied over the decades that brought inflationary disorders, and ended up costing a heavy price, would be avoided, promised Reagan (104). Realizing rapid economic growth had not materialized, Reagan described the deficit as both a symptom and a cause for the nation's economic problems.[63] As such, unless government spending was reduced (by Congress), growth would be sluggish, and failure to act could result in a trillion dollars more in national debt in the next four years alone.

In this address, Reagan outlined a four-part plan to increase economic growth and reduce the deficits: a federal spending freeze, including a six-month freeze in cost-of-living adjustments in various retirement programs and a one-year freeze on military pay and pension programs; controlling so-called uncontrollable spending programs such as food stamps; proposing $55 billion in defense savings over a five-year period; and proposing a standby tax of 1 percent of the gross national product to start in fiscal 1986, but only if Congress did not first approve the spending freeze and budget control programs.

For the second time in recent months, Reagan had proposed the unimaginable—increasing taxes—but only under well-defined conditions that, if present, would be blamed on Congress. Even defense spending was part of deficit reduction. Reagan's only elaboration on this point was that he was given assurances by the defense secretary that the cuts could be safely achieved without endangering America's security. Taxes and defense spending, sacred items in Reagan's economic philosophy, were strictly contingent, thus keeping policy implementation open for interpretation. Pragmatics once again brought Reagan's ideological persona to give in to Reagan's political persona.

Though Reagan reiterated his long-held ideology of restoring "to States and local governments their roles as dynamic laboratories of change in a creative society," little emphasized was a contradictory viewpoint and a major shift relative to the role of the federal government (107). Stated Reagan, "We who are in government must take the lead in restoring the economy" (109). Indeed, dictated by pragmatics, 1983 brought shifts in Reagan's long-held economic philosophy. The recession and the growing budget deficit caused Reagan to be more pragmatic, yet rhetorically, he attempted to show no changes in economic philosophy had occurred.

The principal objective in Reagan's plan was to reduce the deficit, which would, in turn, lead to a sustained recovery. Realizing the strong opposition to the proposed cuts, Reagan claimed that the plan was fair, balanced, and realistic. However, since the economy had not yet fully recovered from the recession, Reagan moved the audience from the present to the future via the promise of a recovery and a revival of economic confidence: "This recovery will bring with it a revival of economic confidence and spending for consumer items and capital goods—the stimulus we need to restart our stalled economic engines" (104). The economy was depicted as going through a temporary slowdown phase, which, with adequate tuning, would be reinvigorated. The engine metaphor seemed to indicate that the recession was temporary, and that it could be fixed with minor repairs.

To conclude, Reagan spoke of the American "can-do" spirit that had always been sustained through good and bad times by a noble vision and hope.[64] "America is on the mend," stated Reagan and since the past proved that there was nothing Americans could not do, a better future was within reach (110). This rhetorical formula, though simple in its construction, was powerful in its patriotic and nationalistic symbolism, since it allowed for the incorporation of ordinary, average Americans to restart the economic engine. This vision, however, was experienced in the present: "From coast to coast, . . . at new construction sites and in churches and community groups, neighbors are helping neighbors. And they've already begun the building, the research, the work, and the giving that will make our country great again" (110).

The Budget: January 1983–January 1984

A few days later, Reagan took the opportunity to preview the budget he was to send to Congress. Deficit, Reagan stated, was a dirty word that he hoped would be a thing of the past (the deficit for 1983 was $176 billion). "But the deficit is going to be large," he warned (140).[65] The budget deficit was caused by the *success* of reducing inflation, which had sent a shock to the system, declared the president. Reagan incorporated a successful cause—reducing inflation—as the culprit in increasing the budget deficit. What Reagan did not say was important as well: he did not blame previous administrations for the budget deficit, but pointed to the success of his economic plan as a likely cause for the deficit. This was the closest Reagan came to taking blame for the growing budget deficit. The success of his economic plan, used here to rationalize a negative economic development, was an admission that the recovery program had indeed brought about an increase in the budget deficit. Reagan thus confirmed the "myth" he just recently attempted to dispel.

Reagan did not hide the severity of the economic situation, yet carefully chosen words stated that the need to "restore" the "neglected" national defense had put pressure on the nation's resources. For the first time, Reagan admitted what he had publicly rejected all along; building the nation's defense was indeed among the causes for the budget deficit. Yet, being a responsible president, justified Reagan, this was something that had to be done. The defense budget, which many attacked for not going through cuts like other programs, was promoted to the level of unique presidential responsibility. Reagan declared, "Where peace and freedom are at stake, we can't afford to gamble," juxtaposing restoration of freedom and peace with neglect and gambling

(140). Noteably, the causality between defense spending and the federal budget deficit was made in a radio address and not in a major address.

With an "America is on the mend" theme, Reagan again outlined his budget proposal including a federal spending freeze, cutting $155 billion in defense spending over the next five years, controlling the growth of spending for entitlement programs without hurting the truly needy, and a stand-by tax in 1986 only if the deficit was to be greater than 2.5 percent of GNP. This speech was unique in its admission of responsibility. Noteably, this approach was taken only as the recession neared its end.

As the economy rebounded, Reagan devoted his February 5, 1983, radio address to discussing the term Reaganomics, a label he stated he did not choose and did not like. "It sounds like a fad diet or an aerobic exercise," he complained.[66] Reagan asserted the term had been used to describe something that had failed, and also to claim he was defensive regarding the worsening budget deficit. Regardless of these accusations, Reagan stated he was willing to take the risk for being perceived defensive, since he did put a stop to the economic mess. This address, as well as other recent speeches, portrayed a somewhat defensive president who sought to redeem himself from the realization that the recession was partly aggravated by his economic program.

As the economic news indicated further improvement, Reagan significantly reduced the number of addresses devoted to the economy. In his May 28, 1983, radio address, on the occasion of the Williamsburg Economic Summit, the president reminded his American auditors that the worst we could now do was to implement a "quick fix" to remaining economic problems that would trigger a new round of inflation.[67] As inflation declined to an annual rate of 3.5 percent and unemployment decreased to 9.8 percent, Reagan could not hide his glee: "Even the gloomiest critics have had trouble denying that things are getting better for you and your families."[68] Reducing his visionary economic rhetoric was the result of the recovery experienced in the present. Put differently, Reagan no longer felt the need to speak in terms of the future now that some of his visions had been fulfilled.

The lull in economic related speeches lasted until October 1, 1983, when in his Saturday radio address Reagan asked whether the economic recovery would last. "I'm bullish on America," he confidently rhetored (1371).[69] His optimism sprang from solid evidence that America had turned the corner toward long-term economic expansion. Hope and confidence were projected as Reagan suggested to the American people, "Let's not be swayed by downbeats who never admit anything's right, never acknowledge the huge problems we inherited, and never admit the progress we've made" (1371). This cautionary statement positioned Reagan as the guardian of his policies that were proven correct and workable. Why did Reagan resort to such statements now that the recovery was being experienced? A likely answer lies in the rhetorical need to constantly present a "villain." Any unexpected setbacks would be blamed on those opposing the administration's economic plan, thus shielding himself from potential accusations.

In his January 21, 1984, radio address, the president's confidence was clearly expressed as he continued his recent rhetorical line of proudly emphasizing a better economic recovery than expected: "Economic forecasting is far from a perfect science. If recent history is any guide, the experts have some explaining to do about what they told us had to happen but never did" (61).[70] Attacking the "doom criers," the president analogized the shape of the economy his administration inherited and the recovery that followed to the "Little Engine That Could."

Reagan attacked the naysayers who had a new gloomy refrain not about the inflation, interest rates, or even the recovery that would not happen, but about a recovery that would not last. According to their argument, the budget deficit would kill the recovery by draining capital needed by business to keep the economy expanding. Indeed, the growing budget deficit began to shape in Reagan a new rhetorical strain, advancing the refutational line he used during the recession: "Well, I happen to believe those who underestimated the strength of this recovery may be wrong about the size of future deficits, too" (61). Self-assured, Reagan implied that since the naysayers were wrong before, they would be wrong this time too.

"A BRIGHT NEW DAWN OF PROMISE AND HOPE"

Aside from the election, the economic recovery, the federal budget, the federal deficit, and the record trade deficit were the major economic news items in 1984. First, the nation's economy continued to surprise even some of the most optimistic forecasts. GNP grew at an annual rate of 6.8 percent, the highest since 1951; inflation fell to an annual rate of 3.7 percent; and unemployment dropped to 7.2 percent.

Second, Congress dismissed Reagan's budget primarily due to the huge increases in defense spending of 13 percent and merely obligatory attempts at deficit reductions. The budget resolution adopted by Congress called for outlays of $932 billion, revenues of $750.9 billion, and a projected deficit of $181.1 billion. However, before both Houses agreed on the budget resolution for fiscal 1985, a deficit reduction package totalling $149.5 billion over three years was passed by Congress and approved by the president. This package included $50 billion in tax increases and a savings of $58 billion in smaller increases in defense spending.[71]

Third, the immediate result of the economic recovery was an unprecedented trade deficit of $123.3 billion in 1984 caused by a resurgent dollar. This deficit nearly doubled the previous record trade deficit set in 1983.

Thanks in large part to the nation's economic recovery, Reagan easily outdistanced Democratic challenger Walter Mondale, winning 525 out of a possible 538 electoral votes. The results of congressional elections were mixed as Democrats gained 2 Senate seats while Republicans picked up 14 House seats.

The State of the Union Address: January 25, 1984

The "America is much improved" theme set the tone for Reagan's third *State of the Union Address* (87).[72] Given his audience, Reagan avoided attacks, preferring instead to speak warmly of Congress, which, despite differences of opinions, helped put a stop to the long economic decline. Renewed energy and optimism were expressed as Reagan stated, "America is back, standing tall, looking to the eighties with courage, confidence, and hope" (87). This speech, perhaps a prelude to the November election, envisioned America's destiny as well as personified the economy around Reagan who stood for all that was right and heroic. To disagree with Reagan was to disagree with America.[73]

Like a good story-teller, Reagan's redemptive narrative was followed by reminding his listeners of the "bad" past. The problems facing America were not the heritage of one person, party, or even one generation, but rather, declared the president, it was the tendency of government to grow. Blame was more neutral and specific "villains" were muted.

His administration, retold the president, faced the worst crisis in America postwar history. The nation lost confidence, families felt helpless in the face of mounting inflation and the indignity of taxes, and an evergrowing web of rules and regulations existed (87). On the international scene, Americans began to feel they were losing the respect of friend and foe. Restoration was presented through the mythical and archetypal statement that "America is too great for small dreams. There was a hunger in the land for a spiritual revival; if you will, a crusade for renewal," but "together we have done it . . . Hope is alive" (88). Reagan's optimism went as far as to state it was alright for Americans to dream. The president fashioned himself as the heroic leader who led the nation to a spiritual rebirth.

On the topic of unemployment, Reagan turned reassuring: "Many of our fellow countrymen are still out of work, wondering what will come of their hopes and dreams," adding, "The heart of America is strong; it's good and true . . . America never was a sick society. We're seeing rededication to bedrock values of faith, family, work, neighborhood, peace, and freedom" (88). In Reagan's philosophy, these economically related terms were clothed in value-laden attributes. With these values,

Reagan offered hope to those still suffering under the economic conditions. Furthermore, Reagan invoked the symbolic name of a household Democrat, Franklin Roosevelt, who said that civilization cannot go back; civilization must not stand still, but in all cases civilization must go forward (88). Thus, for those who still suffered in the present, a vision of a better future was offered.

The still unsolved federal budget deficit brought Reagan to state, "Fear is expressed that government borrowing to fund the deficit could inhibit the economic recovery by taking capital needed for business and industrial expansion" (89). The nation's economy had improved, but an emerging conflict over the federal budget brought Reagan to restate his anti-government stance. Fairness, he contended, dictated that government must not raise taxes to finance the budget deficit. The need, nonetheless, to put blame on identifiable culprits brought Reagan to accuse those not paying their share: "It would be immoral to make those who are paying taxes pay more to compensate for those who aren't paying their share" (90). The solution, in addition to significant cuts in the budget and a structural reform in the tax code, also included a plan to bring the underground economy into honest tax compliance. Reagan reduced the budget deficit to an issue of unfair practices by immoral people. Since he raised taxes, Reagan sought, on numerous occasions, to distance himself from his policy. Here he simplified the issue to that of unscrupulous individuals who had hurt many honest people, thus legitimizing new taxes.

Reagan closed this address with a narrative underlying hope and optimism: "Economic recovery, better education, rededication to values, all show the spirit of renewal gaining the upper hand" (92). Quoting from Carl Sandburg, Reagan stated, " 'I see America not in the setting sun of a black night of despair . . . I see America in the crimson light of a rising sun fresh from the burning, creative hand of God . . . I see great days ahead for men and women of will and vision.' " Added Reagan, "America's best days and democracy's best days lie ahead" (94). The themes of faith, renewal, rebirth, and optimism remained the constant "proofs" of Reagan's projected economy.

Attacks and Counterattacks: March–April 1984

With the presidential election looming on the horizon, his radio address of March 3, 1984, was the first to sound like a campaign speech. While people were paying enough taxes, declared the president, there were those in Washington who took for granted that the federal government had an automatic right to grow at the people's expense. "So, please be a little skeptical when you hear the moaning from Washington's born-again deficit fighters," requited Reagan.[74]

The attack on Democrats intensified as Reagan blamed them for using foggy language like "recovering revenue" or "stopping the revenue drain," sarcastically suggesting it was a choice between a tax increase and a tax increase. Furthermore, Reagan labeled as cruel their idea to eliminate indexing, which would hurt the poor and surviving spouses who owned farms and businesses. Repeating the philosophical view regarding Big Government, the president sought to gain acceptance by convincing the people that though the deficit was a problem, the real problem was not the size of the deficit but the size of the government. By reintroducing this long-held ideological strain in his rhetoric, Reagan sought to minimize attacks on his administration and offer an easily identifiable culprit. Raising taxes, declared Reagan in an effort to implicate Democrats, was a cop-out while cutting waste in government was the proper policy. By arguing forcefully against raising taxes, Reagan sought to deflect his own administration's recent need to raise taxes.

A week later Reagan called the economic recovery the strongest in decades, "from the dark days of despair to a bright new dawn of promise and hope" (333).[75] The metaphor of a "bright dawn" replacing "darkness" and despair presented an attractive juxtaposition. Even earlier when the economy looked quite bad, stated Reagan, he knew that too much pessimism could be deadly. "I merely wanted us to remember that there's a psychological factor in recession, and too much hammering at it makes recession worse" (333). In another rare occasion during his presidency, Reagan used a psychological explanation to confront a negative situation, implying his deep-rooted personal optimism and strength of character. Furthermore, the recession, implied Reagan, was more psychological than real.

Attacks on the Reagan administration for impoverishing the poor and bestowing benefits on the rich brought the president to state in his April 21, 1984, radio address that he was going to swim against the current riptide of criticism. The swimming metaphor transformed Reagan into a lifeguard who prevailed over difficult circumstances to save lives.[76] Acknowledging inflation had eroded the poverty level, Reagan rhetored, who's to be blamed? (585–86).[77] As he was blamed by others, the president turned the accusation against previous administrations for the biggest single tax increase in history (passed in 1977), implying a linkage between more taxes and poverty. Using figures for factual impact, Reagan stated that the rich were paying more taxes now than ever before, and that the rich carried a higher share of the total tax burden (585–86). With a counterargument and some mild proof to justify his own policy, Reagan sought to vindicate himself against the old perception that his party favored the wealthy.

Though the economy showed distinct improvements, the recovery did not trickle down to all segments of society. Unemployment was still high, and the pressure on the White House to assist social programs continued. Reagan attempted to reassure his constituents that everyone would soon enjoy the fruits of the recovery without altering or disrupting his economic program.

THE CAMPAIGN OF CHOICE

Enjoying presidential prerogative and confident the economic rebound was his greatest asset, Reagan's 1984 campaign was limited to speeches that pointed to the success of his economic recovery and blamed Democrats for their pessimistic outlook.

August–November 1984

Late in the summer of 1984, Reagan intensified his attacks on Democrats as his addresses gained an election flavor. He accused the Democrats of saying "no" to America and for having drifted from mainstream thinking.[78] Reagan was angered by the Democrats' refusal to support a constitutional amendment mandating a balanced federal budget, further implying their spending habits. The Democrats, accused Reagan, did not want a spending restraint given their numerous campaign promises. As with recent speeches, the Democrats were described as irresponsible and at times even as un-American. The juxtaposition of his administration's wisdom with the irresponsible Democrats elevated the presidency to the level of a rhetorical myth possessing a unique ethos and qualities that the opposition lacked.[79]

The president honored Labor Day by describing the economic recovery as an American miracle with inflation and tax rates down, attributing to the people their share in a dynamic and exciting future.[80] The economy, added the president, performed well even though inner city areas were yet to benefit from the economic expansion.

Reagan confidently stated the choice was the clearest in 50 years: whether America would continue to champion the great idea of economic growth through individual opportunity, or whether the nation would return to the past that stifled growth (1299).[81] Giving his administration credit for turning the economy around, Reagan claimed he was "determined to keep the mighty engine of this nation revved up to build a future of lasting economic growth" (1299). One of Reagan's main campaign promises was to enact a historic simplification of the tax system that would be fairer and beneficial for all. Not forgetting the other presidential candidate, Reagan stated that the Democratic nominee, if elected, would take us back to the worst misery index of the past, implying tax increases.

Sounding more and more like a candidate, Reagan triumphantly announced in his September 22, 1984, radio address that when he took office in 1981, his administration's goal was to help all people build a new era of lasting economic growth without inflation, "And we're getting closer."[82] Claiming the economy was strong, the president also stated he would like to see the expansion reach every sector of the economy. Reagan acknowledged that steel and agriculture were not enjoying the economic recovery, yet he expressed his confidence that his administration's economic policies would help steel producers rebuild and become stronger, more competitive, and profitable again. Behind this statement, a new economic issue loomed on the horizon: the growing foreign competition and a decline in America's export ability.

In an October 13, 1984, radio address, the choice, according to Reagan was the clearest possible, as 22 months of economic expansion, the strongest in 30 years, was contrasted with the failed policies of the Carter-Mondale administration.[83] The strong economic growth, cautioned Reagan, was not a paper dream, implying the need for faith. The dream, according to Reagan, was a real one. But the dream could not be fully restored, stated Reagan, until every American who wanted a job could find one, and until inflation was down to zero-point-zero. In contrast, stated the president, his opponent had a gloomy vision, thus lacking confidence and the challenge to dream. Adding sarcasm, Reagan ridiculed his opponent for being able to boast of an increase only with regard to inflation, interest rates, and taxes. The economy was captive and entrapped due to the opponent's personal weaknesses while Reagan projected himself as the hero who freed the economy from its captors.[84] Invoking Carter's name was made possible because of Mondale's candidacy, as Reagan contrasted the Carter's years with his achievements.

In his October 27, 1984, radio address, Reagan appealed to America's youth whose enthusiasm, patriotism, and strength of character, he claimed, helped the great renewal of the 1980s. The president stated that he felt a special bond and kinship with the young and their secret for America's success and opportunity. Youth implied future, hope, and continuation, thus, by virtue of their age, youth represented optimism. However, Reagan did not specify what this age group had accomplished in their special link to the economic recovery.

The narrative of recent addresses persisted: "We weren't meant to be a nation divided; we weren't meant to be a nation second-best. We were meant to be, . . . a people with faith in each other, courage to dream great dreams, opportunities to climb higher."[85] Retelling the beginning of the epic, Reagan noted that 1981 was the year for *reversing* the flow of power to Washington and *restoring* sovereignty to the people. Reagan brought to a climax the themes of his rhetoric, that of restoration, his long-standing outlook regarding the role of government and its relationship with the people as the true sovereigns of a democracy.

Reagan stated that the principal difference between the two parties and their candidates was that his was a vision for America that would let the "eagle soar" while the Democrats wanted to return to the days of the "sore eagle" (1756).[86] In yet another juxtaposition, Reagan implied that a vote for him was a vote for America while a vote for the Democrats was against America. His America, he added, was a stronger nation, with a future of peace, filled with hope and new opportunity, "a future where our process is limited only by our own dreams" (1755). America's economy was positioned at the heart of a hierarchical quest whereby its "discovery" would lead to expansion and prosperity.

Address to the Nation on Election Eve: November 5, 1984

On election eve, Reagan addressed the nation, bringing the campaign drama to a climactic end. The dialectic pursued sporadically in recent speeches was fully utilized in this important address. Reagan contrasted the choice between the good and the bad: between going forward with courage, confidence, and common sense, making America strong again, or turning back to policies of malaise that weakened the economy reversing a long-revered tradition of progress (1798).[87] By referring to "malaise," Reagan invoked Carter's name and all that was associated with failed policies, including Carter's vice president. In contrast, with the mighty spirit of free and trusting people under God, the nation would preserve the "golden dream" of America, promised the president.

Reagan unbashfully praised his administration, citing the shock by which the old guard in Washington reacted when he took his case directly to the people. The previous ship metaphor reappeared with the heroic captain (Reagan) together with the American crew making shore safely: "Together we took command of a rudderless ship, adrift in a sea of confusion" (1798). According to Reagan, the American people and his administration took necessary action to turn around years of despair and neglect.

Reagan attributed much to the American people, calling them the real heroes for joining him in a great effort. He ridiculed the Democrats, claiming that where "we" (Republicans) look at a problem and see opportunity, "they" (Democrats) look at opportunity and see a problem; "we" believe in knowing when opportunity knocks while "they" seem determined to knock opportunity.

Reagan repeated the strategy depicting the situation as good but not good enough: "We still have much to do" (1799). No final victory was possible until Americans who wanted a job could find one. Acknowledging the still imperfect situation was a necessity based on the recognition that ignoring areas that still suffered economically would be negatively received by those whose vote Reagan sought. Reagan did not dwell much on negatives but rather moved quickly to claim that even troubled areas would see improvements, stating, "We can and will, because one fact is not debatable: America has made an amazing comeback" (1799). Confidence, jobs, investment, growth, and achievement were the universal marks of success and Reagan's signs of proof.

Reagan quoted John Wayne before his death, stating "Just give the American people a good cause, and there's nothing they can't lick," which presented another variation of the hero theme (1799). Yet the hero Reagan quoted was a fictional one. Whether Reagan believed in such a hero or thought the people would not distinguish between real and fictional heros, Reagan displayed his knack for making mundane issues dramatic.

The small-business men and women, teachers, homemakers, and high-tech entrepreneurs, all economic beings, had brought America *back*, making the nation great *again*. By attributing to the common people the power of restoring America's greatness, Reagan was able to present himself as standing on the side of the people and fighting Big Government for their sake: "All we did was get government out of your way" (1799). The narrative purposefully deemphasized the president's role, portraying Reagan as a helper who was there just to assist and remove that which stood in the way. Yet, such humility was rhetorically powerful since it enhanced the president's heroic role.

The pressure on the Democrats intensified as Reagan rhetorically asked: "What has happened to the Democratic party's concern for protecting the earnings of working people and promoting economic growth?" (1799). In a clear attempt to bring as many Democrats as possible to vote Republican only hours away, Reagan invoked the sacred tenets of his original party and its long tradition of caring and social concerns. But this was not enough. Reagan referred to President John Kennedy's successful program of cutting personal income taxes and giving incentives for industry that resulted in an economic surge. Unfortunately, lamented Reagan, our opponent's team was not in the tradition of John F. Kennedy, or of Harry Truman and Franklin Roosevelt. Reagan implied that Democrats deserted the principles of their own party while Republicans were committed to their principles. Though such a strategy may justifiably be considered ad hominem, it was likely aimed at two distinct audiences: the undecided and Democrats dissatisfied with their party.

Finally, Reagan indicated that the vision he had outlined in 1980 had not come to an end. Specifically, Reagan called for three long-overdue reforms *resisted* by the House: a constitutional amendment to balance the budget and a line-item veto. He also called for further simplification of the tax system. Reagan identified the administration's ultimate objective as a historic task to present to the world an America that was not only strong and secure but more important, an America with a cause and a vision of future and hope. The epic narrative ended on a somewhat jovial, but no less optimistic note of "you ain't seen nothin' yet" (1802). Reagan's campaign theme was a bequest that the people dream old dreams, while claiming that Democrats were unsuitable to govern.[88] If elected, Reagan promised even greater surprises.

CONCLUSION

Reagan's economic rhetoric during the first presidential term was one of optimism, vision, renewal, and restoration. Four years after embarking on a New Beginning, Reagan's first term possessed all the ingredients of a good story, with the bad guy losing and the good guy winning. The story of the economy was that of a difficult beginning with many roadblocks and battles but whose heroes were courageous and whose determination and promise brought victory and redemption from economic malaise.

Reagan's economic rhetoric was rather simplistic from an argumentative perspective yet rich in its figurative and metaphorical usage. Reagan shifted away from the customary presidential appeal to well-defined constituencies, mainstreaming his appeals instead to a universal audience.[89] The American people were defined economically as suffering from taxation, unemployment, and government regulations though they were absolved of any ensuing guilt inherent in the economic situation.[90] Against this despair, Reagan presented himself as the hero who fought for the people and who rescued them from the evil of Big Government.

Reagan offered a radical departure from decades of a benevolent federal system, advocating a New Federalism whereby the government retreats from a welfare state and lessens its involvement in the economy.[91] With this prescription, Reagan sought to lower inflation, increase growth, cut taxes, strengthen defense, and balance the budget by 1984. However, the anticipated growth did not occur as the economy went into a recession. Consequently, the budget was not balanced as predicted. The solution to reducing the budget deficit in 1980 was the elimination of waste, fraud, and abuse; by 1984, the solution had shifted to an emphasis on economic growth. Both solutions were not realistic but rhetorically attractive since they gave a simplified causal formula.[92] Reagan was successful in significantly reducing inflation and, above all, generating the largest tax cut in history. The Omnibus Reconciliation Act of 1981, which cut taxes, reduced social programs, and altered the role of the federal government, was considered a major legislative success for the Reagan administration.[93] In Reagan's populist theme, the government continued to be the enemy of the individual, altering the convention that the government was a provider and helper.[94]

Though his economic rhetoric remained fairly consistent in advocacy and vision, Reagan shifted at key policy points. Reagan departed from Milton Friedman's economic theory on Social Security after the uproar over suggested cuts in benefits.[95] By 1983, a more interventionist policy was implemented, especially in devaluing the dollar as a measure to reduce the trade deficit.[96] Reagan also increased various taxes, not to mention the fact that with less federal help, states increased their own taxes.[97] The significance here is not that Reagan found it necessary to raise taxes but rather that he ignored references to such policies.

The story of Reaganomics is primarily a rhetorical one whereby Reagan incorporated his political viewpoints through sacrifice, scapegoating, redemption, and vision.[98] Reagan, acting as the secular clergyman of the nation, sought to restore traditional values and to integrate the American dream with dominant features of American civil religion.[99] He incorporated myths and ideals to give the nation a purpose after the despair prevailing in the 1970s, and equated faith and courage with patriotism.[100] The prelude to the second presidential term was presented in the 1984 election in which the American people were told to look beyond the "economic recovery."[101] Reagan's economic rhetoric created the perception that the president knew no fear, just optimism and faith, the same ideals he requested from the people.

NOTES

1. James L. Golden, Goodwin F. Berquist, William E. Coleman, eds., *The Rhetoric of Western Thought*, 3d ed. (Dubuque: Kendall/Hunt, 1983), 67–70.

2. Jeffrey K. Tulis, *The Rhetorical Presidency* (Princeton: Princeton University Press, 1987); Roderick P. Hart, *The Sound of Leadership* (Chicago: University of Chicago Press, 1987), xix-xxi.

3. Chaim Perelman and L. Olbrechts-Tyteca, *The New Rhetoric: A Treatise on Argumentation* (Notre Dame: Notre Dame University Press, 1969).

4. Karlyn Kohrs Campbell and Kathleen Hall Jamieson, "Inaugurating the Presidency," *Presidential Studies Quarterly* 15 (1985): 395.

5. Beth A. J. Ingold and Theodore Windt, "Trying to 'Stay the Course': President Reagan's Rhetoric during the 1982 Election," in *Essays in Presidential Rhetoric*, ed. Theodore Windt and Beth Ingold, 2d ed. (Dubuque: Kendall/Hunt, 1987), 400–401; Theodore Windt and Kathleen Farrell, "Presidential Rhetoric and Presidential Power: The Reagan Initiatives," in *Essays in Presidential Rhetoric*, 390.

6. Ibid., 390.

7. For a more complete discussion concerning the content of inaugural addresses see Karlyn Kohrs Campbell and Kathleen Hall Jamieson, "Inaugurating the Presidency," in *Form, Genre, and the Study of Political Discourse*, eds. Herbert W. Simons and Aram A. Aghazarian (Columbia: University of South Carolina Press, 1986), 203–25; Kathleen Hall Jamieson and Karlyn Kohrs Campbell, "Rhetorical Hybrids: Fusions of Generic Elements," *Quarterly Journal of Speech* 68 (1982): 146–57.

8. Campbell and Jamieson, "Inaugurating the Presidency," 404.

9. All references to this speech are from U.S., President, *Public Papers of the Presidents of the United States* (Washington, D.C.: U.S. Government Printing Office, 1982), Ronald Reagan (January 20, 1981), 1–4. Hereafter, *Public Papers*.

10. Richard Reeves, *The Reagan Detour* (New York: Simon & Schuster, 1985), 22.

11. Craig A. Smith, "MisteReagan's Neighborhood: Rhetoric and National Unity," in *Essays in Presidential Rhetoric*, 431.

12. See Robert Lekachman, *Visions and Nightmares: America After Reagan* (New York: Macmillan, 1987), 8.

13. Charles R. Hulten and Isabel V. Sawhill, "The Legacy of Reaganomics: An Overview," in *The Legacy of Reaganomics: Prospects for Long-Term Growth*, ed. Charles R. Hulten and Isabel V. Sawhill (Washington, D.C.: The Urban Institute Press, 1984), 1.

14. Barbara Kellerman, *The Political Presidency: Practice of Leadership* (New York: Oxford University Press, 1984), 225.

15. Windt and Farrell, "Presidential Rhetoric and Presidential Power: The Reagan Initiatives," 391.

16. All references to this speech are from U.S., President, *Weekly Compilation of Presidential Documents* (Washington, D.C.: U.S. Government Printing Office), Ronald Reagan (February 5, 1981), 93–98. Hereafter, *Weekly Compilation*.

17. Robert E. Denton, Jr., and Dan F. Hahn, *Presidential Communication* (New York: Praeger, 1986), 71.

18. All references to this speech are from Reagan, *Weekly Compilation* (February 18, 1981), 130–37.

19. See Richard E. Crable and Steven L. Vibbert, "Argumentative Stance and Political Faith Healing: 'The Dream Will Come True,' " *Quarterly Journal of Speech* 69 (1983): 290–301.

20. Frank Ackerman, *Reaganomics: Rhetoric vs. Reality* (Boston: South End Press, 1982), 40.

21. Windt and Farrell, "Presidential Rhetoric and Presidential Power: The Reagan Initiatives," 392.

22. William F. Lewis, "Telling America's Story: Narrative Form and the Reagan Presidency," *Quarterly Journal of Speech* 73 (1987): 295.

23. Kellerman, *The Political Presidency*, 234.

24. Windt and Farrell, "Presidential Rhetoric and Presidential Power: The Reagan Initiatives," 394; Kellerman, *The Political Presidency*, 236.

25. Reagan, *Weekly Compilation* (April 28, 1981), 478–82.

26. William K. Muir, Jr., "The Primacy of Rhetoric," in *Leadership In the Modern Presidency*, ed. Fred I. Greenstein (Cambridge: Harvard University Press, 1988), 268–71.

27. For a complete description of the major provisions of ERTA see *Congressional Quarterly Almanac 1981* (Washington, D.C.: Congressional Quarterly, 1982), 92–95.

28. All references to this speech are from Reagan, *Weekly Compilation* (July 27, 1981), 814–20.

29. Peter J. Ferrara, "Social Security: Look at Your Pay Stub," in *Assessing*

the Reagan Years, ed. David Boaz (Washington, D.C.: The Cato Institute, 1988), 201–3.

30. Quoted in Samuel Kernell, *Going Public* (Washington, D.C.: Congressional Quarterly Press, 1986), 120–21.

31. All references to this speech are from Reagan, *Weekly Compilation* (September 24, 1981), 1025–31.

32. Denton and Hahn, *Presidential Communication*, 71.

33. The tax cuts of 1981 amounted to a total of $162 billion, including a 23 percent reduction in personal income taxes, a cut in the highest marginal tax rate from 70 to 50 percent, and a cut in the capital gains tax from 28 percent to 20 percent. See Paul E. Peterson and Mark Rom, "Lower Taxes, More Spending, and Budget Deficits," in *The Reagan Legacy*, ed. Charles O. Jones (Chatham: Chatham House, 1988), 218–19.

34. See also Ingold and Windt, "Trying to 'Stay the Course': President Reagan's Rhetoric during the 1982 Election," 404.

35. Denton and Hahn, *Presidential Communication*, 71.

36. David Zarefsky, Carol Miller-Tutzauer, and Frank E. Tutzauer, "Ronald Reagan's Safety Net for the Truly Needy: The Rhetorical Uses of Definition," *Central States Speech Journal* 35 (1984): 113–19.

37. Lester M. Salamon and Alan J. Abramson, "Governance," in *The Reagan Record: An Assessment of America's Changing Domestic Priorities*, ed. John L. Palmer and Isabel V. Sawhill (Cambridge: Ballinger, 1984), 50–53.

38. John K. White, *The New Politics of Old Values* (Hanover: University Press of New England, 1988), 59.

39. Salamon and Abramson, "Governance," 49.

40. Palmer and Sawhill, "Overview," in *The Reagan Record*, 25–28.

41. William A. Niskanen, *Reaganomics: An Insider's Account of the Policies and the People* (New York: Oxford University Press, 1988), 155.

42. White, *The New Politics of Old Values*, 61.

43. Ingold and Windt, "Trying to 'Stay the Course': President Reagan's Rhetoric during the 1982 Election," 402.

44. All references to this speech are from Reagan, *Public Papers* (January 26, 1982), 72–78.

45. Jerry L. Jordan, "Weakening the Dollar: The Tax No One Has to Vote For," in *Assessing the Reagan Years*, 181–82.

46. All references to this speech are from Reagan, *Weekly Compilation* (April 29, 1982), 545–549.

47. See Richard L. Johannesen, "Ronald Reagan's Economic Jeremiad," *Central States Speech Journal* 37 (1986): 79–89.

48. Reagan, *Public Papers* (May 6, 1982), 569–72.

49. Reagan, *Weekly Compilation* (May 22, 1982), 685. The Senate passed a budget resolution that would reduce projected deficits by $358 billion over the next three years. Congress, however, sought to eliminate the third year of the tax cuts, amounting to $150 billion.

50. Reagan, *Weekly Compilation* (May 29, 1982), 728.

51. All references to this speech are from Reagan, *Weekly Compilation* (August 16, 1982), 1035–39.

52. Gregory B. Mills, "The Budget. A Failure of Discipline," in *The Reagan Record*, 119.

53. Fisher Simons, "An Agenda for Tax Policy," in *An American Vision: Policies for the '90s*, ed. Edward H. Crane and David Boaz (Washington, D.C.: The Cato Institute, 1989), 32.

54. Reagan, *Weekly Compilation* (September 4, 1982), 1090–91.

55. All references to this speech are from Reagan, *Weekly Compilation* (September 25, 1982), 1212–14.

56. Hugh Sidney, "Ready to Play Power Poker," *Time* (November 15, 1982), 21.

57. Ingold and Windt, "Trying to 'Stay the Course': President Reagan's Rhetoric during the 1982 Election," 408.

58. All references to this speech are from Reagan, *Weekly Compilation* (October 13, 1982), 1305–10.

59. Walter R. Fisher, "Rhetorical Fiction and the Presidency," *Quarterly Journal of Speech* 66 (1980): 119–26.

60. All references to this speech are from Reagan, *Weekly Compilation* (October 23, 1982), 1383–84.

61. All references to this speech are from Reagan, *Weekly Compilation* (December 18, 1982), 1639–40.

62. All references to this speech are from Reagan, *Public Papers* (January 25, 1983), 103–110.

63. *Reagan: The Next Four Years*, ed. Nancy Lammers (Washington, D.C.: Congressional Quarterly 1985), 62.

64. Smith, "MisteReagan's Neighborhood: Rhetoric and National Unity," 435.

65. All references to this speech are from Reagan, *Weekly Compilation* (January 29, 1983), 140–41.

66. Reagan, *Weekly Compilation* (February 5, 1983), 195.

67. Reagan, *Weekly Compilation* (May 28, 1983), 803.

68. Reagan, *Weekly Compilation* (July 15, 1983), 987.

69. All references to this speech are from Reagan, *Weekly Compilation* (October 1, 1983), 1371–72.

70. All references to this speech are from Reagan, *Weekly Compilation* (January 21, 1984), 61–62.

71. For a detailed description of the package see *Congressional Quarterly Almanac 1984* (Washington, D.C.: Congressional Quarterly, 1985), 144–49.

72. All references to this speech are from Reagan, *Weekly Compilation* (January 25, 1984), 87–94.

73. Paul D. Erickson, *Reagan Speaks: The Making of an American Myth* (New York: New York University Press, 1985), 96–100.

74. Reagan, *Weekly Compilation* (March 3, 1984), 302.

75. All references to this speech are from Reagan, *Weekly Compilation* (March 10, 1984), 333–34.

76. Edwards notes that young Ronald Reagan saved 77 lives on the Rock River. See Anne Edwards, *Early Reagan* (New York: William Morrow, 1987), 14–15.

77. All references to this speech are from Reagan, *Weekly Compilation* (April 21, 1984), 585–86.

78. Reagan, *Weekly Compilation* (August 11, 1984), 1119.

79. Fisher, "Rhetorical Fiction and the Presidency," 119–26.

80. Reagan, *Weekly Compilation* (September 1, 1984), 1209–10.

81. All references to this speech are from Reagan, *Weekly Compilation* (September 15, 1984), 1299–1300.

82. Reagan, *Weekly Compilation* (September 22, 1984), 1349.

83. Reagan, *Weekly Compilation* (October 13, 1984), 1531.

84. See Roger C. Aden, "Entrapment and Escape: Inventional Metaphors in Ronald Reagan's Economic Rhetoric," *Southern Speech Communication Journal* 54 (1989): 384–400.

85. Reagan, *Weekly Compilation* (October 27, 1984), 1669.

86. All references to this speech are from Reagan, *Weekly Compilation* (November 3, 1984), 1755–56.

87. All references to this speech are from Reagan, *Weekly Compilation* (November 5, 1984), 1798–1802.

88. Hart, *The Sound of Leadership*, 206–207.

89. See Windt and Farrell, "Presidential Rhetoric and Presidential Power: The Reagan Initiatives," 397.

90. See Smith, "MisteReagan's Neighborhood: Rhetoric and National Unity," 439.

91. Palmer and Sawhill, "Overview," in *The Reagan Record*, 23.

92. William A. Niskanen, "Reflections on Reaganomics," in *Assessing the Reagan Years*, 10.

93. Richard P. Nathan, "Retrenchment Comes to Washington Society," in "Reaganomics: The New Federalism," *The Reference Shelf*, 55, ed. Carl Lowe (New York: H. W. Wilson, 1984): 28.

94. Reeves, *The Reagan Detour*, 34.

95. Elton Rayack, *Not So Free to Choose: The Political Economy of Milton Friedman and Ronald Reagan* (New York: Praeger, 1987), 187.

96. Jordan, "Weakening the Dollar: The Tax No One Has to Vote For," 176.

97. Mills, "The Budget: A Failure of Discipline," 119.

98. Kenneth Burke, *Permanence and Change*, 3d ed. (Berkeley: University of California Press, 1984), 274–94; William H. Rueckert, *Kenneth Burke and the Drama of Human Relations*, 2d ed. (Berkeley: University of California Press, 1982), 128–62.

99. Erickson, *Reagan Speaks: The Making of an American Myth*, 2–4.

100. Ibid., 88.

101. Hart, *The Sound of Leadership*, 174.

Chapter Six

The Second American Revolution

While Reagan's economic rhetoric during the first term was more temporal, centering primarily around initiating his economic program, recession, recovery, and campaign, the second term centered primarily around specific issues: the budget deficit, tax reform, welfare reform, and international trade. Reagan ended his first presidential term overcoming the recession as well as inducing optimism in the land. The unsolved budget deficit tainted a fairly successful implementation of an ambitious economic program. With his landslide reelection, Reagan entered his second term confident and optimistic.

THE NATION'S DESTINY

The number of major addresses devoted to economic issues subsided while the number of Saturday radio addresses devoted to the economy dramatically increased. These radio addresses gained a similar epideictic stature like many of Reagan's major speeches, characterized by their formality, formulaic, and thematic development.

At the outset of his second term, Reagan reintroduced the theme of a New Beginning to enlist the support of the American people in pushing for further economic programs. Reagan possessed an innate understanding that a good narrative would be well served by a New Beginning theme as well as a dramatic ending.

Despite the ongoing economic recovery, the federal deficit occupied lawmakers for most of 1985. Congress did not meet the provisions of its own budget resolution for fiscal year 1986, which called for spending cuts of nearly $60 billion. The only significant budget reductions were made in the area of defense as Congress approved defense appropriations that for the first time since 1975 constituted a decline in real terms.[1]

On tax matters, Reagan introduced in May 1985 a massive overhaul of the federal tax structure, designed to shift some of the burden away from individuals to corporations and to simplify the existing tax laws. Though the measure died late in the legislative session due to GOP resistance, Reagan was able to revive the bill by speaking directly to the House of Representatives. Reagan's appeal proved successful as the House passed the measure on December 17, 1985. The Senate was to take action on the bill only in 1986.

Second Inaugural Address: January 21, 1985

As the economy experienced a strong recovery, Reagan's rhetoric echoed this resurgence. Whereas Reagan's first *Inaugural Address* had a serious and somber tone, the second was much more optimistic and celebratory. Reagan followed, what he called, a "time of reckoning" theme, dramatizing the "turning point" on the economic front: "We had to look to our past for the greatness and glory. But we, the present-day Americans, are not given to looking backward. In this blessed land, there is always a better tomorrow" (68).[2] Reagan sought to depart from the symbolic past extensively used during his first term, appealing now to destiny. Reagan argued for further acceptance of his economic measures under the premise that the present was good but the future could be better.

Faith, stated Reagan, was the key to economic progress, however, while the "system has never failed us, . . . for a time we failed the system" (67). Reagan implied the faithless were at fault. Contrasting the past (pre-1981) with the accomplishments of his administration, Reagan repeated the theme of his first inaugural, "We allowed taxes and inflation to rob us of our earnings and savings and watched the great industrial machine that had made us the most productive people on Earth slow down and the number of unemployed increase" (67). With the economic ills thus named and the "evils" clearly identified, Reagan's narration built the background for his administration's challenge. "By 1980 we knew it was time to renew our faith, to strive with all our strength toward the ultimate in individual freedom," implying that prior to 1980 the United States had been an economic sinner (67). The pain and frustration resulting from economic "infidelity" were alleviated through the simplicity and purity of faith and hope,[3] implying that those who lacked faith were at fault for the temporary recession, not Reagan.

Following renewal and restoration, Reagan described the current status of the economy as healthy, vibrant, robust, and active. However, success was not good enough: "We will not rest until every American enjoys the fullness of freedom, dignity, and opportunity." (67). With this projection of an even better and prosperous economy, Reagan created the rhetorical formula for the next four years.

Like a scolding parent, Reagan repeated his anti-government argument: "We must never again abuse the trust of working men and women by sending their earnings on a futile chase after the spiraling demands of a bloated Federal Establishment" (68). Calling such a practice a prescription for disaster,Reagan positioned himself on the side of the people who valued fairness and trust, and who distrusted unfair demands by the government.

Reagan also stated that "there is a place for the Federal Government in matters of social compassion" (69). Indeed, Reagan hinted that the government would play a greater role in the economy during his second term, especially in social programs, despite his anti-government stand.

Reagan's vision called for "a new American Emancipation—a great national drive to tear down economic barriers and liberate the spirit of enterprise" (68). The "revolution" called for in the first presidential term was transformed at the outset of the second term to an "emancipation." A Lincoln-like Reagan attempted to project the economy of the next four years as symbolic of ultimate freedom and redemption from bondage and slavery.

Reagan also called for changing the course of 50 years of chronic deficit spending, associating it with previous administrations and their failed economic policies. The specifics of his economic message were simple: further reductions in tax rates and a constitutional amendment to put a cap on the federal budget, reminiscent of Proposition 1. Using Talmudic questioning, Reagan queried: "If not us, who? And if not now, when?" (68) The answer implied the administration's responsibility was to act now with determination and courage instead of the timidity of waiting or preferring others to do the job the president was entrusted with.

Consistent with the inauguration genre, Reagan spoke of the future in positive terms, avoided specifics, and sounded celebratory. However, unlike the first Inaugural Address in which a message of hope was conditioned largely by the situational exigency, the second Inaugural Address was not limited to another variation on the "we did it" theme. Rather, Reagan chose to combine both the success of the past four years with a challenge to take America to further heights.

The Budget: February 1985

Between the Inaugural and the State of the Union addresses, Reagan resumed his more familiar accusatory tone. Two days before submitting his budget to Congress, Reagan stated in a February 2, 1985, radio address that this document was "the most exhaustive effort ever made to rein in government's chronic overspending" (117).[4] Stopping excessive growth of federal spending and putting budget deficits on a permanent downward path were Reagan's essential economic objectives, as he depicted the federal government as unruly and in need of being constrained.

Reagan seemed concerned with the opposition, attempting to inoculate his listeners against counterarguments as he warned people not to listen to statements claiming no progress would be made in bringing deficits down until taxes were increased. "Wrong," claimed Reagan, adding the problem was not taxes but government's overspending. Sarcastically, Reagan stated that "Washington's policy is: 'Heads, I win; tails, you lose" (117). Reagan's harsher language was reserved for the less publicized speeches.

The State of the Union Address: February 6, 1985

Reagan gave the economy his complete attention in this speech, seeking to outline and garner support for completing his economic agenda. The populist appeal was clearly evident as Reagan identified faith, freedom, and values as the guiding stars to hope. Echoing Abraham Lincoln's *Gettysburg Address*, Reagan stated that four years ago "the American people have brought forth a nation renewed, stronger, freer, and more secure than before" (140).[5] These ideals, such as wisdom, vision, and courage, were key to past successes and the conditioning qualities of future achievements. Quoting Proverbs, Reagan noted, "Without a vision the people perish" (141).

The dramatic prologue ushered in Reagan's call for a second American Revolution of hope and opportunity, "a revolution of spirit that taps the soul of America" (141). However, for this vision to materialize, stated Reagan, no constraints could be put on the human mind, no walls could be erected around the human spirit, and no barriers to progress were to be imposed.

To anecdotally prove that indeed the economic achievements were great, Reagan said that in Europe they were calling it "the American Miracle." Stated Reagan, "We stand on the threshold of a great ability to produce more, do more, be more" (141). The economy, added the president, was not getting older but younger and stronger, enjoying 25 straight months of economic growth, a 3-year inflation rate of 3.0 percent, and 7.3 million new jobs in 2 years (141). It did not need rest and supervision but new challenges and greater freedom. This dramatic introduction was meant to link the proposal for a significant tax reform with the freedom metaphor. The word "freedom," Reagan emphasized, was the key to the second American Revolution since a tax reform was meant to free people from government entrapment. Implementing a tax reform, implied Reagan, would make the economy an engine of our dreams, "unleashing the tremendous pent-up power of our economy," promising opportunity for all by liberating the spirit of enterprise (142). The war metaphor, incorporated in the term "revolution," positioned the struggle for freedom as the ultimate objective in Reagan's economic agenda. With this metaphor, Reagan also identified himself with the Founding Fathers as well as contextualizing the tax reform as a struggle for ultimate independence.

Despite the rosy picture, Reagan acknowledged that there were still areas of the country where minorities and teenagers were yet to enjoy the economic recovery. To help those suffering individuals, Reagan supported the Job Training Partnership Act, helping low-income people to own their own homes. However, the government's role, stated Reagan, was limited to creating an atmosphere of freedom; states and localities were responsible for using their tax surpluses for recovery. This statement is paradoxical since in the past Reagan never claimed that government's role was to create freedom, only people could.

The federal deficit was mentioned only in passing as Reagan stated his objection to those saying that growth initiatives had to await actions on deficit reductions (the budget deficit in 1985 reached $196 billion).[6] Making no statements that revealed the extent of this particular concern, Reagan offered economic growth as the solution to reducing the deficit. For example, Reagan stated that every increase of one percentage point of GNP reduced the deficit by about $200 billion over five years (143).

Reagan did outline a general policy for balancing the budget through decreasing government's influence on the total economy. To achieve this goal, Reagan kept his promise not to raise taxes and suggested the budget for 1986 would be frozen at the 1985 level. However, this freeze guaranteed the social safety net for the truly needy, continuing to build military strength, and reducing and even eliminating costly government subsidies. With regard to farm policy, Reagan called for a transition to a market-oriented farm economy.

Seemingly uneasy covering too many specifics, Reagan returned to discussing his vision for America, stating that dreams could become true. The economy, he added, was stronger than ever, with the young leading the way. The Puritan strain in Reagan's rhetoric appeared when he stated that "we've rediscovered that work is good in and of itself," identifying a return to cherished ideals (144). Reagan further stated, "America's economic success is freedom's success; it can be repeated a hundred times in a hundred different nations" (145). Echoing Lincoln again, Reagan stated: "We're not here to congratulate ourselves on what we have done but to challenge ourselves to finish what has not yet been done" (141).

Through the use of metaphors and a dramatic narrative, Reagan gave a speech replete with themes of populism, renewal, restoration, and faith. He extensively used "god" terms such as great, invincible, spirit, wisdom, courage, and compassion. The discourse was positive without the familiar "us" versus "them" dichotomy. In the final account, this highly poetic address, limited on specifics, projected destiny as its main theme. One explanation for such a general address may be that Reagan used this ceremonial occasion as a prelude for future policy-oriented addresses, satisfied with past achievements and attempting at this point to build momentum for a major tax reform. Neither it seemed, did Reagan wish to create a wedge between the administration and Congress, especially relative to passing his tax reform.

Reagan's rhetoric at the outset of this second presidential term was optimistic, celebratory, and positive, extensively incorporating the themes of faith and courage. For the most part, Reagan minimized specific blame, preferring to strengthen identification with Congress in an attempt to get his tax reform. Disturbing economic signs, especially budget and trade deficits, may also have brought Reagan to realize these economic problems could not be solved by rhetorical means alone.

"THE SECOND AMERICAN REVOLUTION"

Central to Reagan's economic agenda was a radical tax reform he wrapped around the second American Revolution metaphor. In addition to advocating a tax overhaul, Reagan focused on the federal budget deficit, welfare reform, the farm crisis, and anti-protectionist legislation.

Address to the Nation: April 24, 1985

Reagan had hoped for smooth sailing, but Congress opposed the administration's budget proposal. With this development, Reagan went public with an angry speech, denouncing the opposition and asking the people for direct support, claiming: "I need your help." The reason for this request was straightforward and dramatic: "Today the United States Senate began a rendezvous with history," as Reagan echoed Franklin Roosevelt's 1936 Acceptance Speech (511).[7] With this exigency, Reagan set the tone for a speech heavy on praise and blame, expressing pride in past achievements, and confidence in the future. Interestingly, the Senate's rendezvous was with history, not with Reagan. Reagan distanced himself from disputes, preferring the conflict be with larger and more symbolic entities such as history. Again, one can observe Reagan's strategy of removing himself from the scene of a potential conflict.

Reagan put his economic ideals in the form of rhetorical questions, asking whether after decades of drift, neglect, and excess, it was possible to put the nation's fiscal house in order, and whether it was possible to assume the existence of a prosperous future by adopting a plan that compelled the federal government to end the dangerous *addiction* to deficit spending (511). Reagan the healer was the one to tidy up the house and put a stop to a dangerous trend by curing government of its ailment. The opposition, however, prevented him from achieving this heroic act, and in this hour of despair, he called on the American people to intercede and put their weight on this crucial issue. In order to ensure public support, Reagan created a strong identification with his American interlocutors through appeals to tradition. Throughout history, he stated, Americans had been willing to meet great challenges and do what was right when destiny demanded it (511).

Reagan's rhetorical arrangement was simple yet compelling. First, Reagan presented questions based on specific premises to which the answers were usually in the affirmative. Next, he presented the general premise in the form of traditional values in order to gain the expected support. To further strengthen his message, Reagan recalled that when he first embarked on the economic challenge, many said it would not work (511). Yet things had turned around after decades of national nightmares.

As the economy prospered, Reagan had the proof he needed to argue for further implementation of his legislative agenda. The ship metaphor returned as the president declared that no longer did the critics call his policies *Reaganomics* (assuming it carried a negative connotation) stating, "the United States is the flagship economy for the world" (511).

The specific call for a complete overhaul of the tax code was identified by Reagan as a "historic moment to shape America's future" (511). Reagan found it attractive to juxtapose history and future with the passing of his tax reform. Less dramatic was Reagan's argument that government considered tax money a gift from the IRS and a magic money machine (511). Unlike this selfish attitude, Reagan's pro-people policy was presented as a moral duty whereby money spent must be justified. Identifying taxes as morally wrong implied that the government that unwisely spent the people's money was inherently immoral.

The prosperous Eisenhower years through the Kennedy years, argued Reagan, resulted in spending increases, yet no one took the next logical step of reducing tax rates or improving other aspects of the economy. Instead, government did the opposite—taking over America—in the name of the Great Society. The consequence of such a trend, added Reagan, was the creation of an enormous weight of federal government spending with a runaway deficit that jeopardized one of every seven family farms and created a great social tragedy (513). Of interest here is Reagan's insertion of the farmers' plight in his lamentation on Big Government, a hint of things to come.

The national debt reaching $1.7 trillion with an ongoing annual interest of $155 billion meant that every person's share was $8,000. The language depicted an administration that did everything possible to solve the problem while big spenders in Congress prevented the task from being accomplished. Stated Reagan: "Surely, there's no faster way to see our prosperity vanish than to yoke the decent, hard-working, taxpaying citizens of this great nation to an automatic spending machine in Washington, D.C." (512).

Reagan presented his economic plan as a small effort that would mean big gains later. The president called for everyone to pitch in together in order to make the future "the best years of our lives" (515). However, cautioned Reagan, if the people refused to pitch in, and the nation returned to the old platform of business as usual, the federal government would destroy the prosperity already in place. The responsibility for not accepting his economic program fell on the people.

As a last attempt to get support for his budget proposal, Reagan dramatized the situation as a crossroad: the hour was late, the task was large, and the stakes were momentous. "I hope history says of us that we were worthy of our past, worthy of our heritage" (515–16). Reagan was fond of incorporating a romantic strain in his rhetoric, the kind that projected a future that was as certain as the American cherished past.[8] Paradoxically, in his second inaugural, when projecting a second American Revolution, Reagan held that no longer did the people need to look at the nation's past for greatness and glory.

Address to the Nation: May 28, 1985

Tax reform was dramatically presented at the outset of this address, as Reagan called for a great historic effort to give the words *freedom, fairness,* and *hope* new meaning and power for every individual in America (703).[9] The tax system that had become an endless source of confusion and resentment must be changed, stated Reagan, with a simple and a fairer tax code that would ensure incentives and rewards for a future of economic growth.

To strengthen this single issue address, Reagan described a past whereby various modifications of the tax code had not improved the tax system; rather, they created a tax system that was "complicated, unfair, cluttered with gobbledygook and loopholes designed for those with the power and influence to hire high-priced legal and tax advisers" (703). The champion of the people sold his tax reform as a historic change to a system that benefited unscrupulous individuals. Reagan established the background for a major tax reform that benefited the middle class and the poor and not necessarily the traditional upper middle class and the wealthy constituencies of the Republican party. Reagan was the restorer of fairness to the people and trust toward the government.

Hints of the tax revolt of the 1970s surfaced in this speech as Reagan explained that those who had lost trust in the government avoided paying their full tax share. Reagan appeared to sympathize with the people for having found clever ways to avoid paying taxes, not casting blame on individuals, preferring instead to blame the government and its tax system.

In his final argument, Reagan called the tax system un-American (three days earlier, Reagan called paying taxes a practice against human nature, offering to make the 1040 tax form an endangered species).[10] By associating taxation with patriotism, Reagan grounded his argument in traditional values, stating that the first American Revolution of 1776 was sparked by the conviction that taxation without representation was tyranny. Similarly, the second American Revolution was one of hope and opportunity, a peaceful one, yet one born of popular resentment (704). Using the symbolism of the War of Independence was a challenge Reagan confidently pursued hoping to promote a fundamental economic issue to the level of great historic consequences.

Acceptance of the tax reform, promised Reagan, would free people from the grip of special interest groups, creating commitment to only one interest group—the people who paid the bill (704). The tax reform would lower tax rates, giving people the incentive to climb higher. The reform would also strengthen the family, which was society's bedrock and the most effective instrument in the economy. Reagan projected tax reform as an extension of his belief in the family, individualism, and common sense, while government control was construed as disruptive and unnecessary, thus anti-family and anti-individualism. "The power to tax is the power to destroy," rhetored Reagan, adding that his tax reform was "the strongest profamily initiative in postwar history" (704–5). Tax reform, explained the president, would offer a ladder of opportunity for every family that felt trapped, thus enabling them to climb out of poverty forever. Despite his continuous calls for cutting welfare, the Reagan administration spared programs aimed at the poor, the needy, and the handicapped from major reductions.[11]

Tax reform would replace the old and tired economy "wheezing from neglect in the 1970s" with a "powerful locomotive of progress carrying a trainload of new jobs" (706). Reagan's vision depicted the acceptance of the tax reform as "a challenge to lift us into a future of unlimited promise, an endless horizon lit by the star of freedom, guiding America to supremacy in jobs, productivity, growth, and human progress," and, "an expression of both America's eternal frontier spirit and all the virtues from the heart and soul of a good and decent people" (707). Reagan attempted to sell his tax reform using the metaphors of youthfulness, the frontier, and the locomotive, all embedded in the romantic ruggedness of the American pioneer spirit.

Between this special address and the 1986 *State of the Union Address,* the economy figured prominently primarily in weekly radio addresses. The topics of discussion covered tax reform, deficit reduction, the growing farm crisis, and resisting protectionist measures.

Tax Reform: June–December 1985

In his June 1, 1985, radio address, Reagan chastised Washington for not taking change (tax reform) very well. It is here, declared Reagan, that the presidency intervenes in trying "to get above the bickering and buttonholding in the cloakrooms and corridors."[12] Transcending himself above politics, Reagan presented himself as the people's lobbyist who had no respect for the Washington bureaucracy and its unwillingness to accept sensible ideas. The negotiations over tax reform were reduced to a simple issue of warranted change versus selfishness.

In his August 3, 1985, radio address, Reagan marked the fourth year after taking the "first giant step toward putting this economy back in your hands" (referring to the 1981 tax reduction bill) (959).[13] Added Reagan, "After being held back so long, a ringing declaration went forth that the dream of economic freedom was alive and well in America's soul" (959). Furthermore, past achievements were the result of people's faith and courage in new opportunities, unlike the panic-stricken Washingtonians who could no longer reach deeper into people's pockets. While unidentified "they" were predicting disaster, the people, said Reagan, began transforming the economy from top to bottom. Against feeding the alligators, he continued, the people sent his administration to drain the swamp. The swamp metaphor was a likely variation on the "clear path" metaphor, juxtaposing the clear road to recovery with a treacherous one. In short, the people made economic change possible, while the Reagan administration served the people.

Prior to the House's decision on tax reform, Reagan took to the air calling for a fair and simpler tax system that would guarantee growth.[14] After the House passed an initial tax reform bill, Reagan stated in late December 1985 that the House had taken to heart what was conveyed in many speeches and what the people said in many telephone calls and telegrams.[15] Reagan implied that the people were right. The pro-growth tax reform was promoted as a people's campaign while Reagan portrayed himself as a humble servant who merely responded to the tax revolt. Yet Reagan was displeased with some serious flaws contained in the bill, expressing his hopes that upon Congress's return to work in early 1986, a final bill would be introduced to provide an unequivocally pro-family, pro-jobs, and pro-future legislation.

Deficit Spending: June–December 1985

As the budget deliberations were in progress, Reagan continued to take his message directly to the public. Considerable progress, indicated Reagan, had been made in achieving spending reductions, bringing down the budget deficit and keeping the economy growing (838).[16] In his June 22, 1985, radio address, Reagan even gave tribute to the Senate for its courage in passing a plan of $56 billion in budget savings. However, the entire legislative branch, accused Reagan, was not planning a true budget savings but simply phantom-cuts stating "no meaningful effort to shrink this gargantuan Federal spending machine" had been set by the Congress (838). Adamantly, Reagan promised to veto any tax increase sent by Congress, and added he would repeat his refusal until he turned blue in the face (839).

When the budget talks did not produce the cuts he advocated, Reagan stated in his July 6, 1985, radio address, "Once again, the budget process has broken down" (875).[17] Simplifying the situation for the people, Reagan warned that the current budget would threaten national security. Against this threat, Reagan depicted congressional spending plans as an orgy, gimmicks, and creative bookkeeping. Positioning the nation's security against a spending orgy juxtaposed the morality of the administration with Congress's immorality.

Still dissatisfied with "business as usual," Reagan sarcastically stated in his July 20, 1985, radio address that he hoped the House budget proposal would get well soon, and suggested he would send to Capital Hill the fine surgeons who helped his recovery from the assassination attempt.[18] In other words, Reagan's medicinal approach suggested Congress required a surgery-like process in order to get back to good health. "Turning blue in the face" and hoping the House budget proposal would "get well soon," were phrases presidents were not in habit of using. Reagan's jargon-like phrases were a conscious attempt to stand near the people through humor and sarcasm.

After the acceptance of the Deficit Control Act of 1985 (the Gramm-Rudman-Hollings legislation), Reagan proudly informed the American people of his enthusiastic support for this historic development. This legislation required the federal government, by law, to lock in a deficit reduction process, leading to a balanced budget (1202).[19] Without cutting defense spending, or breaking the commitment to Social Security, Reagan foresaw a balanced budget by 1990. Rationalizing why earlier promises to balance the budget had not materialized, Reagan described a trend in federal budget spending that reached $100 billion between 1789 and 1962, doubled nine years later, and stood at $900 billion in 1985. The government had spent like a drunken sailor, but now, sounding like a teacher commenting on the maturity of his students, Reagan declared the United States government, at long last, had grown up (1202).

Despite the passage of the Deficit Control Act, Reagan was not completely pleased. The Gramm-Rudman-Hollings amendment came close to his wishes, but the disturbing part of the bill was its lack of specifity with regard to how spending be cut. Reagan asked, "Will we fund wasteful, pork barrel programs at the expense of our national defense? Will we kill off our prosperity with a tax increase?" (1523).[20] On both issues of national security and taxes, he announced his "veto pen is inked up and ready to go" (1523). By presenting himself time and again as a consistent and principled president, Reagan maintained credibility and the opportunity to demand more than either the people or Congress gave him credit for. From an argumentative perspective, Reagan used reasoning by principle, easy to ground on accepted norms and values, and not always easily refutable.

The Farm Crisis in National Addresses August–December 1985

On August 17, 1985, Reagan acknowledged the plight of American agriculture. A host of reasons were identified as causing this crisis ranging from the past grain embargo (implying President Carter's ill-fated policy), double-digit inflation and 21 percent interest rates to federal programs that distorted the market and sent confusing signals to farmers in the form of subsidies and price supports. In this explanation, Reagan did not blame the farmers. On the contrary, he referred to them as the most productive and hardworking and as the backbone of the country. The guilty party was government, and the solution was to free the farmers from discredited programs and government control.[21]

Though farmers accounted for only 3 percent of the work force, farming generated about 18 percent of GNP, declared Reagan, building the rationale for farm aid he had initially resisted (1087).[22] Reagan's justification for farm aid was strong in its emotional appeal as the figures, he announced, "don't tell the whole story. They don't convey the strength and nobility of values, the deep faith in God, and love of freedom and independence, the many years of hard work and caring for friends and neighbors that began on the farm and made America the greatest Nation on Earth" (1087).

Though government aid to farmers was contrary to Reagan's principles, the emphatic discourse was meant to generate sympathy for their plight and to justify a policy shift. Modifying his anti-government rhetoric (aiding farmers), Reagan needed to minimize this apparent inconsistency. Using supportive arguments that, expectedly, relied on traditional values, Reagan stated, "The strength of our farmers has always been the strength of their dreams," adding that to lose the farmers was to lose the heart and soul of America (1087). With these compassionate appeals, Reagan asked Congress to help farmers, yet he rejected protectionist bills that would have worsened their situation. In late 1985, Reagan lended a hand to the farmers but only in accordance with his obligation to cut deficit spending (the farm credit system policy).[23]

Anti-Protectionism: August–September 1985

Growing protectionist pressure brought Reagan to suggest that such measures were almost always destructive and that advocates of protectionism often ignored its huge costs that outweighed its benefits. Protectionism, explained Reagan, usually ended up weakening the protected industry while free trade meant fair trade (1025).[24] The pressure for such restrictive measures, voiced by business and industry through Congress, the very sectors that had helped reinvigorate the economy, brought Reagan to avoid naming any particular group advocating protectionism.

Reagan attempted to tackle the issue of the trade deficit by dispelling the myth behind protectionist measures. While in 1980 the United States had a trade surplus and only 99 million had jobs, today in 1985, stated Reagan, with a trade deficit, almost 107 million Americans had jobs (1025). Reagan sought to refute the charge that protectionist measures would increase employment. The reasoning, however, was misleading since other factors may have lead to increased employment while Reagan attempted to show that the trade deficit had not hurt employment, even implying it had caused some benefits. Reagan warned he would oppose any protectionist legislation, stating: "We must not retreat into the failed policies of the past, whether they be protectionism or higher taxes" (1025–26). Reagan associated cutting taxes with opposing protectionist measures but did not explain how these seemingly divergent issues were tied together.

As for those looking at the trade deficit with alarm, Reagan rhetored that the United States' share of world exports had not declined. Reagan further explained that the trade deficit was not the result of rising imports, but was due to a decline in United States' exports, claiming that the strength of the U.S. dollar and the vibrant economy made U.S. exports expensive, while low taxes and low inflation made America an attractive place to invest.[25]

It is noteworthy that on September 22, 1985, the administration changed its policy toward the exchange rate, deliberately depreciating the dollar by holding down interest rates in the U.S. This move was indicative of the administration's conscious attempt to reduce the trade deficit and counter protectionist legislation in Congress. However, no clear public statement revealed this interventionist policy.[26]

On both tax reform and deficit reduction, Reagan was able to further advance his economic agenda. Congress passed the Deficit Control Act of 1985 (Gramm-Rudman-Hollings), and the Senate approved the initial pro-growth tax reform. Expectedly, Reagan's discourse was optimistic, with freedom and fairness serving as foundational values. As for trade barriers, Reagan strongly opposed protectionist measures, advancing arguments by principle and definition and attempting to convey strong resistance to any disruption of the principle of free trade. With regard to the farm crisis, Reagan shifted his policy of refusing to bail out troubled farmers by enacting legislation to aid farmers. This shift was achieved through the use of empathy to minimize the perception of inconsistency.

TOWARD A RADICAL TAX REFORM

Congress passed and Reagan signed into law on October 22, 1986, the most significant rewriting of federal tax laws since 1942. The new tax laws shifted close to $120 billion from individual tax liability to corporations as the measure sought to address the growing imbalance between individual and corporate tax burdens. The Tax Reform Act of 1986 also greatly reduced the progressivity of personal and corporate income taxes. Specifically, the top personal income tax rate declined from 50 to 28 percent, and the top corporate income tax rate was reduced from 46 to 34 percent.[27]

Aside from tax reform, the congressional budget resolution for fiscal year 1987 met the $144 billion deficit ceiling prescribed by Gramm-Rudman-Hollings, as Congress was finally able to reach agreement on an $11.7 billion deficit reduction bill in addition to $11 billion in increased revenues from the Tax Reform Act of 1986. Reagan, however, strayed far from budget negotiations as he feared an election year tax increase could cause serious damage to congressional Republicans' reelection chances. Reagan's absence from the budget talks mattered little though, as Democrats regained control of both Houses of Congress.

State of the Union Address: February 4, 1986

The state of the Union was stronger than last year, stated Reagan, adding, "Tonight we look out on a rising America, firm of heart, united in spirit, powerful in pride and patriotism. America is on the move!" (135).[28] However, reminded the president, not long ago the situation was urgent as the greatest country on Earth turned into a land of broken dreams. Who was to be blamed? The government, answered Reagan, for growing beyond the people's consent, "threatening to crush the very roots of our freedom" (135). America's comeback was the result of the people's heroic efforts, quiet courage, common sense, and undying faith. What specifically the "people" did was not addressed, yet Reagan implied the people had faith in him and his administration.

Reagan offered the discourse of hope overcoming misery. "Private values must be at the heart of public policies," sounded Reagan, adding that history is made by people of vision and courage (136). Reagan sought to make radical changes (creating history) through the conviction that courage, faith, and vision were essential ingredients of persuasion.

The United States was a miracle, declared the president, adding, "We have done well, but we cannot stop at the foothills when Everest beckons" (136). The objective, he spelled out, was to redefine the role of government; not to control, not to demand or command, not to contain, but to help in time of need, to create opportunities so that all could climb toward economic power and justice (136). Reagan had argued throughout his political life for less government. Yet, six years after he became president, a shift had taken place. Reagan had allowed the government some role, and it seemed that the role was more significant than the language revealed. Political initiatives such as the growing coordination with the United States' major trading partners on economic and monetary policy, devaluing the dollar to reduce the trade deficit, and increased support for certain welfare programs were reflective of a more interventionist government, the kind Reagan had publicly opposed.[29]

Against calls to raise taxes, Reagan repeated that the large budget deficit was due not to undertaxing but to government overspending. Yet the government, stated Reagan, could not reduce the deficit by taking from the truly needy. However, Reagan called on government to revise or replace programs enacted in the name of compassion but that in essence degraded and discouraged individuals and families. With this argument Reagan transcended the intuitive perception that social programs brought about positive results. The sought social reform was couched in compassionate language so as to minimize its effect. Echoing Franklin Roosevelt, Reagan stated welfare programs were "a narcotic, a subtle destroyer of the human spirit" (138). Instead, Reagan called for escaping the spider's web of dependency, building social programs on the principle of how many recipients could become independent of welfare. The entrapment metaphor associated with social welfare issues depicted an unwarranted situation that could be resolved only through independence.

Reagan's remaining objectives were the approval of a line-item veto on budget spending and a continued commitment to national defense. With the authority of the line-item veto, Reagan stated he was willing to take responsibility, adding, "I'll make the cuts, I'll take the heat" (136). Reagan portrayed himself as a bold, confident, and daring president. He reiterated his long-held view that defense spending was not just another budget expense but the government's prime responsibility: "Keeping America strong is as vital to the national security as controlling Federal spending is to our economic security" (137). This analogy is quite intriguing since it equated the importance of spending cuts with the importance of building the nation's security, precisely what Congress opposed.

The address concluded with the familiar visionary call where "no victory is beyond our reach, no glory will ever be too great" (140). Poetically, Reagan portrayed the American dream as "a song of hope that rings through night winter air; vivid, tender music that warms our hearts when the least among us aspire to the greatest things: to venture a daring enterprise" (139). Heroism, courage, and hope were the ingredients of the American dream. "Confident in our future and secure in our values, Americans are striving forward to embrace the future," was Reagan's principal vision (137).

For almost a year, no major economic addresses were delivered. The primary issues Reagan addressed in his radio addresses touched on cuts in spending and a tax reform.

Deficit Reduction: February 1986–January 1987

The general outline of the 1986 *State of the Union Address* was given detailed consideration in Reagan's first radio address of 1986. Reagan's number one priority in the budget debate was "to cut the fat out of the Federal budget and to stop anyone trying to cut the heart of your family budgets" (195).[30] Reagan was for cutting the federal budget, reducing taxes, and against cutting the family budget (imposing taxes). "But a funny thing happened on the way to Capitol Hill," delighted Reagan with a take on a popular play (195). Those who spoke the loudest about the need to cut deficits suddenly cried "foul" when real cuts became apparent. Paternalistically, Reagan answered those calling for raising taxes: "Let me give you some facts about how a little cooperation and common sense can put us on a glide path to a balanced Federal budget" (195). Not through raising taxes, but by holding a little garage sale to get rid of Conrail, Amtrak, and raising some $2 billion in user fees. Even defense was not off limits, declared Reagan, agreeing to cut $3 billion below the level Congress consented to in August (195). In raising user fees and making cuts even in defense spending in order to reduce the budget deficit, Reagan the politician prevailed over Reagan the ideologue.

The budget talks of 1986 were tied, in part, with the open question regarding the Gramm-Rudman-Hollings limits on the federal deficit. Only after the Supreme Court put in Congress's hands the decision on deficit reductions did the Reagan administration ask Congress to meet the target deficit of no more than $144 billion.[31]

As the September 30 deadline for passing the budget neared, Reagan went on the attack in his September 27, 1986, radio address. Reagan contrasted Congress's irresponsibility with the fairness of his administration, claiming that the simple activity of balancing a checkbook was something Congress had difficulty performing. With Congress unable to produce a responsible budget (no details were supplied), Reagan expressed frustrations at the fiasco of the last minute throwing together of a continuing resolution—a collection of pet projects and wasteful spending that would never make it into a real budget. For six months, contended Reagan, Congress dragged its feet, refusing to send the appropriations bills necessary to keep government running (1287).[32] The only appropriation bill passed, ridiculed Reagan, was the one funding the legislative branch. In the name of truth and fairness, Reagan attacked Democrats for blaming taxpayers for causing the deficit since they paid little taxes. Calling such accusations hogwash, Reagan repeated his accusation that overspending and not undertaxing was the cause for deficits (1287). Reagan portrayed a struggle between Congress and the people and not between Congress and his administration, thus removing himself from the immediate scene.

The "fiasco" of the September 27 message regarding the budget process was intensified in November to a "disgrace."[33] Congress failed to send the White House an appropriation bill bringing the government close to a shut down. Reagan suggested that the budgetary process was simply unworthy of the legislature of the greatest democracy in the world, and that no private company would be permitted to behave the way the United States conducted its fiscal business.

Deficits stem from "our failure to remember that government consumes wealth, it doesn't create it," Reagan stated (1609). This viewpoint, added Reagan, was contrary to the economic theory he had studied in college. Accordingly, when bad times occurred, the only way to restore prosperity was to spend our way out of it with massive new government programs paid for by borrowing. But, countered Reagan, "Everybody knows you can't spend yourself rich any more than you can drink yourself sober" (1609). Reagan anecdotally argued against government spending, reducing a complex issue to an oxymoron. Reagan seemed to suggest that common sensical and simple solutions were more worthy than any sophisticated academic advice (i.e., Keynesian principles).

The expanded discourse over the budget deficit pointed to a certain exigency that Reagan attempted to address. Though more spending was included in the proposed budget (for the elderly, law and drug enforcement, AIDS research, health care, and air traffic safety), Reagan stated he was disappointed to learn that the Democratic leadership had declared their first priority was to pass a budget-busting clean water bill vetoed last year. "Well, now, I'm in favor of clean water, but the only thing clean in this bill is its name."[34] The objection to the billions requested was handled anecdotally, minimizing the perception the president was against the substance of the bill. "You can't have it both ways," he lectured the Democrats, adding "You cannot decry deficits and then pass budget-busting legislation" (3). For Reagan, the easy refutation was pointing out the apparent inconsistency.

Tax Reform in National Addresses: May–December 1986

As tax reform neared approval, Reagan could not hide his satisfaction, proudly announcing that "America today stands poised to lift off into a new age of opportunity powered by one of the most exciting economic changes of my lifetime" (609).[35] Indeed, Reagan took this victory as a personal achievement of a lifelong pursuit. At the core of the tax code proposal was the simplicity of having only two tax rates: 15 and 28 percent, with over 80 percent of the people in the former tax bracket. The 6 million poor, explained Reagan, would be exempted from paying taxes altogether (609–10). In addition, the tax reform eliminated tax deduction for IRAs and many tax shelters, but increased the amount of personal deductions.

One side effect of the much publicized tax reform, explained Reagan in his July 26, 1986, radio address, was a slower growth during the second quarter of 1986 (1005).[36] Reagan claimed that the legislative process on the Hill had caused some investment hesitation in the business sector. However, once the new ground rules regarding the new tax laws were known, he expected business to really start moving.

Reagan did not even wait for the final approval and signing of the tax reform bill to sound like a winner. When he took office, stated Reagan, "The economy had about as much energy as a hound dog on a hot summer day" (1006). Some said, he continued, that the economy would never get on its feet, yet now the economy is strong, robust and with the tax reform the future would be bright (1006).

In August, after the conference negotiation on the Hill approved the Tax Reform Act of 1986, Reagan could not hide his vindication. "We're about to score the winning run, not just of the game but of the whole season," Reagan proudly announced (1122).[37] The president reminded his audience of the long and arduous struggle, and despite the chorus of pessimists, "America is built on a can-do spirit" (1122). No longer, stated Reagan, would taxes be used to make economic and social policy, but rather, market forces would shape the economy. With more money left in the hands of individuals, Reagan promised the tax reform to be the most effective anti-poverty program, in addition to encouraging risk-taking, innovation, and enterprise (1122–23).

After finally signing the Tax Reform Act of 1986 in late October, Reagan called it "a victory for fairness," assuring a new era of growth and opportunity.[38] This achievement and many others were hard fought, reminded Reagan, yet there was still a cloud hanging over the economy: the possibility that a tax-and-spend mentality will return to Washington and take us back to those bad old days. It can happen, warned Reagan, and we need to be on our guards. The paranoid formula of describing hard-fought battles complete with sacrifice and redemption coupled with a warning was often present in Reagan's rhetoric as a safeguard against policy reversals. The war metaphor was employed again; this time, however, to describe victory (as distinct from earlier war metaphors used to advance an upcoming political initiative). Reagan's use of war metaphors was preserved for the toughest and most radical of Reagan's economic issues. The war metaphor, unlike the path or the medicinal metaphors, implied a hard-fought battle replete with risks, dangers, and heroic efforts.

In closing the book on 1986, Reagan briefly recounted the year, complete with "long-lasting events that the political pundits don't remember or may not have noticed" (1673).[39] For Reagan, the tax reform became his single most significant achievement during his presidency. Immensely proud of this achievement, Reagan stated that though many said "the tax reform was an impossible dream . . . we showed the cynics our system still works," and that despite "gloom and doom," the country was moving forward (1674).

Some have called his effort the "Reagan revolution," causing him to smile, chuckled the president. The values may have been revolutionary, he stated, but they were from a revolution much older than he was—the revolution of 1776.[40] Humbly, Reagan presented himself as the agent-restorer who simply believed in traditional values but was not their inventor.

"THE FOURTH AND FINAL QUARTER"

The success of the tax reform did not reduce Reagan's energy in pushing for a complete implementation of his economic program. Reagan's discourse, continuously optimistic, also attempted to shield his administration from any perception of real economic decline due to an uncontrollable budget deficit and growing world competition.

Up until October 19, 1987, leaders of both Houses of Congress were unsuccessful in persuading Reagan to meet with them for an "economic summit" to enact deficit reduction legislation. Black Monday though finally persuaded Reagan to acquiesce to congressional demands. To placate fears in the financial markets over future record deficits, the two sides compromised on November 20, 1987, to a two-year deficit reduction plan totalling $76 billion in spending cuts and tax increases. Reagan got the best of the compromise since the deficit reduction package agreed upon was less than the amount of savings required by the congressional budget resolution adopted on June 24, 1987.

News was also made in 1987 on Gramm-Rudman-Hollings. Specifically, Reagan signed a new version of the bill on September 23, 1987, which eased the federal deficits permissible under the 1985 law and promised a balanced budget by fiscal year 1993 instead of 1991.

The economic expansion continued in 1987, setting a record in October for the longest peacetime expansion in U.S. history. In addition, more good news came in the form of a reduction in the federal deficit from $220 billion in fiscal year 1986 to $148 billion in fiscal year 1987.

State of the Union Address: January 27, 1987

With the lowest inflation in a quarter of a century, low unemployment, and a boom in construction, economic indicators pointed to a strong economy. But for Reagan going strong was not good enough: "Let's roll up our sleeves and go to work and put America's economic engine at full throttle" (60).[41]

Due to the economic progress, "America is at peace tonight, and freedom is on the march" (60). The restoration of the nation's defenses and leadership in the world, explained Reagan, were the direct result of economic viability. However, though the world was safer, it was not safe enough. Further investments in defense were required. According to Reagan, any effort to undercut the national security and the U.S. negotiating leverage would also mean a threat to the economic vitality (61–62). Positioning the economy at the top of his political hierarchy, other political aspects were associated with and depended upon economic strength.

Facing the federal deficit, Reagan resorted to dramatic narrative. Calling the deficit outrageous and the budget process a sorry spectacle, Reagan maintained the need to stop pushing onto the next generation the excesses of government. By simply stating and repeating these messages time and again, Reagan attempted to shield himself from accusations regarding the administration's responsibility for the huge deficit. At fault, argued Reagan, was the process and not just the substance of budgetary issues. Calling the process cumbersome and nightmarish, Reagan's solution was the line-item veto "so we can carve out the boondoggles and pork, those items that would never survive on their own" (62).

Given suggestions by the House to postpone the Gramm-Rudman-Hollings deficit reduction target, Reagan stated that the American people were tired of hearing the same old excuses. Reagan also rejected new taxes, repeating his principal conviction that deficits were not the result of not paying enough taxes but were due to government overspending (62). Though the issue was the budget deficit, Reagan hardly touched on the nature of the deficit or gave any details regarding the budget proposal and the projected deficit.

Similar to his California policy of welfare reform, Reagan called for a new national welfare strategy through state-sponsored, community based projects. "This is the time to reform this out-moded social dinosaur and finally break the poverty trap" (62). Independence, freedom, and self-support were the values Reagan espoused to advance this welfare reform. To illustrate, Reagan touched on his special concern for the elderly who had to face the intolerable choice between bankruptcy and death. Reagan suggested legislation that would "free" the elderly from the fear of catastrophic illness. More specifically, Reagan pointed to the welfare dinosaur consisting of some 59 major programs that costed more than $135 billion in 1985. To solve this cumbersome system, Reagan proposed a national welfare strategy that would offer reform through state-sponsored, community-based demonstration projects (62). As in his approach to the budget deficit, Reagan identified the welfare system as problematic, not the principle of welfare. Yet Reagan's sympathetic language indicated his support for the socially disadvantaged despite his long-standing opposition to increased funding for welfare.[42]

On the topic of America losing her competitive edge, Reagan claimed that such a trend would not happen if actions were taken soon. By "acting now" through funding of research, fighting unfair trade practices, and helping farmers, Reagan called for government to promote America's ability to compete, in order to "enter the next century having achieved a level of excellence unsurpassed in history" (63). Not to be overlooked was Reagan's call for the government to promote America's competitiveness. Whether an inconsistency or a purposeful shift innocently presented, this statement is significant. Similar to his shift in aiding the socially disadvantaged, Reagan departed from his anti-government zeal and offered a more interventionist role for the government in offsetting growing world competition.

Through lower taxes and a smaller government, Reagan claimed, the government had its ways of freeing people's spirits. But this was not enough. Now, claimed Reagan, the nation needed to strive for excellence, since "excellence is what makes freedom ring" (63). The bicentennial of the Constitution returned Reagan to the revolution theme; "Our revolution is the first to say the people are the masters and government is their servant" (64). By projecting a government that served the people, Reagan incorporated his modified stand regarding the role of government, though on the surface this statement seemed to offset the impression of the previous statements whereby the government would play a greater role in various domestic programs. The call for excellence was also meant to counter the growing perception that America was losing to international competition.

Consistent with the revolution theme was the "We the people" anaphora Reagan chose in giving homage to farmers, children, hostages, entrepreneurs, and builders. By addressing several important constituencies that had been on the public agenda in recent months, Reagan highlighted groups that had either enjoyed the administration's special consideration or were on the administration's list of concern. Interestingly, hostages were included with the economic-related constituencies. Perhaps the pressure on the White House to resolve the hostage situation and the administration's inability to offer hope in this particular issue brought Reagan to hide this "consistuency" in the larger economic context where hope and progress had materialized.

Reagan concluded his address with a vision, stating, "America isn't finished. Her best days have just begun" (65). The vision, unlike many others, was positioned against a growing perception that the United States had lost the economic competition with other countries, increasing social problems such as crime and drugs, and a budget deficit that made America the biggest debtor nation.

Welfare Reform: February–August 1987

Using the theme of "up from dependency," the current welfare system, Reagan argued, was "one long and sorry tale of disappointment" (123).[43] To prove his point, Reagan rationalized that during the prosperity of the 1950s, poverty declined, however, when government began to spend millions on welfare programs, poverty stopped declining (123–24). Reagan attributed poverty to government's program the very thing government programs sought to solve. By challenging conventions through the switching of causality, Reagan sought not only to advance his own theory about the solution to social problems but more important, to redefine the role of social policies.

The solution, highlighted in earlier speeches, called on the family to provide a strong support system. However, Reagan acknowledged that the family unit had declined, again attributing this development to the welfare system. Reagan called for a welfare system that would lift people out of poverty without wasting money on unworkable solutions. Finally, he offered faith in the family, faith in individual dignity, and faith in the federal system of government as the keys to a new welfare system (124). In actuality, no real solution was offered here. The family Reagan spoke of was to relieve the government from responsibility, but this was not a convincing argument as Reagan himself acknowledged the decline of the family unit.

Economic indicators, according to Reagan, had shown a decline in poverty, reversing a trend begun in 1979. However, Reagan added, more had to be done to reduce poverty and dependency, arguing that by changing the welfare system and its reliance on federal approaches dictated from Washington, improvements could be made.[44] Programs such as the Low-Income Opportunity Improvement Act promised that people would be encouraged to be self-sufficient. Dependents would be required to engage in some work instead of making dependency on welfare their employment.

In essence, Reagan called for a welfare reform that intervened early in order to prevent dependency. Reagan presented an idea that on the surface was sensible and logical, yet avoided the complexity of its implementation. More important, the premise of "Up From Dependency" as the only solution was only anecdotally supported. No real proof was supplied showing that less funding would solve poverty instead of further hurting the poor.

America's Competitiveness: February–July 1987

The sense that America was not measuring up in the world market became even more acute in Reagan's February 21, 1987, radio address when he suggested that people move away from such general notions. Instead, Reagan preferred people to understand the problem as precisely as possible. Such a statement was uncharacteristic since Reagan did not flatly reject the pessimistic sentiment, but rather gave it a more focused explanation thus limiting its potentially negative impact.

Even more revealing was Reagan's contention that it may not be the best thing for America to be "the tallest one around just because everybody else is flat on his back."[45] By redefining the situation, Reagan sought to transcend, or at least minimize, the growing pessimism of a declining United States. What is intriguing about Reagan's statement is his attempt to establish an argument of relativity; that relative to other nations, the United States was still a vibrant nation while other nations were lazy (lying flat on their back). Reagan sought to solve a problem by changing perceptions. He suggested that Americans look at the new trend not as "threats" but as "challenges," precisely because a challenge corresponded with Reagan's rhetoric of hope, faith, and optimism, whereas threats implied weakness.

As the pressure to legislate trade barriers continued, Reagan devoted yet another radio address to this topic. Reagan stated on May 16, 1987, that he did not "believe the American people are afraid of competition."[46]

The underlying theme was the challenge posed by competition. Implying the value of courage, Reagan spoke at length about one successful company (Harley-Davidson) that requested its special tariff be removed so that they could meet their competition head on. The challenge, according to Reagan, lay in improving products and increasing exports, but above all, it was dependent on the courage of individuals.

In June, Reagan put forward a stronger case against the perception of an economically declining America. Despite the impression other countries were performing better, Reagan assured his audience that the economy was outperforming the economies of America's trading partners. The grounds for this statement was the 4 percent of real economic growth, about the same as that of Japan, and a much better rate than that of European countries. Also, America's economic growth prompted economic growth throughout the world, claimed Reagan.[47]

To prove the United States was still in command of its international trade, Reagan stated that by teaching Japan a lesson (imposing economic sanctions over semiconductors), the United States had sent a clear sign to its trading partners. The president who strongly opposed trade barriers made an about face. His tough and threatening language was thus meant to offset a policy shift.

Based on the economic principles espoused by the United States, Reagan proudly announced that the Venice summit agreed to work against trade barriers and reduce subsidies for agriculture with the objective of eliminating them altogether by the year 2000. The participants in the summit also reached an agreement on the premise "that the economic progress we've made together has enabled the democracies to rebuild their defenses, keep peace in the world, and strengthen our alliances."[48] Against the recent pessimistic mood of declining world influence and economic viability, Reagan presented the nation as a world leader, with a powerful economic system admired and emulated by other nations. Against growing pessimism, Reagan affirmed his optimism in America.

On July 11, 1987, Reagan had good news in the form of economic indicators (manufacturing productivity of 3.5 percent, exports increased by 14 percent while imports declined by 5 percent). With these figures, Reagan declared America's competitiveness was strengthening as the nation had turned the corner on the trade deficit (799).[49] However, just as America was making progress, Congress, stated Reagan, was trying to set us back, analogizing the situation to "closing the barn door when the horse is trying to get back in" (799). Instead, suggested Reagan, Congress ought to open markets, not close them; expand trade, not put up roadblocks (780). Congress, according to Reagan, was the sole stumbling block to a stronger U.S. economy.

Deficit Reduction: February–October 1987

As in previous speeches, Reagan differentiated the budget process from the budget deficit. The budget process "is as rife as it ever was with favoritism and special pleading" (200).[50] Without reform, stated Reagan, economic prosperity would never be safe, spending would increase, and the nation would be back where it was seven years earlier with federal spending running wildly out of control (200). The proposed budget was sound, and with a balanced budget "America could greet the future confident that the monster of deficit spending was locked away forever in its cage" (200). Implied in the monster-in-the-cage entrapment metaphor was the notion that reducing and eliminating the deficit meant freedom from terror and uncertainty.

A strong conditioning factor had returned to this address as Reagan claimed that a prosperous future was dependent on congressional action. On March 21, 1987, Reagan called the budget process "more like a magic show. It's wink and blink and smoke and mirrors and pulling rabbits out of hats, but almost all that ever comes up are designs to hide increases for the special interests" (289).[51] Reagan attacked Congress for fooling him and the people through an unacceptable process, charging that Congress's "enhanced recission authority," which allowed for overturning the president's veto by a simple majority, was a sneaky way to bring certain spending through the back-door (289–90).

Expressing his displeasure with the Senate adopting certain procedures that made it easier to exceed the Gramm-Rudman-Hollings spending target, Reagan dismissingly stated, "Maybe your reaction is the same as mine: Here we go again."[52] Congress, blamed Reagan, refused to exercise any budget discipline, adding that the only solution still lay in a constitutional amendment that would mandate a balanced budget. Reagan's sarcasm proved more pointed than any lengthy explanation.

Being fond of associating his convictions with those of the Founding Fathers, Reagan told of Thomas Jefferson, who was troubled by one omission in the Constitution: the lack of a limitation on the federal government's borrowing. Our Founding Fathers, noted Reagan, knew from firsthand experience how tyranny abused the fiscal powers of government, and how excessive taxing can lead to inflated currencies and economic hardships.[53] By identifying with the Founding Fathers, Reagan argued that what they knew was not only true but that it was time to honor their foresight.

Reagan spelled out two objectives: First, the need to work together with Congress in reforming the budget process, putting a stop to delays and broken commitments. This would be accomplished through a vote on a constitutional amendment mandating a balanced budget. Second,

Reagan asked for the people's immediate help in pressing House representatives to agree to a responsible deficit reduction package. Otherwise, his veto pen would put a stop to big spending bills. Reagan added he was ready to talk and consult, but not if the objective was additional spending, more taxes, and less defense (677). Reagan would play but only by his rules.

When Congress outlined its budget proposal, Reagan resumed his attack on elusive big spenders. For awhile, stated Reagan, the big spenders seemed to have gone underground, but now they had resurfaced like cicadas, threatening to overrun Congress. No one wanted to repeat the mistake of one presidential candidate who called for higher taxes, stated Reagan (a likely reference to Walter Mondale), but now the tax-and-spend crew was back calling for new spending without any embarrassment (716).[54] His administration was willing to work with those in Congress who would work in good faith. However, the current budget was a bad one. To illustrate the waste included in the budget, Reagan pointed out the absurd purchasing by the government of underwater property, or subsidizing 100,000 acres in Texas owned by none other than the prince of Liechtenstein (716). With these two ad absurdum examples, Reagan rhetorically questioned how some in Congress could still claim they could not find anywhere to cut, except the defense of the nation.

Being keen on dramatic effects, Reagan proposed yet another constitutional amendment in the form of an economic bill of rights attempting to invoke the sentiment of the original Bill of Rights. Such a bill, stated Reagan, would guarantee that the people not be too heavily burdened by big government, by excessive taxes, by skyrocketing inflation, and by high interest rates.

America's Economic Bill of Rights

The underlying principle in this bill was that economic freedom and political freedom were inextricably linked (768).[55] The objectives included: the freedom to work, freedom to enjoy the fruits of one's labor, freedom to own and control one's property, and the freedom to participate in a free market. In order to achieve these freedoms, Reagan outlined several initiatives, including: reducing subsidized government competition with private citizens; reducing the burden of government regulation; protecting individuals from government's overborrowing, excess spending, and overtaxing; reforming the present welfare system; and encouraging American workers and businesses to fully participate in an increasingly complex world economy (768–70).

Calling such a statement a bill of rights added the constitutional prestige and formality to Reagan's long-held economic principles. Nothing new was added to this list, except for the emphasis put on the premise that economic issues lay at the foundation of political issues. Put differently, a nation's economy, in Reagan's (and Milton Friedman's) view, holds together its political and social dimensions.[56]

On the following day's July 4, 1987, radio address, the timing of the economic bill of rights became clear as it was meant to intertwine with the Fourth of July celebration. The economic bill of rights, stated Reagan, was a package of fundamental economic reforms written in the shadow of Thomas Jefferson. The specific purpose of the bill, however, was less impressive than the stature given to it. Reagan sought to guarantee "truth in spending," a required full disclosure of vital details of pending budget legislation.[57] Reagan attempted to make it impossible for Congress to approve spending without having to justify or disclose purposes and recipients of funding.

By late September, Reagan announced that he expected the federal deficit to drop by 30 percent, a savings of about $65 billion. But the good news was dampened by Congress passing a budget the president disagreed with. Reagan was also displeased with Congress tying the signing of the budget bill to massive cuts in national defense (1077).[58] Congress, blamed Reagan, consistently brought government to the edge of default before facing its responsibility. Two weeks prior to the October crash of the stock market, Reagan prophetically warned that congressional brinksmanship threatened the holders of government bonds, and that instability would occur in financial markets as the federal deficit increased (1077).

After the stock market crash, Reagan assured both domestic and international audiences of the soundness of the American economy. With a 3.8 percent increase in the GNP and an inflation rate of 1 percent for the last quarter, Reagan called the economic growth historic and astonishing, despite the market's volatility.[59] Reagan asked the public to remember that corrections and fluctuations would occur, adding that nothing would go wrong if consumers did not overreact, and that there was no reason to lose confidence in the economic expansion.

Only in late October did Reagan connect the crash of the stock market with an unsound fiscal policy espoused by Congress. Reagan reminded his audience of his warning that the economic expansion could end and the economy could be sent into a tailspin. The stock market was giving the nation some warning, declared Reagan. With this "sign," Reagan hoped spending cuts could finally become a reality, adding, "deficit cuts, like diamonds, must be forever."[60]

Though the economy displayed positive indicators, underlying problems emanating primarily from the budget deficit threatened to leave a less than perfect economic legacy. Reagan, the ever image-conscious politician, continued to project optimism, vision, and confidence. The crash of the stock market gave Reagan the opportunity to sound vindicated, attributing the crash to years of waste and irresponsible spending.

"WE'RE NOT FINISHED YET"

Reagan's rhetorical approach to the final stage of his presidency was exceptionally optimistic and celebratory. The theme that there was still much to be done presented an energetic and motivated president, who after seven years was tirelessly going strong, willing to campaign even though he was no longer a candidate. What he could not complete economically, Reagan sought to complete rhetorically, presenting a confident and idealized United States whose economic mission had finally been actualized.

Despite rumors of economic downturn in 1988, the nation's economy continued its seven year resurgence as GNP grew at an annual rate of 3.8 percent and the economy moved toward "full employment" at an annual rate of 5.3 percent. Reagan's final year as president proved to be relatively productive as welfare underwent major reforms, a massive trade bill was signed into law, and the nation's first catastrophic health care bill was enacted.

The welfare reform measure Reagan signed on October 13, 1988, bore at least one major similarity to his 1971 welfare reforms: a work requirement for adult welfare recipients. This law was the first ever federally mandated work requirement.

In response to the nation's 1988 trade deficit of $152 billion, Reagan signed on August 23, 1988, the Omnibus Trade Bill. Though the bill contained no sharp reversals of the United States' trade policy, it did rework existing solutions to unfair trade practices abroad and import surges detrimental to American firms.

The State of the Union Address: January 25, 1988

Reagan opened this speech pointing to the success of the past seven years stating, "We're not finished yet," but humbly added he would leave the reciting of his administration's accomplishments to history (85).[61] Retelling the beginning of his economic quest, Reagan proudly reminded that seven years ago his administration brought ideas such as individual rights and a free market as an engine of economic progress. These ideas were part of a larger notion that the strength of the individual, family, neighborhood, and community comprised the concept of "We the people" and the foundation of the idea "that the people grant government its rights, and not the other way around" (85). In

Reagan's ideology, the correct vision was proven successful, and the people were depicted as heroic and the true agents of change.

The joint efforts of Congress and the administration, stated Reagan, resulted in bringing "down" spending, tax rates, inflation, and unemployment. Other successes included the "rise" in family income and seeing the poor "climb" out of poverty. Economic success was metaphorically depicted following upward and downward paths (Heaven and Hell), highlighting negative aspects as declining while positive ones were increasing.

Reagan outlined four objectives: taking steps to keep the economy strong and growing by maintaining low inflation and full employment, attacking social problems by ensuring the economic independence of the poor, continuing the exciting economic and democratic revolutions around the world, and preserving a strong national security to protect peace (86). In recent addresses Reagan introduced the notion that a causal relationship existed between economic development and political changes. Later in this address Reagan stated that the United States' greatest contribution to the world was the promotion of freedom as the key to economic growth. Reagan equated freedom with economic viability, further enhancing his contention regarding the manifestation of economic freedom in the movements for political freedom around the world.

The budget deficit remained a distraction for Reagan. Yet, even here, Reagan was able to highlight a positive development—a change in the prevailing perception that deficits created prosperity. Finally, he declared, there was an agreement that the deficit would not make us rich (thus proving that Keynesians were wrong). This consensus, he claimed, brought Congress and the administration to cut spending. However, cautioned Reagan, repeating the message of the first *State of the Union Address*, "The Federal Government is too big, and it spends too much money" (87). Reagan warned he would fight any attempt to renege on the budget agreement, including using his veto power.

Reagan also repeated his attack on the budget process, calling the deadlines and continued resolutions a monstrosity. To illustrate the point, Reagan pointed out the 1,053 pages in the budget appropriation bills (physically present by the podium for visual impact), and calling the 43 pound document behemoths. Even worse, the administration was given only 3 hours to read the entire budget and that 300 people had to be employed in order to finish reading it in the alloted time, otherwise, the government would have been shut down. Congress, lectured Reagan, should not repeat such an unacceptable process. Reagan positioned the administration at the receiving end of the budget process, unable to act appropriately and always at the mercy of Congress' spending spree. Nearing the end of his administration, realizing the budget deficit could not be reduced, Reagan took advantage of this symbolic address to dramatically "prove" his point about the budget process as the cause for the deficit.

As a solution, Reagan envisioned a joint effort whereby priorities were set and spending was accomplished within available revenues. Also, Reagan repeated his request for a line-item veto, defining it as "the right to reach into massive appropriation bills, pare away the waste, and enforce budget discipline" (87). To prove his point about waste, Reagan chose ridicule, alluding to unacceptable spending "tucked away behind a little comma here and there," such as cranberry research, and the study of crawfish (87).

Reagan argued that a balanced budget and a reduction in the deficit would prevent the government from ever again ravaging the family budget, thus creating a causal link between family suffering and the budget problem. Government, continued Reagan, should never again legislate against the family and the home (88). By identifying the family as the sufferer and the government as the victimizer, Reagan projected himself and his administration as compassionate and caring.

Government was also at fault for the failing of social programs. "With the best of intentions, government created a poverty trap that wreaks havoc on the very support system the poor need most to lift themselves out of poverty: the family" (88). The solution, declared Reagan, was to be found in community and local efforts such as innovative welfare programs that required recipients to work and effective child support enforcement practices. Government, lectured Reagan, ought "to show a little humility" in nurturing the many "sparks of genius" in many communities (88). Thus Reagan identified the solutions to social problems to exist on the local level.

Reagan took the step here to depict current economic decisionmaking as historically comparable to the writing of the Constitution or to Lincoln's Gettysburg Address, since the principle involved was that of affirming the role of government of and by the people. Reagan stated, "It is up to us now to decide whether our form of government would endure and whether history still had a place of greatness for a quiet, pleasant, greening land called America" (91). Not only invoking great symbols like the Constitution or a great President, Reagan also used Lincoln's phrasing to dramatize the importance of economic issues. Reagan thus consistently identified historical significance as the rationale for advancing his political and economic agenda.

Calling Washington, D.C., a city of hope in the land that is free (in earlier years Reagan referred to it as the Puzzle Palace on the Potomac), Reagan concluded with a vision of America as a shining city on a hill. Hope and faith were the themes of this address and the grounds for implementing the last item on the list of what was already accomplished—deficit reduction. "Let's make this (year) the best of 8 . . . right to the finish line," called Reagan (86).

International Trade: March–November 1988

Reagan's March 12, 1988, radio address was uncharacteristically long as Reagan set out to counter pessimistic perceptions regarding the economy. Throughout his seven years in office, stated Reagan, "professional doomsayers have latched onto one issue after another as evidence of an American decline" (335).[62] Trade was the most recent subject of lamentation by (unidentified) advocates who were using this issue to argue for more government involvement in private business, and to argue for protectionist barriers. But the doom merchants, declared Reagan, were wrong, stating, "The United States economy remains the most dynamic and exciting one on the globe" (335). The "proof" for this assertion came in the form of clearing two "myths": First, the trade situation had improved more quickly than people realized (the trade deficit had dropped 18 percent since the third quarter of 1986). The second "myth," that Congress could pass a law that would reduce the trade deficit (protectionist measures) without hurting prosperity, was also untrue as it would pose a threat to the nation's export boom. When in possession of a positive economic indicator such as the improving trade deficit, Reagan was quick to use it as a myth-dispelling proof. Labeling the opposition's assertions a myth added cynicism to an already suspecting president.

Reagan advocated a compromise that would increase international competitiveness and increase trade, jobs, and productivity. "It is still possible to write a bill that I can sign," stated Reagan (335). The draft for the bill, he reminded, already eliminated a number of troublesome provisions such as illegal quotas, budget-busting giveaways, yet many obstacles remained.

What Reagan did not spell out on March 12, he detailed a day earlier during a briefing in the White House to selected business leaders. Reagan opposed retaliatory provisions that would be in violation of the General Agreement on Tariffs and Trade (GATT), as well as to provisions that restricted a company's right to close facilities and relocate, and those that required disclosure of trade arrangement. Behind these issues was Reagan's concern with measures that would discourage foreign investment in the United States.[63] For the national audience, Reagan's version was general and generous in its attack on Congress, whereas the specifics were spelled out to more selective audiences. The details of his objection were revealing nonetheless. Supporting foreign investment in the U.S. became economically necessary in part by the argument for fair and free trade but more important it was a form of infusing capital into the economy. Yet the growing concern about losing to foreign competition was not an issue Reagan was willing to admit to a national audience.

On March 26, 1988, Reagan stated that "Congress will stay on course and that we will settle on a bill that avoids the great danger of choking off international trade and slowing down economic growth."[64] Reagan juxtaposed strength and faith with surrender, doubt, and defeatism. Growth was the principal objective in resisting trade barriers, but beyond this important economic objective, the word "growth" as an "ultimate" term already expressed optimism and hope.

Commenting on the threat of foreign investment, Reagan gave assurances that there was nothing to be afraid of. Foreign investment, he said, was only 12 percent of U.S. public debt, down from 16 percent in 1978. Unable to ignore the growing foreign investment in the United States, Reagan rationalized that such investment brought a host of benefits, including jobs and lower interest rates. America, claimed Reagan, lived in a global economy, a term he had recently introduced into his public addresses.[65] Rhetorically, Reagan gradually shifted public awareness toward a growing interdependent world in which the U.S. was an important partner but no longer autonomous.

The "economy is strong" continued to be Reagan's theme, reassuring Americans against perceptions of losing economic superiority. The American people, stated Reagan, were misinformed because the good news was not reported, and they did not hear that the trade deficit had turned around (525).[66] The bearer of bad news (the media) was the implied scapegoat. "The fearmongers had their heyday last October, when the stock market fell 508 points in 1 day," predicting a dire future for the U.S. economy (525). The fearmongers, accused Reagan, spread predictions of depression, recession, catastrophe, and calamity while the economy had clear signs of strength (unemployment at 5.5 percent and GNP at 4.8 percent). At issue was the trade bill still under negotiation. Reagan's position was that he would not sign a bill that reversed the progress made in the last five years. He agreed with some provisions such as repealing the windfall profit tax, but disagreed with other provisions. Stated Reagan, "As long as I'm President, we're going to keep traveling the road we're on, one of free and fair trade" (525).

After three years of hard work, he had no choice but to send the bill back to Congress. Congress, claimed Reagan, sent him a trade bill that threatened to destroy jobs and reverse policies of seven years (617).[67] At the heart of his objection was the provision that required businesses to give advance notice of layoffs or plant closings; not that he rejected the notification, stated Reagan, after all it was the humane thing to do, but government, he argued, should not dictate rules and regulations. Advance notification should be decided in bargaining between labor and management, not by arbitrary rule enforced by Washington (617).

Reagan raised his objection to the trade bill to a personal level, stating he felt strongly about this issue, perhaps because he was once a union president who negotiated with management without the need for Washington to act. Philosophically, Reagan stated the real issue was the kind of government the nation wanted. After seven years of limited government and the longest peacetime expansion, there was no need for big government (617). Not only did Reagan argue against big government, but he also continued to advocate a causal relationship between limited government and economic prosperity.

In the Declaration of Independence, the Founding Fathers, stated Reagan, charged the British, among others, with cutting the colonies' trade with all parts of the world. That year, Adam Smith wrote about the folly of protectionism. In Reagan's assessment, America's most recent experiment with protectionism, the Smoot-Hawley act of 1930 proved disastrous, having led to the Great Depression (1569).[68] Two years later, he added, he had casted his vote for Franklin Roosevelt who opposed protectionism, thus reminding Democrats of their misplaced heritage. Yet, the recent trade deficit had led some misguided politicians to call for protectionism. In fact, stated Reagan, more jobs were created while maintaining free trade (1569). By associating the anti-tax revolutionary spirit with his own views on protectionism, Reagan was able to ground his discourse on tradition, wisdom, and heroism, the themes he had always found appealing.

Part of the problem, continued Reagan, was in using "words" such as "war" to talk about trade, while an alliance that benefited both countries would have been a more accurate description (1569). Reagan's understanding of war metaphors may have been the result of his own use of such vocabulary. But Reagan may have had another reason for making this point. Today, he said, protectionism was used as a cheap form of nationalism, "a fig leaf for those unwilling to maintain America's military strength and who lack the resolve to stand up to real enemies: countries that would use violence against us or our allies" (1569). In other words, the war metaphors, complained Reagan, were used by advocates of protectionism, namely Democrats, to disguise their opposition to a strong defense.

Deficit Reduction: February–December 1988

In mid-February, Reagan submitted the fiscal year 1989 budget, which included a reduction of $75 billion in spending over two years (237).[69] If Congress upheld the pressures during election year to increase spending (implying Congress' inherent weakness and spending habits to buy votes), Reagan promised solid results. Reagan predicted that the savings in budget spending as a percentage of the GNP would be cut by half relative to 1983 (237). To appease those opposing cuts, Reagan stated that the budget remained firm in supporting domestic programs as well as funding the minimum required to hold the country safe. Anything less, added Reagan, would jeopardize the national security.

On October 1, 1988, Reagan informed the people of a major victory regarding the budget process. The process that was so inappropriate that not even Congress knew what was in it had finally ceased. For the first time in many years, announced Reagan, the budget work had been done on time. "We won," Reagan announced victoriously. Even defense appropriations, despite the opposition of many liberals to Strategic Defense Initiative (SDI), looked good, he added. The last 24 hours of budget negotiations proved historic, declared Reagan, marking the end of the "Perils of Pauline" budget games Congress played for so long (1247).[70] Yet Reagan was not completely satisfied with the budget decisions, especially with the textile protectionist bill and cuts in funding for federal agencies that enforced the drug laws. Ridiculing the Democrats, Reagan stated, "It's time the liberals realize that the fight against drugs is not 'Pee Wee's Big Adventures' but a serious and dangerous business" (1247).

On December 17, 1988, prior to submitting his final budget, Reagan resumed his attack against an unbalanced budget and the inadequacy of the budget process. Reagan ignored the apparent inconsistency between congratulating Congress in October for finishing the budget work on time and resuming his attack on the budget process. The verdict was in, he announced (without explaining whose verdict he presented), claiming the current system did not work. Since 1982 he had requested Congress to take back unneeded funds more than 460 times, and in 83 percent of the cases, Congress refused, telling him, "spend it all."[71] In chastising Congress's wasteful habits, Reagan called to restore the constitutional balance and repair the system (in 1974 Congress stripped the president of his ability to refuse to spend funds).

Campaigning Again: February–October 1988

Though not campaigning for himself, Reagan campaigned for his party. Throughout his remaining year in office, Reagan attacked "the other party," contrasting it with numerous "George and I" references. In the 65th straight month of the longest peacetime expansion in U.S. history, Reagan confidently and jovially noted that some of his opponents were very concerned about the state of the economy, adding he did not blame them. "If I were in their shoes, I'd be worried too" (444).[72] With 16 million new jobs, low inflation, and a GNP that exceeded expectations, Reagan added sarcasm to his campaign messages. The opponents, continued Reagan, had convinced themselves that record growth and vibrant job creation were bad news. "And they say it's all the fault of Reaganomics" (444). Reagan replied he was willing to take the blame or credit for the growth but humbly added that would be unfair since all he did was to get government out of the people's way. Though he sought to project humility, Reagan's more enduring projection of himself during the presidency was that of the nation's savior.

Forewarning the American people of the upcoming Democratic convention, Reagan predicted the economy would prove to be a central issue. Rhetorically inoculating his hearers against Democrats and their polemic, Reagan reminded the people of two important facts: upon arriving in Washington, the economy was in a mess, and that his administration's policies brought economic growth.[73] For years, stated Reagan, two basic philosophies regarding the economy had been put into effect: the liberal view, suspicious of free markets and private enterprise, preferring government to intervene in the economy through taxing, regulating, and spending more of the people's money; and his administration's philosophy, which put its trust in the people and did not trust big government, thus preferring tax cuts, less government regulations, and giving people incentive to grow, to invest, and to innovate.

On August 13, 1988, Reagan sought to enchant his radio listeners by stating that "the leadership of the other party has my Irish up" (1055).[74] Reagan was angered by the Democrats' talk about being in a recession, if not in outright depression. While the other party had been talking, "George Bush and I've been hard at work, putting into practice the ideals you believe in, the ideals that, at her heart, America has always stood for: strong defenses; low taxes and limited government; compassion and fair play" (1055–56). Reasoning through patriotism and tradition continued to be Reagan's favorite rhetorical proofs.

After the successful agreement on the fiscal 1989 budget in early October, Reagan ridiculed Democrats for congratulating themselves for handling the budget. The truth of the matter, continued Reagan, was that his administration stopped Congress from saying "The dog ate my homework," implying the irresponsible way Congress had handled the budget (1325).[75] Reagan used the teacher-student analogy, depicting the student as mischievous, adding that the liberals were still big spenders, and no matter when they handed in their homework, they still called their paper "tax and spend."

Against the possibility that Democrats may have politically scored over the recent budget agreement, Reagan attempted to strengthen the perception that when the issue was spending Democrats had not changed. Reagan reminded the people that only Congress could decide how much the government could spend, and since Congress was controlled by liberals, the Democrats were the villains. Reagan associated the term "liberals" with all that was bad with the economy.

In his final radio address prior to the presidential election, Reagan invoked his predecessor's name. Jimmy Carter, blamed Reagan, increased federal spending by 17 percent, twice as fast as the economy grew as a whole. This indicator, coupled with waste, fraud, deteriorating services, and abuse in a number of agencies, proved that the government had gotten too big to control. Blaming Carter and contrasting his administration's successes with the failures of the Carter administration, simplified for the citizenry the stakes and the choices, the way Reagan wanted the people to see them. Though eight years later, referring to Carter may have been seen as shallow, Reagan's logic typified oral cultures, whereby a single anecdote or a story serves as adequate evidence for a conclusion.[76]

Farewell Address to the Nation: January 11, 1989

This final address was redemptive, poetic, and emotional, befitting the occasion of a departing president who was about to step down from the political stage. This address was designed as the final chapter in a story that for many began eight years earlier and for Reagan himself some four decades ago.

Reagan began on a personal note, establishing an identification with the American people: "We've been together 8 years now, and soon it'll be time for me to go" (63).[77] Reagan said he had saved some thoughts for a long time, one of which he wanted to share with the American people. The presidency had set him apart from the people while often he wanted to stop the car and reach out from behind the glass and connect. Now that the presidential "constraints" were soon to be lifted, Reagan sought to emphasize he was all along a citizen politician.

Two themes were projected throughout the address: highlighting the progress made in the last eight years, and giving tribute to the American people who were responsible for the progress. Restoration and rediscovery served as the foundational values of the people who made the progress come true. In the 1980s, declared Reagan, "we rediscovered" freedom, and established this precious of all values as the consummation of the long quest. It had been quite a journey this decade, "we" held together through some strong seas but at the end "we" reached our destination. The sea metaphor implied heroic efforts shared by both captain and crew during some rough sailing. "We" made a difference, stated Reagan, in creating two triumphs: the economic recovery and the recovery of our morals. For Reagan, the economy was a secular religion, thus compatible with issues of morality. The beginning, continued Reagan, was a humble one, recalling that during the first economic summit with U.S. allies, he felt like the new kid in school while "it was all François this and Helmut that," and that at one point he leaned in and said, "My name's Ron" (54). That year, the narration continued, his administration ignited an economic comeback and the recovery began. During the next economic summit things had changed, everyone was quiet, and then one of them broke the silence and said, "Tell us about the American miracle" (54). The narration depicted by Reagan presented a simple yet powerful hero who succeeded from humble beginning through courage and determination.

During 1980, recalled Reagan triumphantly, his economic program was described as something that would end in an economic collapse. Yet, all predictions proved wrong. During that process, Reagan said he won the nickname "the great communicator," yet he never thought it was his style or his words that made the difference. Rather, claimed Reagan, it was the content of the message that made the difference, adding, "I wasn't a great communicator, but I communicated great things" (54). Though Reagan tried to distance himself from his flattering label, his humility worked to enhance his credibility. As for calling his economic program the "Reagan Revolution," Reagan preferred to view it as the great discovery of values and common sense. Reagan sought to gain the perception of the restorer, and in so doing, could comfortably use values and traditions as the commonplaces for his arguments. It was common sense, said Reagan, that told us that with big taxes on something, people would produce less of it. So taxes were cut and people began to produce more. Consequently, the economy bloomed like a plant.

According to Reagan, the first principle in guaranteeing economic success was believing in ourselves, then the future would be ours. A simple notion presented in a causal manner was the key to the economic recovery. The success was even greater than predicted. "We meant to change a nation, and instead, we changed a world" (54). In this final address, Reagan attributed the success of America to the trend his administration had begun for advocating free markets around the world. These (unidentified) countries rediscovered that the moral way of government was the practical way. Through economic progress and prosperity, Reagan sought to prove that democracy was morally good, thus superior to other political systems.

His anti-government views brought Reagan to reflect on the fork in the river he met in the middle of his life. Reagan confessed he never had the intention to go into politics but ventured into this arena because he wanted to protect something precious—putting a stop to the ways government behaved. "Ours was the first revolution in the history of mankind that truly reversed the course of government, and with three little words: "We the People" (55). Further stated Reagan, "I was a citizen politician, and it seemed the right thing for a citizen to do" (55). With unselfish motives, a mission, and faith, Citizen Reagan presented to the American people his version of his involvement in political life. Through this description, as well as in many others, Reagan empowered the people as the counterpoint to big government, and minimized his role in turning the economy around. Behind this political philosophy was also a rhetorical strategy that put the responsibility of acceptance or rejection of Reagan's plan on either the people or on the government. With the simple statement that people were not free unless government was limited, Reagan reduced his economic and political philosophy to a principle.

Not mentioning the budget deficit would have been a curious omission, yet Reagan minimized its effect. He stated his regrets over the deficit problem but added that the final address was not for arguments, thus he would hold his tongue (56). Reagan offered an observation—that in all his victories he never used his troops, or his regiments; the people won his victories. Reagan positioned the word victories (twice) in close proximity to the deficit problem, and repeated the strategy of empowering the people while burying the deficit issue between the many successes of his administration. Not to be overlooked is the notion that if the people were responsible for the many victories, they were also responsible for the failure to balance the budget.

The final part of the farewell address was a tribute to faith and destiny. Using the words and thoughts of John Winthrop (who borrowed from the book of Matthew in the New Testament), Reagan's discourse turned poetic:

> I've spoken of the shining city all my political life, but I don't know if I ever quite communicated what I saw when I said it. But in my mind it was a tall proud city built on rocks stronger than oceans, wind-swept, God-blessed, and teeming with people of all kinds living in harmony and peace, a city with free ports that hummed with commerce and creativity, and if there had to be city walls, the walls had doors and the doors were open to anyone with the will and the heart to get here. That's how I saw it, and see it still (56–57).

Furthermore, Reagan described the shining city as an economic entity:

> More prosperous, more secure and happier than it was 8 years ago. But more than that; after 200 years, two centuries, she still stands strong and true on the granite ridge, and her glow has held steady no matter what storm. And she's still a beacon, still a magnet for all who must have freedom, for all the pilgrims from all the lost places who are hurtling through the darkness, toward home . . . [W]e've done our part . . . We did it. . . . We made a difference. We made the city stronger. We made the city freer, and we left her in good hands (57).

Reagan was leaving the scene content and able to forward a vision beyond his own administration. Reagan understood the human craving for a victorious hero, and he gave the American people a story with a happy ending. The eight years were described by Reagan in a legend-like manner with the hero overcoming many obstacles, succeeding, loved by the people and never forgetting the humble beginning. Behind the attribution of greatness to the nation and its people, Reagan took measures to project humility.

This address ended the story about a long journey and its quest. "Truth" had prevailed and the story had a happy ending. Reagan fashioned himself as the hero of his romanticized vision of America, he was the hero of the Shining City.[78]

CONCLUSION

During the second presidential term, Reagan's rhetoric was redemptive and redundant. In contrast to his governorship, Reagan had accomplished most of what he had set out to achieve. The major success during his second presidential term was the passage of the radical Tax Reform Act of 1986. Reagan did not solve the budget deficit, though he witnessed a decline in the trade deficit. In welfare reform, Reagan was able, late in his presidency, to pass a work requirement bill for welfare recipients. Also, late in his second term, Reagan signed a trade bill to guarantee fair trade practices.

Reagan pushed hard for a complete implementation of his economic plan using discourse that reflected his personal stake in the nation's economy. Reagan had not changed his innately optimistic nature, but where he knew he could not get the legislation he sought, he tended to advance attacks and blame, and when he won he sounded vindicated. At the root of all the economic ills, Reagan identified the federal government. Accordingly, economic rhetoric reduced complex problems to a simplified drama whereby the virtuous people fought a bad government.

Though the issues covered were predominantly economic, his economic rhetoric was often sermonic and ceremonial, simple in its praise, blame, discussion of problems, and their causes and solutions. The discourse was often reductionist, lending itself to metaphorical developments, and thematically appealing to traditional values of restoration, courage, and hope. Reagan spared his national audience many details and specifics that often revealed policies different than those publicly advocated.

The description and analysis of Reagan's economic rhetoric reveals some significant shifts during the second term. As in his first term, Reagan emphasized the budget process as unacceptable, confused, and in need of an overhaul. This approach afforded Reagan the opportunity to continue attacking Congress without having to debate the merit of specific budgeted items. This rhetorical shift may have helped Reagan fend off attacks against him for cutting funds, however, it did not result in deficit reduction. The frequent argument for a constitutional amendment to limit government's spending did result in one measure of success: the Gramm-Rudman-Hollings bill, which put in principal a "lid" on how much the government could spend. Reagan did not succeed in getting the line-item veto he often requested. Even the Gramm-Rudman-Hollings bill, soon after its passing, was in jeopardy, as Congress and the White House could not agree on how to keep spending under control. Reagan also took the constitutional route in presenting a Bill of Economic Rights as a way to dramatize his concern for the nation's economic welfare. However, beyond its initial presentation and explanation, the bill did not resurface in his discourse.

Numerous legislative issues were a continuous attempt by Reagan to create fundamental changes affecting the nation's economic system. Reagan sought to change both the product as well as the process. However difficult an issue was politically, rhetorically, Reagan often identified a "villain" who stood for all that was undesirable, and in contrast, presented the administration's solution as the desirable one. During the second term in office, Reagan engaged in more extensive explanations of economic issues, often identifying causal relationships that narrowed down potential solutions. These explanations masked at times policy difficulties and sought to defend the Reagan administration from any blame.

Economists suggest that U.S. trade policy turned very protectionist during the Reagan presidency, primarily as the result of strong congressional pressure, yet the free trade rhetoric was the consistent message the administration sent.[79] A related policy shift that did not receive rhetorical treatment was the monetary measures the administration took to solving the budget and trade deficits. The decision to devalue the dollar against other currencies received no clear rhetorical expression. The significance of this interventionist approach lay in the greater role Reagan assigned to the government. Only in passing did Reagan's discourse acknowledge that government had some economic responsibilities. Concerned with criticism and the inconsistency such a shift may have caused, Reagan's major speeches were mute on the issue.

Reagan left the scene well liked by the American people. As Roderick P. Hart states, presidents create a scene that itself argues in behalf of the president's argument.[80] Reagan mastered this practice with scenes that were primarily metaphorical, laced with strong values that depicted America as an economic entity and the people as economic beings. Reagan remained an outsider to the Washington scene, close to the people and serving as their advocate against the impersonal bureaucracy. His economic rhetoric was reflective of his personal approach to political issues and his antagonism toward the government.

Reagan's economic rhetoric during his final four years dwelled on the success and argued for more while underlying problems were often minimized and even ignored. Though Reagan remained optimistic, he had to counter the growing perception that America was losing its competitive edge. The budget deficit, increased foreign investment in the United States, and the U.S. becoming the largest debtor nation could not be ignored but neither could they be solved by rhetorical means alone. Reagan tried to minimize this perception, reaffirming Americans' belief in their ability to compete, and reassuring them of a better future.

NOTES

1. See *Congressional Quarterly Almanac 1985* (Washington, D.C.: Congressional Quarterly, 1986), 14.

2. All references to this speech are from U.S., President, *Weekly Compilation of Presidential Documents* (Washington, D.C.: U.S. Government Printing, 1985), Ronald Reagan (January 21, 1985), 67–70. Hereafter, *Weekly Compilation*.

3. See Richard E. Crable and Steven L. Vibbert, "Argumentative Stance and Political Faith Healing: 'The Dream Will Come True,' " *Quarterly Journal of Speech* 69 (1983): 290–301.

4. All references to this speech are from Reagan, *Weekly Compilation* (February 2, 1985), 117–18.

5. All references to this speech are from Reagan, *Weekly Compilation* (February 6, 1985), 140–46.

6. As quoted in Daniel J. Mitchell, "Stemming the Flow of Red Ink: How to Stop the Federal Spending Crisis," in *An American Vision: Policies for the '90s*, ed. Edward H. Crane and David Boaz (Washington, D.C.: The Cato Institute, 1989), 32.

7. All references to this speech are from Reagan, *Weekly Compilation* (April 24, 1985), 511–16; See Ellen Reid Gold, "Ronald Reagan and the Oral Tradition," *Central States Speech Journal* 39 (1988): 168.

8. See Walter R. Fisher, "Romantic Democracy, Ronald Reagan, and Presidential Heroes," *Western Journal of Speech Communication* 46 (1982): 303.

9. All references to this speech are from Reagan, *Weekly Compilation* (May 28, 1985), 703–7.

10. Reagan, *Weekly Compilation* (May 25, 1985), 695.

11. Paul E. Peterson and Mark Rom, "Lower Taxes, More Spending, and Budget Deficits," in *The Reagan Legacy*, ed. Charles O. Jones (Chatham: Chatham House, 1988), 226.

12. Reagan, *Weekly Compilation* (June 1, 1985), 731.

13. All references to this speech are from Reagan, *Weekly Compilation* (August 3, 1985), 959–60.

14. Reagan, *Weekly Compilation* (December 14, 1985), 1501.

15. Reagan, *Weekly Compilation* (December 21, 1985), 1523.

16. All references to this speech are from Reagan, *Weekly Compilation* (June 22, 1985), 838–39.

17. All references to this speech are from Reagan, *Weekly Compilation* (July 6, 1985), 875–76.

18. Reagan, *Weekly Compilation* (July 20, 1985), 923.

19. All references to this speech are from Reagan, *Weekly Compilation* (October 5, 1985), 1201–03.

20. All references to this speech are from Reagan, *Weekly Compilation* (December 21, 1985), 1522–23.

21. Reagan, *Weekly Compilation* (August 17, 1985), 989–90.

22. All references to this speech are from Reagan, *Weekly Compilation* (September 14, 1985), 1087–88.

23. Reagan, *Weekly Compilation* (December 7, 1985), 1471–72. On December 23, 1985, the administration signed the Farm Credit Amendment Act of 1985, which ensured a steady supply of credit to farmers to guarantee the safety and soundness of the system. See U.S. President, *Public Papers of the Presidents of the United States* (Washington, D.C.: U.S. Government Printing Office, 1985), Ronald Reagan (December 23, 1985), 1498. Hereafter, *Public Papers*.

24. All references to this speech are from Reagan, *Weekly Compilation* (August 31, 1985), 1025–26.

25. Reagan, *Weekly Compilation* (September 7, 1985), 1047–48.

26. The "weekly currency" policy was spelled out in the Plaza Agreement, which stated that "further orderly appreciation of the nondollar currencies against the dollar is desirable." In plain English, this statement called for devaluing the dollar against other currencies. The play on words is interesting since the key term in the statement is "appreciation," a rather positive and innocuous term for what in essence is depreciation. See Jerry L. Jordan, "Weakening the Dollar: The Tax No One Has to Vote For," in *Assessing the Reagan Years*, ed. David Boaz (Washington, D.C.: The Cato Institute, 1988), 182–83; Poole suggests that during the 1986 State of the Union Address, Reagan referred to the need to have a stable dollar at home and reliable exchange rates around the world, and that with this statement the Reagan administration began coordinating economic and monetary policy with U.S. trading partners. See William Poole, "Monetary Policy: Monetarism to Fine-tuning," in *Assessing the Reagan Years*, 169.

27. For detailed description of the Tax Reform Act of 1986 see *Congressional Quarterly Almanac 1986* (Washington, D.C.: Congressional Quarterly, 1987), 494–504.

28. All references to this speech are from Reagan, *Weekly Compilation* (February 4, 1986), 135–40.

29. See, Poole, "Monetary Policy: Monetarism To Fine-Tuning," 169.

30. All references to this speech are from Reagan, *Weekly Compilation* (February 8, 1986), 195–96.

31. Reagan, *Public Papers*, (July 7, 1986), 927.

32. All references to this speech are from Reagan, *Weekly Compilation* (September 27, 1986), 1287–88.

33. Reagan, *Weekly Compilation* (November 8, 1986), 1549.

34. Reagan, *Weekly Compilation* (January 3, 1987), 3.

35. All references to this speech are from Reagan, *Weekly Compilation* (May 10, 1986), 609–10.

36. All references to this speech are from Reagan, *Weekly Compilation* (July 26, 1986), 1005–06.

37. All references to this speech are from Reagan, *Weekly Compilation* (August 23, 1986), 1121–23.

38. Reagan, *Weekly Compilation* (October 25, 1986), 1454.

39. All references to this speech are from Reagan, *Weekly Compilation* (December 27, 1986), 1673–74.

40. Reagan, *Weekly Compilation* (January 3, 1987), 2.

41. All references to this speech are from Reagan, *Weekly Compilation* (January 27, 1987), 59–65.

42. See Peterson and Rom, "Lower Taxes, More Spending, and Budget Deficits," 224–26.

43. All references to this speech are from Reagan, *Weekly Compilation* (February 7, 1987), 123–24.

44. Reagan, *Weekly Compilation* (August 1, 1987), 894.

45. Reagan, *Weekly Compilation* (February 21, 1987), 181.

46. Reagan, *Weekly Compilation* (May 16, 1987), 541.

47. Reagan, *Weekly Compilation* (June 13, 1987), 666.

48. Reagan, *Weekly Compilation* (June 15, 1987) 675.

49. All references to this speech are from Reagan, *Weekly Compilation* (July 11, 1987), 799–80.

50. All references to this speech are from Reagan, *Weekly Compilation* (February 28, 1987), 199–200.

51. All references to this speech are from Reagan, *Weekly Compilation* (March 21, 1987), 289–90.

52. Reagan, *Weekly Compilation* (May 2, 1987), 469.

53. Reagan, *Weekly Compilation* (May 23, 1987), 578.

54. All references to this speech are from Reagan, *Weekly Compilation* (June 20, 1987), 716–17.

55. All references to this speech are from Reagan, *Weekly Compilation* (July 3, 1987), 768–70.

56. See Elton Rayack, *Not So Free to Choose: The Political Economy of Milton Friedman and Ronald Reagan* (New York: Praeger, 1987), 9–10, 78.

57. Reagan, *Weekly Compilation*, (July 4, 1987), 775.

58. All references to this speech are from Reagan, *Weekly Compilation* (September 26, 1987), 1077–78.

59. Reagan, *Weekly Compilation* (October 24, 1987), 1227.

60. Reagan, *Weekly Compilation* (October 31, 1987), 1258.

61. All references to this speech are from Reagan, *Weekly Compilation* (January 25, 1988), 85–91.

62. All references to this speech are from Reagan, *Weekly Compilation* (March 12, 1988), 335–36.

63. Reagan, *Public Papers* (March 11, 1988), 323.

64. Reagan, *Weekly Compilation* (March 26, 1988), 405–6.

65. Reagan, *Weekly Compilation* (April 9, 1988), 444–45.

66. All references to this speech are from Reagan, *Weekly Compilation* (April 23, 1988), 525–26.

67. All references to this speech are from Reagan, *Weekly Compilation* (May 14, 1988), 617–18.

68. All references to this speech are from Reagan, *Weekly Compilation* (November 26, 1988), 1568–69.

69. All references to this speech are from Reagan, *Weekly Compilation* (February 20, 1988), 237–38.

70. All references to this speech are from Reagan, *Weekly Compilation* (October 1, 1988), 1246–47.

71. Reagan, *Weekly Compilation* (December 17, 1988), 1643.

72. All references to this speech are from Reagan, *Weekly Compilation* (April 9, 1988), 444–45.

73. Reagan, *Weekly Compilation* (July 16, 1988), 945.

74. All references to this speech are from Reagan, *Weekly Compilation* (August 13, 1988), 1055–56.

75. All references to this speech are from Reagan, *Weekly Compilation* (October 15, 1988), 1325–26.

76. Gold, "Ronald Reagan and the Oral Tradition," 170.

77. All references to this speech are from Reagan, *Weekly Compilation* (January 11, 1989), 53–57.

78. Amos Kiewe and Davis W. Houck, "The Rhetoric of Reaganomics: A Redemptive Vision," *Communication Studies* 40 (1989): 107.

79. See William A. Niskanen, "U.S. Trade Policy: Problems and Prospect," in *An American Vision*, ed. Edward H. Crane and David Boaz (Washington, D.C.: The Cato Institute, 1989), 55.

80. Roderick P. Hart, *The Sound of Leadership* (Chicago: University of Chicago Press, 1987), 131.

Chapter Seven

The Reagan Legacy

Edwin Black contends that the association between stylistic tokens and one's ideology is hardly coincidental or arbitrary but rather points to a strong link between style and outlook.[1] The Reagan style and outlook, though varied over 38 years, attests to Black's contention. Ronald Reagan's political outlook was conditioned largely by his economic viewpoint. His economic rhetoric sprung not from any existing ideological foundation but rather from a personal ideology based largely on a set of principles coupled with a pragmatic and a common-sense approach to contemporary problems. Whether the issue was the spread of communism, welfare reform, the environment, social unrest, or the nation's security, Reagan positioned these and other issues in an economic context. In like manner, individualism was defined as the freedom to enjoy the fruits of one's labor while the nation's security was contingent on economic supremacy and free trade.

Reagan "brought home" issues of national and international concern by associating their impact on issues the average citizen was daily occupied with, namely, work and earning power. Taxes, employment, welfare, trade, the budget deficit and government's role in the economy comprised the list of economic issues governments usually must deal with. Reagan understood the people's concern with these basic issues and consistently incorporated them in his public discourse. Reagan added a rhetorical twist to these issues by wrapping them around the metaphors of freedom, enterprise, choice, individualism, pride, national heritage, and a vision for a glorious future.

To this day and into the foreseeable future, the merits of Reaganomics have been and will continue to stir controversy among economists and laypersons alike. It is noteworthy to observe if with hindsight the Reagan administration did achieve its initial goals. The Reagan administration was successful in lowering the rate of inflation and unemployment. However, while the rate of inflation dropped drastically in 1981, the nation endured a painful recession. The administration also was successful in cutting tax rates in 1981 and 1986 though taxes did increase in 1982, 1983, 1984, and 1987. The Reagan administration's objective of reducing government regulation had seen some successful showcase undertakings (de-monopolizing of AT&T, dismissing air traffic controllers), yet the bureaucracy bloated rather than decreased.

The Reagan administration was successful in securing an increase in the defense budget that had been scaled back drastically during the Carter administration. However, one of the fundamental economic objectives that the Reagan administration did not achieve was balancing the federal budget. In fact, the federal deficit has swelled to immense proportions partially due to the decrease in tax revenues. Though he was unable to solve all economic problems, Reagan offered a reasonable diagnosis of what was wrong with the economy.[2]

While President Reagan presented the nation's economy as improving people's conditions, facts also pointed at a regression and declining economic strength. (By 1989, income distribution between rich and poor was back to the level it was in 1947).[3] The assumption behind the "supply-side" approach Reagan advocated did not materialize, as the supply of goods and services did not result in the anticipated increased consumption, new markets, and new prosperity.[4] Reagan offered a vision that represented the American heritage, yet, Reaganomics may prove just a phase in stopping the growth of government.[5]

We will leave, however, this debate concerning the relative costs and benefits of Reaganomics to others more qualified in the fields of public policy and economics. Our concern has been with the persuasive nature of Reagan's economic rhetoric, its roots, progression, principles, strategies, and situational factors.

Reagan's presidential persona, a source of fascination for many, developed over 40 years in public view. By covering four decades of economic rhetoric, we attempted to present the development of Reagan's economic rhetoric from inception to the final moments of his presidency. Accounting for Reagan's lifelong pursuit of addressing economic issues has led us to several observations regarding his pre-presidential and presidential economic rhetoric, as well as comments covering Reagan's economic discourse in general.

PRE-PRESIDENTIAL ECONOMIC RHETORIC

Reagan's initial involvement with economic issues was limited to tax policies and their "unfair" impact on the movie industry. Out of this well-focused issue, Reagan developed an economic program that would carry him all the way to the presidency. The principle argument in Reagan's early involvement with political and economic concerns was free enterprise. Yet this guiding principle with its focus on taxes and government's unnecessary intrusion, couched in moralistic language, was often infused with conspiratorial reasoning.

During the 1950s and early 1960s, Reagan associated the issues of government spending and taxes with themes of a socialist and communist conspiracy as his economic rhetoric was situated in the red scare mentality, thus fully capitalizing on public sentiment. Reagan's economic rhetoric was apocalyptic with the conspiracy theme used exclusively as a fear appeal. Against this development, Reagan's solutions were highly moralistic and principled, often incorporating war metaphors and strong religious themes. His anti-government arguments and constant accusations against liberals for causing the economic apocalypse characterized Reagan's early economic rhetoric as negative. The frequent simplification of good vs. evil and the framing of complex issues in such a way that only Reagan's solutions were the sensible ones would prove beneficial in later years.

Thus against the "immorality" of high taxation on actors and actresses, Reagan offered the alternative of proportional taxation, warranted on the biblical notion of tithing. Reagan added to the morality issue a conspiratorial slant. In front of partisan gatherings, Reagan delivered the right-wing version of "The Speech," accusing liberals of purposefully planning the overthrow of the United States. The proof of this end was manifested economically ("foot-in-the-door" legislation). In the moderate version of "The Speech," designed to distance himself from the extremist label, Reagan implied an impending communist takeover only because of the ineptitude of the federal government—not purposeful like the right-wing version.

Less government, the all-encompassing master metaphor Reagan developed during his pre-gubernatorial speeches, was further shaped during his gubernatorial years. Beneath the less-government principle, Reagan incorporated specific principles including tax rebates, reforms, and cuts; welfare reform; and spending cuts. This rather limited list of economic issues all springing from a root metaphor, the appeal of simplified issues, and hence simplified discourse, proved to serve Reagan well throughout his political life.

During Reagan's first term as governor, after failing to appreciate the give and take of politics and hence his highly partisan rhetoric, a more pragmatic persona emerged due primarily to his unpopular ideological persona. Reagan championed spending increases in mental health, education, and welfare payments to the truly needy, yet still tried to project the image of a fiscal conservative. Reagan also developed during this period the strategy of emphasizing the role of the people if the state were to prosper, thus removing himself from ultimate responsibility. Reagan also extensively scapegoated others for various economic ills, further removing himself from responsibility.

Reagan's second term as governor proved more successful than the first term. Reagan became more skilled politically primarily by realizing the need to compromise. He was successful at getting some of his legislation passed despite a Democratic majority in both houses. Yet Reagan lost on Proposition 1, not without returning to his more extreme and apocalyptic rhetoric as defeat grew imminent. Reagan's rhetoric showed his lack of faith in the people as well as him blaming Democrats for a conspiracy by subverting Proposition 1. At one point Reagan even dismissed his Creative Society as the ideal solution.

Free enterprise and supply-side logic were evident in much of Reagan's discourse. Trying to cut taxes yet increasing government revenues was Reagan's guiding principle. His notion of a vertically structured society also hinted that free enterprise meant inequality in income.

Reagan was undeterred in publicly stating that state government did not have sufficient funds for all programs. Neither was he politically inhibited to publicly announce cuts in funding to programs such as tuition or to increase progressive taxes. When the situation required a change of policy, Reagan did not hesitate to make an about face and announce a compromise or even acceptance of developments he disagreed with. Reagan the pragmatic politician often accommodated Reagan the ideologue, resulting in a practical approach to economic issues. At times, Reagan was even proud of showing his practical side and his willingness to compromise principles for the sake of a common good. Thus when he faced inconsistencies such as arguing against taxes yet raising them or arguing against government involvement in welfare, yet suggesting taxing inheritance, Reagan's rationalization had the public good transcending selfish interests. Governor Reagan developed a keen insight into how to rationalize policy decisions with discourse that overcame narrowly structured issues to appear beneficial to the common good.

Overall, economic issues during the governorship period were of a specific sort and called for discourse addressed to more specific constituencies. Reagan's rhetoric, in this context, often sounded extreme, harsh, and riskier than the discourse addressed to a national audience. This discourse rarely incorporated heroes and visions. Neither did Reagan develop speeches around distinct themes. On the contrary, his speech was usually specific and direct.

Reagan's presidential campaign speeches were primarily a modified version of his governorship speeches. Given the national audience, Reagan tamed somewhat his more extreme rhetoric but kept intact his principles. Though the anti-government rhetoric remained familiar, Reagan introduced the features of trust and hope into his economic discourse embodied in the values of faith, family, neighborhood, work, and freedom. This inventional variation was a precursor to the full blown visionary and optimistic rhetoric of his presidency.

Reagan's initial campaign rhetoric proved counterproductive. His 1975 federalism speech, advocating more say and autonomy in the hands of state and local governments was severely attacked. Consequently, Reagan sought in 1976 to compensate for "The $90 Billion Speech." As the campaign went on, Reagan's defensive discourse turned more offensive, attacking Gerald Ford's economic policies. When defeat became apparent, Reagan turned away from specific issues to discussing values.

Though the federalism issue of the 1976 campaign was not repeated in the 1980 campaign, Reagan did not change his basic convictions but rather modified them to appear more appealing. For the sake of attracting more Democratic votes and further distancing himself from the extreme conservative label, Reagan's economic rhetoric was structured around the fulfillment of his earlier predictions. The strategy of pointing at the unmanageability of the Washington bureaucracy, slow growth, high inflation, budget deficits, and high taxes, issues he had raised time and again, helped Reagan in presenting his policies as the better choice. Reagan modified his earlier anti–Social Security stand, proposing a voluntary approach, appealing to women and the working class, thus expanding the traditional Republican constituency.

Reagan repeatedly compensated for the pro-wealthy bias of supply-side tax cuts by emphasizing that they would benefit the lower- and middle-income classes the most. In this way Reagan did not break from his conservative constituency while at the same time he included the more traditional Democratic constituency in his economic planning. Reagan also suggested that Jimmy Carter was guilty of a conspiracy that was purposefully designed to ruin the economy. Reagan thus resumed some of his early extreme rhetoric. The contrasting effect of the optimistic Republican candidate and the gloom and doom Democratic one further crystalized the choice the voters were going to make.

Through trial and error, Reagan learned the lesson of carefully adjusting ideas to audiences. He began his political life warning of an imminent danger to the political system and was now ready to head the government he frequently criticized. One of the most distinct features of Reagan's discourse during almost 30 years of addressing political issues was the gradual moderation of his discourse. Reagan learned the need to compromise, to appease, to scapegoat, and to placate. Yet, during climatic situations, Reagan's more extreme rhetoric would surface, representing his true character.

PRESIDENTIAL ECONOMIC RHETORIC

Reagan entered the White House experienced and confident. He had learned from his earlier mistakes, and he was ready to implement his economic policies, using cautious and consistent discourse. As Barbara Kellerman has noted, "Ronald Reagan was able to get what he wanted when he wanted it because of the nature of the times and the opposition, but also because he did many things right."[6] Reagan, claims Kellerman, avoided the hard sell, and his speeches were firm but not abrasive, persuasive but not to the point of being hostile. Reagan had the ultimate marketing personality.[7]

Reagan's popular appeal was not indicative solely of his abilities to communicate effectively with the people but also by the fear the opposition had in opposing him. Reagan often used threats when the opposition disagreed with his plans, knowing that his initial success and popularity could turn the people against Congress. Reagan's most pervasive rhetorical objective was to reach the people and he did so above Congress's head. Despite the hardships of the recession and temporary loss of popularity, Reagan was well liked because his rhetoric had a popular appeal to it. During bad times, people need to be comforted as they seek to know that not all is lost, that things will get better. Optimism and hope are the essential ingredients of any religion. Reagan understood human nature and gave the people the secular sermon many needed to hear.

Reagan embarked on the presidency by introducing the theme of a New Beginning to signify a radical change from existing political notions and practices. In consistently pushing his less-government principle, Reagan sought to reform the tax system and Social Security, as well as making drastic reductions in government spending. Reagan was successful during the first term in halting the growth of government in nondefense spending and in passing the radical tax reforms of 1981. However, the strong objections of many Social Security recipients to any cuts resulted in a policy shift whereby the planned reform had to be eliminated and even denied. Reagan also shifted his less taxes policy a year after passing the largest tax reduction in the nation's history. A larger than predicted budget deficit in 1982 brought Reagan to ask for significantly increased revenues.

Of unique interest is the recession of 1981–1982, which caused Reagan enormous discomfort. Reagan's discourse was uplifting and confident (never admitting failure). Reagan did not risk major rhetorical shifts during this period, preferring instead to maintain the role of optimistic president who, in the face of difficult times, had to be perceived as confident and assured. The Carter experience may have taught Reagan the danger of rhetorical shifts that depress rather than assure. Reagan realized the presidential role of taking the nation beyond the here-and-now by projecting optimism and future prosperity. With hindsight, Reagan's rhetorical choice proved successful as his post-recession rhetoric was not only optimistic but also redemptive of overcoming an economic downturn.

During his second term, Reagan reintroduced the theme of a radical change, this time, however, the goal was more limited but significant nonetheless. The Second American Revolution ushered the most radical overhaul of the tax system, the Tax Reform Act of 1986. Reagan also got the legislation that put a limit on federal spending but was unsuccessful in passing a constitutional amendment to balance the budget. Welfare reform in the form of a work requirement on the part of welfare recipients and a major trade bill concluded Reagan's economic agenda. Yet despite the many successes, the Tax Reform Act of 1986 did not result in higher revenues; rather, just as in 1981–82, it contributed to the more than $1 trillion debt accumulated during the Reagan years.

Despite midstream changes and inconsistencies on issues such as cutting tax rates but increasing revenues or calling for limiting federal help to farmers yet helping them during the farm crisis, Reagan attempted to appear rhetorically consistent and principled. By incorporating metaphors such as "fairness," the "truly needy," "restoration," and "renewal," Reagan appealed to most Americans but especially to blue-collar Americans, the poor, and farmers, not always among the Republican constituency. These metaphors were used not just as simple points of reference and identification but also as strategic definitions that advanced Reagan's agenda. The metaphors were present, even necessary, in order to compensate for the lack of substantive progress. By speaking about the spirit of renewal, restoration, and projecting a glorified vision, Reagan used the cherished past to mold confidence in the future. High interest rates, taxes, and unemployment could be mitigated by transcending the past into the future. To complement this rhetorical approach, Reagan also used moralistic discourse to ground important economic objectives such as cutting tax rates, reducing spending, or reforming social programs.

Reagan's story-telling character was based on a metaphorical linkage between the familiar and the unfamiliar. By using his "less government" master metaphor, Reagan was able to transcend the problems in the situation by associating contemporary experience with people's cherished values and traditions. This master metaphor allowed Reagan to comfortably use other attractive metaphors such as "Founding Fathers," "new beginning," and "second revolution." The presidential speech consistently promised hope and optimism provided the people accepted his economic proposals. The presidential economic rhetoric portrayed a rosy picture far beyond what the situation merited and was frequently characterized by both its redemptive and visionary themes.

The presidential economic rhetoric was overall cohesive, consistent, optimistic, reassuring, and cautious. This is not to say that economic indicators were as consistent, optimistic, and reassuring as the rhetor depicted them to be. In the face of policy shifts, such as raising taxes or devaluing the dollar, Reagan remained literally aloof and even silent. Consistency was Reagan's major concern as he arduously kept the image of a principled president.

Whereas economic issues in California were of a specific sort, the economy took an expected national flavor, thus less specific for Reagan as president. Reagan also presented the more consistent ideological persona and minimized his pragmatic political persona. Reagan was a strategic speaker who was conscious of his rhetorical continuity. He often previewed his important speeches and later reiterated their main points. He skillfully integrated minor speeches with major ones to keep his agenda in public view as well as building a long relationship with the American people. If he had to appear more forthcoming, Reagan would do so primarily in his radio addresses where exposure and reaction were usually limited.

FOUR DECADES OF ECONOMIC RHETORIC

Ronald Reagan was a rhetorical phenomenon in American politics. His predilection to assume that with effective discourse he could achieve most if not all of his economic plans gave rise to rhetoric rich with conditional promises, not all of which were politically feasible. Reagan's uniqueness rests not on his ability to resort to the rhetoric politicians are expected to use, but rather that he usually captured the correct sentiments of the moment, be it fear of communism or despair in the face of malaise, to projecting hope and dreams during a recession.

With a rather simple set of economic principles, Reagan forged political ideas that proved appealing. His anti-government campaign was the beginning and the end of his political philosophy. The issues he was concerned with never changed throughout his "political" life. The programmatic rhetorical skeleton Reagan employed remained by and large consistent. His narrative consisted of a balancing act between the past, present, and future, serving to forge a dramatic course, to warn of danger, to cherish the past, or to lament of its absent values in the present. His frequent metaphors of a ship at sea, road/path, war, and medicine were used dialectically to either warn of danger or to project hope and confidence.

The story-telling character of Reagan's discourse was a natural result of his affinity with simplified discourse and his ability to reduce complex economic issues to story-like features with the customary villain and hero depiction. Organizing his rhetoric around the dichotomies of "good" and "bad," "fair" and "unfair," "hero" and "villain"—the stuff that good stories are made of—came naturally to Reagan. Accordingly, major economic problems were given simple solutions most people could identify with. Values and morals were frequently identified as the rationale for advancing economic principles. Reagan's ideology was essentially a set of principles embedded in his moralistic, practical, and pedagogical outlook on life.

Though scholars and journalists have commented on Reagan's skill at empowering the people, we feel that Reagan created the perception of empowering the people. Reagan put much, if not most, of the responsibility in improving economic conditions on the people's acceptance or rejection of his proposed policies. However, in this so-called empowering game, Reagan actually empowered himself by distancing his persona from disaster and setbacks, yet never minded attributing success to the people. This aspect is consistent with the fact that in both his pre-presidential and presidential speeches, Reagan never took blame but was quick to take credit or give tribute to the people. The scene/agent ratio was the strategy Reagan used to conditioning success or failure on the larger scene (the public, Congress, the other party, the other candidate, etc.). Put differently, Reagan created a rhetorical scene that included in it the people, their representatives, and the government whereas Reagan himself was never part of the scene, but rather an outsider who offered to make changes for the good of the people. Reagan skillfully structured his discourse around this scene/agent ratio whereby the scene was to be modified if the agent and his message were to be accepted.

The most distinct feature of his rhetorical transformation was Reagan's gradual leaning toward more generalized discourse. The presidential discourse, in particular, was distinctly generalized, even vague on key economic issues. The populist theme in his discourse often masked disturbing details and deflected troubling news. This development raises an ethical question. Should the people be satisfied with generalized discourse uttered by the president or should they demand the chief executive present more accurate and informative speech? In the age of instant media coverage, the abundance of presidential images, and immediacy of experience, presidential speech in particular is disappointingly generalized, simplified, and watered down in an effort to maximize impact and minimize damage. The rhetorical treatment of image is clearly achieved at the expense of more informative and educational speech.

Throughout his political life, during his extremist period to the end of his eight years in the White House, through the "thousand years of darkness" vision to the "Shining City on a Hill" vision, Reagan's rhetoric always kept a promise to improve, to build, to correct, and to do better. Reagan told his numerous audiences they would have more and enjoy more if certain conditions were to be met. Reagan appealed to the people by tailoring his economic rhetoric to public sentiments regarding inflation, taxation, employment, individualism, and freedom. Reagan also kept constant his main economic principles of lowering taxes, increasing growth, and limiting government involvement in people's lives. The result of this cojoining of viewpoint and expression resulted, in part, in Reagan's successful speech making. Reagan's consistent advocacy and promises coupled with signs of real economic growth gave the nation the confidence needed in a free market society, while growing economic problems were deemphasized and even ignored. Clearly, more informative speech would have been beneficial in the long run, and with hindsight perhaps even advantageous to the Bush administration, which found itself caught in the rhetorical trap of the Reagan administration.

Reagan's popular appeal, to the extent that people prefer to hear of less taxes, less inflation, and more growth, was compatible with his economic programs and thus he possessed the formula for political success. Reagan may have been an ideologue, but he was also a practical politician, skilled in adjusting his ideas to people. The seeming flip-flop on issues of principle ought not to be narrowed down to an aspect of mere expediency. Reagan's compromises, political shifts, and accommodating discourse were the mark of an adept politician who understood the limits of his ideology and the need in the political arena to find a more pragmatic course of action.

The longest peacetime economic expansion in American history (1983–1990) must not be limited to Reagan's economic policies but can be partially attributed to his rhetoric of optimism and vision. The interdependency between productivity, investment, and revenue, and any ensuing policies thereof, are insufficient in maintaining a certain economic performance. Optimism, confidence, and vision are necessary ingredients of economic performance as well. After many experiences in addressing economic issues, Reagan appreciated the role of intangibles in the nation's economy and consequently developed a knack for an economic rhetoric that was unique in its simplicity yet powerful in its appeal. The "invisible hand" may very well be rhetorically shaped.

NOTES

1. Edwin Black, "The Second Persona," *Quarterly Journal of Speech* 56 (1970): 109–19.

2. Isabel V. Sawhill and Charles F. Stone, "The Economy," in *The Reagan*

Record: An Assessment of America's Changing Domestic Priorities, ed. John L. Palmer and Isabel V. Sawhill (Cambridge: Ballinger, 1984), 71.

3. Richard Reeves, "Reagan's Legacy: Rich Gained, Poor Lost," *The Philadelphia Inquirer* (September 1, 1990), A7.

4. Ibid.

5. William A. Niskanen, *Reaganomics: An Insider's Account of the Policies and the People* (New York: Oxford University Press, 1988), 333.

6. Barbara Kellerman, *The Political Presidency: Practice of Leadership* (New York: Oxford University Press, 1984), 245.

7. Ibid., 249–50.

Selected Bibliography

Ackerman, Frank. *Reaganomics: Rhetoric vs. Reality*. Boston: South End Press, 1982.

Aden, Roger C. "Entrapment and Escape: Inventional Metaphors in Ronald Reagan's Economic Rhetoric." *Southern Speech Communication Journal* 54 (1989):384–400.

Arnold, Carroll C. *Criticism of Oral Rhetoric*. Columbus: Charles E. Merrill, 1974.

Balitzer, Alfred A., ed. *A Time for Choosing: The Speeches of Ronald Reagan, 1961–1982*. Chicago: Regnery Gateway, 1983.

Berthold, Carole A. "Kenneth Burke's Cluster-Agon Method: Its Development and an Application." *Central States Speech Journal* 27 (1976):302–9.

Birdsell, David S. "Ronald Reagan on Lebanon and Grenada: Flexibility and Interpretation in the Application of Kenneth Burke's Pentad." *Quarterly Journal of Speech* 73 (1987):267–79.

Bitzer, Lloyd F. "The Rhetorical Situation." *Philosophy and Rhetoric* 1 (1968):1–14.

Black, Edwin. "The Second Persona." *Quarterly Journal of Speech* 56 (1970): 109–19.

———. *Rhetorical Criticism: A Study in Method*. New York: Macmillan, 1965.

Blair, Carole. "From 'All the President's Men' to Every Man for Himself: The Strategies of Post-Watergate Apologia." *Central States Speech Journal* 35 (1984):250–60.

Blankenship, Jane, Marlene G. Fine, and Leslie K. Davis. "The 1980 Republican Primary Debates: The Transformation of Actor to Scene." *Quarterly Journal of Speech* 69 (1983):25–36.

Boaz, David. ed. *Assessing the Reagan Years*. Washington, D.C.: The Cato Institute, 1988.

Bormann, Ernest G. "A Fantasy Theme Analysis of the Television Coverage of the Hostage Release and the Reagan Inaugural." *Quarterly Journal of Speech* 68 (1982):133–45.

Boyarsky, Bill. *Ronald Reagan, His Life and Rise to the Presidency*. New York: Random House, 1981.

Brock, Bernard, and Robert L. Scott. "An Introduction to Rhetorical Criticism." In *Methods of Rhetorical Criticism: A Twentieth-Century Perspective*, ed. Bernard L. Brock and Robert L. Scott, 2d ed., rev. Detroit: Wayne State University Press, 1980.

Burke, Kenneth. *Permanence and Change*. 3d ed. Berkeley: University of California Press, 1984.

———. *The Philosophy of Literary Form*. 3d ed. Berkeley: University of California Press, 1973.

———. *The Rhetoric of Religion*. Berkeley: University of California Press, 1970.

———. *A Rhetoric of Motives*. Berkeley: University of California Press, 1969.

California Journal 5. (November 1974).

California Journal 5. (August 1974).

California Journal 5. (February 1974).

California Journal 4. (September 1973).

California Journal 4. (August 1973).

California Journal 4. (February 1973).

California Journal 3. (June–July 1972).

California Journal 3. (May 1972).

California Journal 2. (December 1971).

California Journal 2. (July–August 1971).

California Journal 2. (June 1971).

California Journal 2. (May 1971).

California Journal 2. (February 1971).

Campbell, Karlyn Kohrs. *The Rhetorical Act*. Belmont, CA: Wadsworth, 1982.

Campbell, Karlyn Kohrs, and Kathleen Hall Jamieson. "Inaugurating the Presidency." *Presidential Studies Quarterly* 15 (1985):394–411.

Cannon, Lou. *Reagan*. New York: G.P. Putnam's Sons, 1982.

———. "The Reagan Years." *California Journal* 5 (November 1974):360–66.

———. *Ronnie and Jessie: A Political Odyssey*. New York: Doubleday, 1969.

Congressional Quarterly Almanac 1988. Washington, D.C.: Congressional Quarterly, 1989.

Congressional Quarterly Almanac 1987. Washington, D.C.: Congressional Quarterly, 1988.

Congressional Quarterly Almanac 1986. Washington, D.C.: Congressional Quarterly, 1987.

Congressional Quarterly Almanac 1985. Washington, D.C.: Congressional Quarterly, 1986.

Congressional Quarterly Almanac 1984. Washington, D.C.: Congressional Quarterly, 1985.

Congressional Quarterly Almanac 1983. Washington, D.C.: Congressional Quarterly, 1984.

Congressional Quarterly Almanac 1982. Washington, D.C.: Congressional Quarterly, 1983.

Congressional Quarterly Almanac 1981. Washington, D.C.: Congressional Quarterly, 1982.

Crable, Richard E., and Steven L. Vibbert. "Argumentative Stance and Political Faith Healing: 'The Dream Will Come True,' " *Quarterly Journal of Speech* 69(1983):290–301.

Crane, Edward H., and David Boaz, eds. *An American Vision: Policies for the '90s*. Washington, D.C.: The Cato Institute, 1989.

Denton, Robert E., Jr. *The Primetime Presidency of Ronald Reagan*. New York: Praeger, 1988.

Denton, Robert E., Jr., and Dan F. Hahn. *Presidential Communication*. New York: Praeger, 1986.

Dickinson, Gregory L. "Creating His Own Constraint: Ronald Reagan and the Iran-Contra Affair." Master's thesis, University of California, Davis, 1990.

Edwards, Anne. *Early Reagan*. New York: William Morrow, 1987.

Erickson, Paul D. *Reagan Speaks: The Making of an American Myth*. New York: New York University Press, 1985.

Fisher, Walter R. "Romantic Democracy, Ronald Reagan, and Presidential Heroes." *Western Journal of Speech Communication* 46 (1982):299–310.

———. "Rhetorical Fiction and the Presidency." *Quarterly Journal of Speech* 66(1980): 119–26.

Friedman, Milton. *Capitalism and Freedom*. Chicago: University of Chicago Press, 1982.

Gadamer, Hans-Georg. *Philosophical Hermeneutics*, trans. and ed. David E. Linge. Berkeley: University of California Press, 1976.

Galbraith, John Kenneth and Paul W. McCracken. *Reaganomics: Meaning, Means, and Ends*. New York: The Free Press, 1983.

Gold, Ellen Reid. "Ronald Reagan and the Oral Tradition." *Central States Speech Journal* 39 (1988): 159–76.

Golden, James L., Goodwin F. Berquist, William E. Coleman, eds. *The Rhetoric of Western Thought*. 3d ed. Dubuque: Kendall/Hunt, 1983.

Goldwater, Barry. *The Conscience of a Conservative*. Shepherdsville: Victor, 1960.

Goodnight, G. Thomas. "Ronald Reagan's Re-formulation of the Rhetoric of War: Analysis of the 'Zero Option,' 'Evil Empire,' and 'Star-Wars' Addresses." *Quarterly Journal of Speech* 72 (1986):390–414.

Greenstein, Fred I., ed. *Leadership in the Modern Presidency*. Cambridge: Harvard University Press, 1988.

Gurevitch, Michael, Tony Bennett, James Curran, and Janet Woollacott, eds. *Culture, society and the media*. London: Methuen, 1982.

Hankins, Sarah Russell. "Archetypal Alloy: Reagan's Rhetorical Image." *Central States Speech Journal* 34 (1983):33–43.

Hart, Roderick P. *Modern Rhetorical Criticism*. Glenview: Scott Foresman & Company, 1990.

———. *The Sound of Leadership*. Chicago: University of Chicago Press, 1987.

———. *Verbal Style and the Presidency*. Orlando: Academic Press, 1984.

Hoftstadter, Richard. *The Paranoid Style in American Politics and Other Essays*. Phoenix ed. Chicago: University of Chicago Press, 1979.

Hulten, Charles R., and Isabel V. Sawhill, eds. *The Legacy of Reaganomics: Prospects for Long-Term Growth*. Washington, D.C.: The Urban Institute, 1984.

Hyman, David N. *Public Finance: A Contemporary Application of Theory to Policy*. 2d ed. New York: Holt, Rinehart & Winston, 1987.

Ivie, Robert L. "Speaking 'Common Sense' about the Soviet Threat: Reagan's Rhetorical Stance." *Western Journal of Speech Communication* 48 (1984):39–50.

Jamieson, Kathleen Hall and Karlyn Kohrs Campbell. "Rhetorical Hybrids: Fusions of Generic Elements." *Quarterly Journal of Speech* 68 (1982): 146–57.

Johannesen, Richard L. "Ronald Reagan's Economic Jeremiad." *Central States Speech Journal* 37(1986):79–89.

Jones, Charles O., ed. *The Reagan Legacy*. Chatham: Chatham House, 1988.

Kellerman, Barbara. *The Political Presidency: Practice of Leadership*. New York: Oxford University Press, 1984.

Kernell, Samuel. *Going Public*. Washington, D.C.: Congressional Quarterly Press, 1986.

Kiewe, Amos, and Davis W. Houck. "The Rhetoric of Reaganomics: A Redemptive Vision." *Communication Studies* 40(1989):97–108.

Kimzey, Bruce W. *Reaganomics*. St. Paul: West, 1983.

Lammers, Nancy, ed. *Reagan: The Next Four Years*. Washington, D.C.: Congressional Quarterly, 1985.

Lekachman, Robert. *Visions and Nightmares: America After Reagan*. New York: Macmillan, 1987.

Lewis, William F. "Telling America's Story: Narrative Form and the Reagan Presidency." *Quarterly Journal of Speech* 73(1987):280–302.

Lowe, Carl, ed. "Reaganomics: The New Federalism," *The Reference Shelf* 55. New York: H. W. Wilson, 1984.

McCloskey, Donald N. *The Rhetoric of Economics*. Madison: University of Wisconsin Press, 1985.

McGee, Michael Calvin. "The 'Ideograph': A Link Between Rhetoric and Ideology." *Quarterly Journal of Speech* 66(1980):1–17.

Medhurst, Martin J. "Public Address and Significant Scholarship: Four Challenges to the Rhetorical Renaissance." In *Texts in Context: Critical Dialogues on Significant Episodes in American Political Rhetoric*, ed. Michael C. Leff and Fred J. Kauffeld. Davis: Hermagoras, 1989.

———. "Postponing the Social Agenda: Reagan's Strategy and Tactics." *Western Journal of Speech Communication* 48(1984):262–76.

Moore, Mark P. "Reagan's Quest for Freedom in the 1987 State of the Union Address." *Western Journal of Speech Communication* 53(1989):52–65.

Niskanen, William A. *Reaganomics: An Insider's Account of the Policies and the People*. New York: Oxford University Press, 1988.

Noonan, Peggy. *What I Saw at the Revolution*. New York: Random House, 1990.

Palmer, John L. and Isabel V. Sawhill, eds. *The Reagan Record: An Assessment of America's Changing Domestic Priorities*. Cambridge: Ballinger, 1984.

Perelman, Chaim, and L. Olbrechts-Tyteca. *The New Rhetoric: A Treatise on Argumentation*. Notre Dame: Notre Dame University Press, 1969.

Phelan, James. "Can Reagan Win California?" *The Saturday Evening Post*, 4 June 1966, 89–93.

Phifer, Gregg. "Two Inaugurals: A Second Look." *Southern Speech Communication Journal* 48(1983):378–85.

Preston, Thomas C., Jr. "Reagan's 'New Beginning': Is It the 'New Deal' of the Eighties?" *Southern Speech Communication Journal* 49 (1984):198–211.

Procter, David E. "The Rescue Mission: Assigning Guilt to a Chaotic Scene." *Western Journal of Speech Communication* 51 (1987):245–55.

Rayack, Elton. *Not So Free to Choose: The Political Economy of Milton Friedman and Ronald Reagan*. New York: Praeger, 1987.

Reagan, Ronald. *Speaking My Mind*. New York: Simon & Schuster, 1989.

———. Introduction by Richard M. Scaife. *Ronald Reagan Talks to America*. Old Greenwich: Devin Adair, 1983.

———. *The Creative Society*. New York: Devin Adair, 1968.

———. with Richard G. Hubler. *Where's the Rest of Me*? New York: Dell, Sloan and Pearce, 1964.

Reeves, Richard. "Reagan's Legacy: Rich Gained, Poor Lost." *The Philadelphia Inquirer*, 1 September 1990, A7.

———. *The Reagan Detour*. New York: Simon & Schuster, 1985.

Ritter, Kurt W. "Ronald Reagan and 'The Speech': The Rhetoric of Public Relations Politics." *Western Speech* 32 (1968):50–58.

Rogin, Michael P. *Ronald Reagan, The Movie*. Berkeley: University of California Press, 1987.

Rueckert, William H. *Kenneth Burke and the Drama of Human Relations*. 2d ed. Berkeley: University of California Press, 1982.

Rushing, Janice Hocker. "Ronald Reagan's 'Star Wars' Address: Mythic Containment of Technical Reasoning." *Quarterly Journal of Speech* 72 (1986):415–33.

Scheele, Henry Z. "Ronald Reagan's 1980 Acceptance Address: A Focus on American Values." *Western Journal of Speech Communication* 48 (1984):51–61.

Sidney, Hugh. "Ready to Play Power Poker." *Time* 15 November 1982, 21.

Simons, Herbert W., and Aram A. Aghazarian, eds. *Form, Genre, and the Study of Political Discourse*. Columbia: University of South Carolina Press, 1986.

Slade, Steve. "Ronald Reagan's Simple Answers." *Progressive* 40 (March 1976):18–21.

Stuckey, Mary E. *Getting Into the Game: The Pre-Presidential Rhetoric of Ronald Reagan*. New York: Praeger, 1989.

Thurow, Lester C. *The Zero-Sum Solution: Building a World-Class American Economy*. New York: Simon & Schuster, 1985.

Tulis, Jeffrey K. *The Rhetorical Presidency*. Princeton: Princeton University Press, 1987.

Weaver, Richard M. *The Ethics of Rhetoric*. Chicago: Regnery Gateway, 1953. Reprint. Davis: Hermagoras, 1985.

Welch, Robert. *The Blue Book of the John Birch Society*. Copyright by the author, 1961.

White, John K. *The New Politics of Old Values*. Hanover: University Press of New England, 1988.

Will, George. "The Economy of Leadership." *Newsweek*, 27 August 1984, 84.

Wills, Garry. *Reagan's America: Innocents At Home*. Garden City, N.Y.: Doubleday, 1987.

Windt, Theodore, and Beth Ingold, eds. *Essays in Presidential Rhetoric*. 2d ed. Dubuque: Kendall/Hunt, 1987.

Woodward, Gary C. "Reagan as Roosevelt: The Elasticity of Pseudo-Populist Appeals." *Central States Speech Journal* 34 (1983):44–58.

Zarefsky, David, Carol Miller-Tutzauer, and Frank E. Tutzauer. "Ronald Reagan's Safety Net for the Truly Needy: The Rhetorical Uses of Definition." *Central States Speech Journal* 35(1984):113–19.

PUBLIC ADDRESSES

U.S. President. *Weekly Compilation of Presidential Documents*. Washington, D.C.: U.S. Government Printing Office, 1989. Ronald Reagan, 1989.

U.S. President. *Weekly Compilation of Presidential Documents*. Washington, D.C.: U.S. Government Printing Office, 1988. Ronald Reagan, 1988.

U.S. President. *Weekly Compilation of Presidential Documents*. Washington, D.C.: U.S. Government Printing Office, 1987. Ronald Reagan, 1987.

U.S. President. *Weekly Compilation of Presidential Documents*. Washington, D.C.: U.S. Government Printing Office, 1986. Ronald Reagan, 1986.

U.S. President. *Weekly Compilation of Presidential Documents*. Washington, D.C.: U.S. Government Printing Office, 1985. Ronald Reagan, 1985.

U.S. President. *Weekly Compilation of Presidential Documents*. Washington, D.C.: U.S. Government Printing Office, 1984. Ronald Reagan, 1984.

U.S. President. *Weekly Compilation of Presidential Documents*. Washington, D.C.: U.S. Government Printing Office, 1983. Ronald Reagan, 1983.

U.S. President. *Weekly Compilation of Presidential Documents*. Washington, D.C.: U.S. Government Printing Office, 1982. Ronald Reagan, 1982.

U.S. President. *Weekly Compilation of Presidential Documents*. Washington, D.C.: U.S. Government Printing Office, 1981. Ronald Reagan, 1981.

U.S. President. *Public Papers of the Presidents of the United States*. Washington, D.C.: U.S. Government Printing Office, 1990. Ronald Reagan, 1988.

U.S. President. *Public Papers of the Presidents of the United States*. Washington, D.C.: U.S. Government Printing Office, 1988. Ronald Reagan, 1986.

U.S. President. *Public Papers of the Presidents of the United States*. Washington, D.C.: U.S. Government Printing Office, 1988. Ronald Reagan, 1985.

U.S. President. *Public Papers of the Presidents of the United States*. Washington, D.C.: U.S. Government Printing Office, 1985. Ronald Reagan, 1983.

U.S. President. *Public Papers of the Presidents of the United States*. Washington, D.C.: U.S. Government Printing Office, 1983. Ronald Reagan, 1982.

U.S. President. *Public Papers of the Presidents of the United States*. Washington, D.C.: U.S. Government Printing Office, 1982. Ronald Reagan, 1981.

Reagan, Ronald. *Birmingham Campaign Speech* (October 9, 1980).

———. *Philadelphia Campaign Speech* (October 7, 1980).

———. *Iowa Campaign Speech* (September 30, 1980).

———. *Sunnyvale, California, Campaign Speech* (September 25, 1980).

———. *National Television Address* (July 6, 1976).

———. *National Television Address* (March 31, 1976).

———. *Excerpts of Remarks Made in Manchester, New Hampshire* (February 21, 1976).

———. *Remarks to the Southern Republican Conference Banquet* (December 13, 1975).

———. *Candidacy Announcement* (November 20, 1975).
———. "Let The People Rule" (September 26, 1975).
California. Governor's Office Press Releases. Ronald Reagan. *Collected Speeches.* Sacramento, CA., 1974.
California. Governor's Office Press Releases. Ronald Reagan. *Collected Speeches.* Sacramento, CA., 1973.
California. Governor's Office Press Releases. Ronald Reagan. *Collected Speeches.* Sacramento, CA., 1972.
California. Governor's Office Press Releases. Ronald Reagan. *Collected Speeches.* Sacramento, CA., 1971.
California. Governor's Office Press Releases. Ronald Reagan. *Collected Speeches.* Sacramento, CA., 1970.
California. Governor's Office Press Releases. Ronald Reagan. *Collected Speeches.* Sacramento, CA., 1969.
California. Governor's Office Press Releases. Ronald Reagan. *Collected Speeches.* Sacramento, CA., 1968.
California. Governor's Office Press Releases. Ronald Reagan. *Collected Speeches.* Sacramento, CA., 1967.
"A Time for Choosing." In Anne Edwards. *Early Reagan.* New York: William Morrow, 1987, 561–70.
"Encroaching Control." In *A Time for Choosing: The Speeches of Ronald Reagan, 1961–1982,* ed. Alfred A. Balitzer. Chicago: Regnery Gateway, 1983, 21–38.
"On Taxation." In Congress. House of Representatives. Committee on Ways and Means. *General Revenue Revision.* 85th Cong., 2d sess., 27 January 1958, 1980–1993.
"The Basic Hollywood Speech." In Ronald Reagan. *Speaking My Mind.* New York: Simon & Schuster, 1989, 18–21.

Index